Interdisciplinary Learning Through Dance

101 MOVEntures

Lynnette Young Overby, PhD

Michigan State University
East Lansing, Michigan

Beth C. Post

Discovery and Explorer Elementary Schools
Williamston, Michigan

Diane Newman

Happendance Professional Company and School
Okemos, Michigan

HUMAN KINETICS

Library of Congress Cataloging-in-Publication Data

Overby, Lynnette Young.
    Interdisciplinary learning through dance : 101 moventures / Lynnette Young Overby, Beth C. Post, Diane Newman.
            p. cm.
    Includes bibliographical references.
    ISBN 0-7360-4642-9 (soft cover)
    1. Movement education—Study and teaching (Elementary)—Curricula. 2. Dance for children—Study and teaching (Elementary)—Curricula. 3. Interdisciplinary approach in education. I. Post, Beth C., 1954- II. Newman, Diane, 1949- III. Title.
    GV452.094 2005
    372.86'8'044—dc22

                                    2004028483

ISBN: 0-7360-4642-9

The Web addresses cited in this text were current as of November 24, 2004 unless otherwise noted.

Acquisitions Editor: Judy Patterson Wright, PhD; **Developmental Editor:** Jennifer Sekosky; **Assistant Editor:** Ragen E. Sanner; **Copyeditor:** Jan Feeney; **Proofreader:** Amie Bell; **Permission Manager:** Dalene Reeder; **Graphic Designer:** Nancy Rasmus; **Graphic Artist:** Dawn Sills; **Photo Manager:** Kelly J. Huff; **Cover Designer:** Keith Blomberg; **Photographer (cover):** Kelly J. Huff; **Photographer (interior):** Kelly J. Huff, unless otherwise noted. Photos on pages 3, 8, 17, 20, 26, 48, 65, 109, 126, 138, 226, and 230 © Charles Knickerbocker. Photos on pages 31, 51, 53, 131, and 164 © Human Kinetics. Photo on page 303 © Linda McCausey; **Art Manager:** Kelly Hendren; **Illustrator:** Tim Offenstein, unless otherwise noted. Art on page 287 © Denise Lowry; **Printer:** United Graphics.

We thank Cerro Gordo Elementary School in Cerro Gordo, Illinois, for assistance in providing the location for the photo shoot for this book.

"Bebop Beat" on the MOVEntures CD is an original composition by Stan Jensen of Michigan State University. Music clearances for CD and DVD through: The Prairie Production Group (Champaign, IL), ProMusic, Inc. (Boca Raton, FL), and Human Kinetics (Champaign, IL).

Printed in the United States of America   10 9 8 7 6 5 4 3 2 1

Human Kinetics
Web site: www.HumanKinetics.com

United States: Human Kinetics
P.O. Box 5076
Champaign, IL 61825-5076
800-747-4457
e-mail: humank@hkusa.com

Canada: Human Kinetics
475 Devonshire Road Unit 100
Windsor, ON N8Y 2L5
800-465-7301 (in Canada only)
e-mail: orders@hkcanada.com

Europe: Human Kinetics
107 Bradford Road
Stanningley
Leeds LS28 6AT, United Kingdom
+44 (0) 113 255 5665
e-mail: hk@hkeurope.com

Australia: Human Kinetics
57A Price Avenue
Lower Mitcham, South Australia 5062
08 8277 1555
e-mail: liaw@hkaustralia.com

New Zealand: Human Kinetics
Division of Sports Distributors NZ Ltd.
P.O. Box 300 226 Albany
North Shore City
Auckland
0064 9 448 1207
e-mail: blairc@hknewz.com

To our parents, who encouraged us to pursue a unique profession; to the classroom teachers who inspired us; to our students, who are a constant source of imagination, energy, and enthusiasm for learning; and to our families, whose love sustains us every day.

Contents

MOVEnture Finder

(continued)

(continued)

Preface

"**I** am a teacher, not a dancer. How can I possibly teach dance in my classroom when I know little about it and am not comfortable doing it?"

It does sound intimidating, doesn't it? Though movement is one of the most natural things humans do (we use it to communicate nonverbally even before birth), the idea of moving in the classroom makes many teachers break into a nervous sweat. Images leap to mind of students out of control, freed from their desks to create rhythmic mayhem, weakening the reserve of even the staunchest educator. So movement education has been relegated to the gym and identified primarily with the pursuit of sports. But what about movement for its own sake? Movement that, through self-expression and body awareness, becomes *dance*?

Teachers often think they have to be able to dance in order to use it in the classroom. But that is not the case. Teachers only have to be able to *appreciate* dance for the learning it lends, just as they appreciate music, or history, or the magic of the written word. As educators, we are responsible for *directing* the learning of our students, not necessarily being able to excel at every aspect ourselves. So "How can I teach dance?" is not the right question. The real question is "How can you not?"

Dance is successful in the classroom because it harnesses the innate desire harbored by every child: *to move*. Furthermore, dance is uniquely suited to support conceptual learning because the dance vocabulary is expressed in terms of the body, space, time, and force—concepts also fundamental to understanding the universe. Scientific inquiry defines the physical universe using these same fundamentals: a particle (body or mass) travels at a certain speed (time), through a given distance (space), with a distinct energy (force). And although dance can teach such fundamentals in exciting ways, its most powerful contribution to learning may be the wonderful web of connections it provides to understanding our place within that universe—an understanding of what it is to be human, to belong to a society, to respect and appreciate "otherness."

Engaging in dance captures the whole person. It is more than just hands-on learning—it is minds-on, bodies-on learning. Through the creative lesson plans developed for *Interdisciplinary Learning Through Dance: 101 MOVEntures*, classroom teachers will find a wealth of opportunities for teaching both curricula and dance as art. Our intention is to support teachers in their desire to bring more cross-disciplinary approaches to their learning environments. As educational research and experience has shown, the development of critical-thinking skills does not support the simplistic linear model on which our traditional teaching of the "3 Rs" is based. With all the new information about multiple intelligences, learning styles, and the power of hands-on experiences, we know that learning exhibits a marvelous complexity, requiring broad integration of multilevel experiences, information, and cognition. Teachers are becoming more adventurous, demanding more flexibility in approaches, more models for learning, more support not only to achieve specific grade requirements but to prepare and engage children in the joy of lifelong learning.

Inspired by these teachers' willingness to mold a new view, we created *Interdisciplinary Learning Through Dance: 101 MOVEntures* to support their journey. Classroom teachers, physical education teachers, and teacher educators will find useful examples and models for systematic development and implementation of an integrated curriculum that uses dance methodologies.

Interdisciplinary Learning Through Dance: 101 MOVEntures consists of a teaching manual for teachers of kindergarten through fifth grade and an accompanying compact disc and DVD. The manual provides the basic language of dance, the "how-tos" for lesson planning, classroom-management techniques, and assessment choices. Beyond these basics, the major thrust of this book is its wealth of lesson plans, each designed as a special movement adventure, or "moventure." Chapters cover the core areas of physical education (which introduces the language and elements of dance), language arts, math, social studies, science, and music, theatre, and visual arts.

Every lesson identifies the national standards and benchmarks for both dance and the core curricular subject area addressed. The CD provides music to accompany certain lessons, and the DVD offers visual support for the application of teaching methods as well as a demonstration of sample lessons with real students in real classrooms.

Suggestions for further lesson planning and curricular development are also included and, where applicable, audio, visual, and written resources are referenced.

Teachers will benefit from having field-tested models of lessons ready for implementation. These lessons are based on several years of classroom teaching as well as teaching teachers at both national and international professional-development institutes. As part of the editing process, education consultants who specialize in each curricular area have reviewed the lessons. The Moventure program has been received at professional conferences with enthusiastic response from participants who, moved by a spirit of adventure and curiosity, were attracted to something with such an unusual title. Their written evaluations revealed that they were attracted to a session that allowed learning while moving around

because they were tired of the sitting-and-listening format of most conference sessions. How much better they now understand why children, who *love* to move, become restless with the limitations of life at a desk! With the simple act of pushing back the furniture and creating open space, more than space constraints are unleashed. Excitement buzzes, hearts pound, creative juices flow, and ordinary perceptions are expanded. Scary? Yes! It's always scary (and thrilling) to be poised at the precipice of discovery!

For some students, expression through the performing arts and entertainment industry will be their lifetime calling. But the traditional method of training through costly private dance classes, music lessons, or drama workshops excludes many children. That is why the arts need to be considered core curriculum in every school. Otherwise, we are leaving out an entire segment of learners who may be gifted in arts or entertainment but do not have the financial resources to become competent. This is not only a loss to the individual but also a loss to us all.

To the teacher, the power of dance may be its usefulness as an instructional tool; but to the student, dance offers a playful way to learn. As teachers become confident in directing and incorporating dance activities, their students will be able to read about, think about, write about, and dance about the things they are learning. Teachers win, and students win, as they share the process of dancing across the curriculum.

So go ahead. Take a chance. Teach your classes with dance.

Acknowledgments

There are always those who lend their expertise and wisdom to the development of such a project as *Interdisciplinary Learning Through Dance: 101 MOVEntures*. Without the help of these people, this effort would never have come to fruition. We gratefully acknowledge the contributions of numerous people, including our colleagues in dance education, our curriculum and technical consultants, and our students. First and foremost, we salute the body of knowledge pioneered by our colleagues—dance educators everywhere—who, through their leadership and innovation, have developed us as much as we have developed ourselves.

We are also greatly indebted to our Michigan consultants: Joyce Krause of Detroit Schools (physical education), Deborah Sharpe of Haslett Schools (language arts), Helen Shipley of Haslett Schools (mathematics), Evelyn Dungey of Lansing Schools (social studies), Connie Crittenden of Williamston Schools (science), and Ana Cardona of the Michigan Department of Education (visual and performing arts). These people patiently reviewed all Moventure lessons for alignment with the National Standards and general readability from a classroom teacher's point of view. In addition, we are grateful to Marcey Siegel and Nicolea Broadrick for their final review of lesson content.

Other important people gave singular contributions of time and expertise. Michele Root-Bernstein, coauthor of *Sparks of Genius*, aligned the Moventure lessons with the thinking tools discussed in her book. Charles Knickerbocker chased us from site to site in order to photograph our students. Brian Post lent his computer savvy throughout the book-writing process, and Marlo Quintel lent us her typing skills. Judy Patterson Wright, Jennifer Sekosky, and Ragen Sanner, our editors at Human Kinetics, patiently walked us through the project while offering advice and support. Doug Fink, our DVD director, and Roger Francisco, our Audio Services Manager, at Human Kinetics. And finally, we would like to thank all the students at Happendance School in Okemos, Williamston Elementary Schools, and Red Cedar Elementary School in East Lansing for their joyful participation during the dance videography and photography sessions.

How To Use This Book

Interdisciplinary Learning Through Dance: 101 MOVEntures is designed to assist teachers in identifying and classifying the connections between curricular concepts and dance through the basis of national standards and Michele and Robert Root-Bernsteins' thinking tools. This book encourages you, the classroom teacher, to find new connections and create lesson plans that will further link concepts shared among disciplines.

So what is a Moventure? The word *Moventure* is coined from the words *movement* and *adventure*. It came about in a serendipitous moment as the three authors searched for a nontechnical term to describe the lively process of connecting dance and curriculum. A Moventure lesson is intended to be a playful way to engage students and teachers alike as they embark on the journey of learning together.

MOVEnture Format

Moventure lessons provide a map for the systematic delivery of standards-based curriculum. These chapters are organized by curricular area with the lessons aligned by difficulty, from easiest to most challenging. Each lesson has 10 parts.

- **Grade Levels.** The grade levels give you a general idea of the complexity of the tasks included in the lesson.
- **Length of Lesson.** Approximate amount of time required to implement the lesson (and number of sessions in the case of splitting the lesson into multiple components) is indicated here.
- **Materials.** This section of the lesson is a list of materials required.
- **National Standards.** At the heart of each lesson are the National Standards for Dance

Education and at least one other curricular area. In creating the lessons based on the standards, we have aligned the objectives, activities, and assessments to provide a clear guide for instruction. Appendix B provides a thorough listing of each standard used within the lessons.

- **Objectives.** The objectives indicate what students should learn during the lesson and are the basis for the assessment.
- **Introduction.** This part of the lesson contains information that promotes an understanding of and motivation for the forthcoming movement experience.
- **The Moving Adventure.** This section of the lesson includes specific tasks and activities. Teaching cues promote learning by providing specific feedback statements. The moving adventure will often conclude with an application that includes creating and performing.
- **Assessment.** The conclusion of the lesson lasts a few minutes and includes suggestions for reviewing the focus of the lesson that was emphasized during the moving adventure. Assessment may be in the form of questions from you or a demonstration by students. The students may also be asked to do other tasks, such as interview grandparents or write a story.
- **Assessment Forms.** The assessment forms range from checklists for students' use to rubrics for teachers' use. The templates for the assessment forms listed in this section are included in appendix A.
- **Extensions.** The purpose of the extensions is to take each lesson to the next level with factors you can manipulate: different movement, music, and activities (such as drawing, writing, and observing and responding).

Throughout the lessons you will also notice this symbol inserted within the text. A one- or two-word description follows the symbol. This alerts you to a link between a certain instruction and the 13 thinking tools identified by Michele and Robert Root-Bernstein in their book *Sparks of Genius*. The thinking tools are included to reflect the cognitive processing students will experience that is specific to each lesson. Appendix C contains a list of the thinking tools and a description of their relevance to teaching dance.

An additional component that should be a key part of every Moventure lesson is time for reflection. After each lesson, take time to reflect on the lesson by answering questions that will lead to an improved understanding of teaching and learning. The following are examples of questions:

- Did I accomplish the objectives? Why or why not?

- Were the students positively engaged in learning most of the time?

- How can I improve my teaching in the next session?

Audio and Visual Aids

Dance most obviously connects with music. For many of the Moventure lessons (but not all), musical accompaniment is recommended and included on the CD. Look for the appropriate musical selection identified in the "Materials" section near the beginning of the lesson. Look for this icon to identify lessons that have recommended musical selections on the accompanying CD. A complete song list is available on pages 296-297.

The DVD allows for a closer look at how to use a Moventure with your class. Certain lessons, such as Universal Circle Dance, 20th-Century Celebration, and Dance of the Four Elements, are enhanced by an easy-to-follow visual aid. Other video clips demonstrate the important components necessary for a successful Moventure, including management techniques, safety and spatial criteria, and closure activities. The DVD clip is noted in the "Materials" section near the beginning of any lesson for which it is used. Look for this icon to identify lessons that are shown on the accompanying DVD.

Summary

Interdisciplinary Learning Through Dance: 101 MOVEntures is designed to offer a more comprehensive method by which to reach and teach the whole child, every child. Within these pages are treasures to be discovered: the joy of children moving, sparks of creative expression, and the wondrous expansion of learning through the Moventure lessons themselves. But let us not forget who is guiding the daily adventure of seeking new knowledge—you, the classroom teacher. So grab your gear and get moving!

chapter 1

Connecting Dance and Curriculum

Dancers communicate through movement. As the painter communicates with paint, and the musician with a violin, the dancer communicates with her instrument, her body. At the epitome of artistic expression, the dancer and the dance become one. Dance is the oldest of the art forms and has been used throughout history for many purposes: as a form of religious expression, as a means of celebration, as a rite of passage, and as a means of passing cultural and social traditions on to the next generation.

Creative Dance

Creative dance, a term usually offered to describe dance for children and the focus of this book, provides all participants with the opportunity to enhance their abilities to think and move in new and satisfying ways. Creative dance is intended to develop the creative, physical, mental, and artistic aspects of a person in a nonperformance setting. The student explores and creates as a process, not as a product.

Throughout history, dance has been a vehicle for the communication of many diverse and universal concepts. This text builds on the ability of dance to communicate and connect. Not only is dance a discipline with specific content, but it is also a tool for synthesizing and transforming other disciplines.

An Interdisciplinary Approach

Interdisciplinary approaches make good sense because most of the problems encountered in life require specific knowledge and broad application. In other words, we must understand the concepts of a particular discipline in order to solve problems that extend beyond that discipline. According to education researchers Mansilla, Miller, and Gardner (2000), "students demonstrate interdisciplinary understanding when they integrate knowledge and modes of thinking from two or more disciplines in order to create products, solve problems, and offer explanations of the world" (p. 18). Problems may occur in interdisciplinary work when the disciplines are not afforded equal status. To ensure such status is addressed, most lessons in this text are designed to connect the learning and application of concepts in dance with primarily one other discipline. To teach with this approach requires a general knowledge of the discipline you are teaching, plus a basic understanding of dance concepts. For example, in the lesson on dinosaurs in chapter 7, knowledge of the characteristics and evolution of dinosaurs, along with a basic understanding of the elements of dance, are both necessary for integrating the scientific concept (dinosaurs) and the dance concepts (space, time, force, and body movement). However, it is not necessary to feel comfortable with all aspects

of dance in order to make it a part of your class. You can learn with your students!

Many of the lessons in this book have been presented during professional development workshops with teachers and as part of a creative dance university course. Though many teachers begin the sessions with only a vague understanding of dance concepts, through the dance experiences they are able to explore these concepts, experience an integrated lesson, and design a lesson based on the vocabulary of dance and a curricular area of their choice. For example, teachers have designed interdisciplinary science lessons about the life cycle of a butterfly, states of matter, properties of light, simple machines, characteristics of rocks, clouds, and ecosystems. Success at developing such lessons, using the Moventure format, increases confidence in planning for integrated learning experiences.

Many teachers have found success using the Moventure program through a workshop or university course.

"Students learn much more when they're allowed to use their bodies and movement instead of just reading books, articles, materials, and bibliographies to make these activities possible."

Elaine Flore, middle school language arts teacher

"The Moventure workshop was exhilarating for me because it made me more aware of how the arts are an important component in teaching."

Jill Campbell,
elementary and middle school counselor

"Prior to my participation in creative movement and learning, I believed that dance was a specialized activity in which only certain people could be successful. Now, however, my opinions about dance have changed. Now, I understand dance to be a communicative effort. Whether the communicative intent is personal or social, the creative dancer uses his or her knowledge of the elements of dance (body, space, force, and time) to express thoughts and feelings. It is almost as if the elements of dance are words and that, once defined and exemplified, a student may express oneself more fully by employing the elements of dance rather than spoken words."

Connie Shorter,
teacher of students with mental disabilities

"My children picked up the elements of dance really well! I was able to teach a lesson on the water cycle as well as a cross-curricular lesson that incorporated most of the subject areas. The children were able to grasp the concepts taught even better by using movement."

Malika Snipe, kindergarten teacher

"Upon beginning this class, I was a little apprehensive about this course and how I could make it a viable part of my classroom. However, after trying and sharing the things I've learned with my students, I now see that not only does it help with their comprehension of material, but it also unleashed their creativity."

Donna Jefferson, fourth-grade teacher

"It has been exciting using creative movement in my class. The confidence that creative movement brings makes my students more successful. I see creative dance as an essential tool to enhance students' learning."

Ruth Boykin, fourth-grade teacher

"I recently made body movements to go along with the alphabet, and my students and I learned the spelling words for the week by dancing out the spellings of the words. My children became excited about spelling because they know that if they use the dance to learn the words, they will get most of the words on the test correct, and in return they

Dance offers students a playful, creative way to learn.

feel confident and successful about themselves in the classroom."

Lakennethia T. Vaughn, special needs teacher

Standards-Based Instruction

Forty-seven states have aligned their curricula with the National Standards and Benchmarks (Bonbright and McGreevy-Nichols 1999). Teachers and students are becoming increasingly accountable for mastery of the materials in the documents of the national and state standards, the purpose of which is to ensure a high level of achievement by all students. Appendix B contains listings of the standards for dance, physical education, language arts, mathematics, social studies, science, theater, music, and visual arts. Moventure lessons identify which specific standards are addressed through the activity presented. When properly implemented, these lessons offer students the opportunity to apply knowledge that transcends the disciplines.

Each lesson allows the teacher to address at least one national standard through creative dance. For example, in Dancing Dreams, lesson 33 in chapter 4, the students simultaneously meet standards in language arts and in dance. The Moventure approach is not an "add-on" of more time and more content to teach. Rather, the philosophy is to save time by teaching more content, more meaningfully.

Thinking Tools

In their book *Sparks of Genius: The Thirteen Thinking Tools of the World's Most Creative People* (1999), the Root-Bernsteins present a well-documented series called thinking tools (see appendix C). The thinking tools reflect underlying abilities necessary for the understanding and expression of disciplinary content. Few curricula acknowledge the importance of imagination—or of imaginative skills such as abstracting, analogizing, and recognizing and forming patterns—to conceptual understanding. Robert and Michele Root-Bernstein (2000) suggest that education in these skills is absolutely essential for students who are destined for any and every creative endeavor:

If we want to educate students capable of invention within their chosen fields, we must do two things: first, provide them with a rich repertoire of creative mental tools such as imaging, abstracting, empathizing, or play-acting, kinesthetic thinking, analogizing, and modeling; second, train them in the skills needed to translate what they learn through those tools into formal, symbolic languages such as words, dance, music, or mathematics. (p. A64)

Thinking tools learned in the arts, or in creative movement as presented in this book, are transferable to other disciplinary areas so that recognizing and forming patterns in dance enhances the understanding of patterns in social studies or mathematics. Thinking tools create a truly transdisciplinary curriculum in which all content areas link to one another at the level of imaginative thinking, problem solving, and creative expression.

The lessons in this book make explicit the specific thinking tools exercised in each learning experience. For example, in a lesson that uses dance to deliver math concepts, recognizing and forming patterns may be listed as the thinking tools most relevant to the plan. In such case, they link the two subject areas both imaginatively and cognitively. Indeed, with these tools in mind, dance does not simply illustrate math; the patterns of dance as well as those of math become one and the same, but differently expressed. Exercising and emphasizing tools for thinking one or two at a time will enhance the ability of all students to think well beyond the lessons in the book because these tools, most easily learned in the arts, are transferable to other content areas such as social studies and science. Along with the standards-based objectives, the thinking tools are offered here as another layer of learning that teachers can identify and use as time and comfort allow. The thinking tools within each lesson are easily recognizable, as the names of the applied thinking tools appear alongside this symbol.

Summary

It is our hope that the lessons in this book provide a model for teachers and teacher educators to build on. With educational theory and the national standards as our guide, we have demonstrated the many ways that concepts in dance illuminate the concepts in other disciplines, and vice versa. The model will be complete when dance becomes an integral part of the curriculum.

chapter 2

Guiding the Dance Experience

Dance is a discipline equal to the other disciplines presented in this text. Classroom teachers have the opportunity to teach all subjects, including the arts, as a part of the regular curriculum. Unfortunately, many classroom teachers have little to no experience with creative dance during their preservice training. It is imperative, therefore, to begin this adventure with successful teaching and learning experiences. These experiences will build the confidence of the teacher and the competence of the learners. The following teaching strategies and classroom-management techniques are suggested as ways to ensure a successful beginning to interdisciplinary dance education.

Tools for Teaching Dance

As with any type of teaching, dance teaching requires specific skills, strategies, and techniques that ensure the success of the program. Knowing your options for using interdisciplinary dance in your classroom will help you feel confident when approaching this material, which may be new to you and your students.

Creating a Dance Environment

Dance can take place in many spaces; you do not necessarily need a gymnasium. A classroom, with desks and chairs pushed to the boundaries, can be more than adequate. When more space is required, empty classrooms, gymnasiums, multipurpose rooms, carpeted library areas, and even an outdoor location can be used.

Once you have selected the lesson and location, refer to the materials list, gather supplies, select music to be used, and plan for assessment. Remember, safety first! As you prepare for your lesson, consider the following issues:

- **Warm-up and cool-down.** To prevent injuries, a warm-up including a series of locomotor movements (such as walking, running, skipping, or otherwise increasing heart rate and body temperature) followed by gentle stretching is a healthy way to begin a lesson. The following examples from chapter 3 can be used as warm-ups prior to another moventure or activity, or as complete lessons in their own right: Shake and Freeze (lesson 1), Silly Dance (lesson 2), and Towers (lesson 18). Ending a lesson with a few stretches and relaxation, known as a cool-down, will enable the students to focus on preparing for the next classroom activity. Examples of Moventures that can be used as cool-downs are Mirroring (lesson 5), Flower Dance (lesson 8), and Ahh! Relaxation (lesson 12).

- **Appropriate footwear.** Athletic shoes are most appropriate for this type of activity. For the youngest elementary children in particular, nothing supplants the sheer joy of dancing in bare feet, provided the floors are clear and clean.

- **Appropriate clothing.** The clothing worn by most children today is appropriate for active participation. Restrictive clothing, such as tight jeans and tops, or clothing that is too revealing, such as short skirts and dresses, would be inappropriate.

- **Rules.** You must clearly state and enforce rules of behavior to ensure a safe environment. Immediately caution students who purposely bump into other students or do not follow instructions. Consequences may include a warning for a first offense, a five-minute separation from the class with the student actively observing for a second offense, and elimination from the activity for the duration of the class time for a third offense.

Typical Teaching and Learning Formations

Students need to understand the concepts of moving in both personal and general space. They should also be able to form circles, select partners, and create small groups. Establish boundaries in the movement space. Use orange cones, furniture, or other easily visible markers to delineate the dance area.

- **Self-space.** Students stand in one spot, testing that they are not too close to furniture, walls, or another student by turning with their arms outstretched. In self-space (also called "personal space"), students work individually, making sure to keep their space separate from other students' spaces as they move.

- **Scattered formation.** Students work in self-space individually, with partners, or in small groups positioned randomly throughout the activity space. A scattered formation allows students to explore ideas improvisationally and work independently.

- **Lines.** Students can form lines through locomotor or nonlocomotor movements, or the students can be frozen in space. Lines are appropriate when teaching specific movements in structured dances.

- **Circles.** Circles are similar to lines in that they can be formed in space in many ways. Circles are useful at the beginning and end of a lesson. They are also used when teaching simple folk dances.

- **Share through performance.** Students can learn a great deal through simple observation. For example, half the class can perform as the other half watches, and then the two groups can switch roles. Sharing through the performance gives students the opportunity to express themselves.

- **Movement centers or stations.** You can establish special stations that encourage independent work on specific content. For example, you could establish a station on the time line of dance through history (see 20th-Century Celebration, lesson 64, in chapter 6), where students can study historical events and dances of the decades.

Signals

Though physical education teachers often use a whistle, dance teachers prefer a musical instrument or verbal command to cue students. A clear signal, such as a drumbeat, or the statement "Ready, go!" or "Begin" can start a movement activity. You can use the command "Freeze!" or a drumbeat to end an activity or get the students' attention. The students must be required to stop, listen, and hold their shape solidly when you give the signal to freeze. Use the command "Unfreeze" or "Relax" to require students to dissolve their frozen position as they look at you for further directions. Music can replace the drumbeat as a signal to start and stop. When the music begins, students may begin the movement activity. When the music stops or fades gradually, students may stop in likewise fashion.

The "Go" and "Freeze" mirroring activity is a good example of a way to help your students understand the importance of listening, following instructions, and maintaining body control. Give the signal "Go" to students to begin the activity and "Freeze" to end it. Sample instructions may be, "When I say, 'Go,' I would like each of you to mirror me. Follow me exactly, as if you are looking in a mirror. Ready, go!" The students will begin to follow your movements. After about 30 seconds, say, "Freeze."

Other suggestions include using a double drumbeat as a signal to freeze. Or, try the approach used by one of the authors: Say, "Yo, students!" and students respond, "What's up?" followed by a countdown of 5-4-3-2-1. By the time you reach 1, all students should be focused on you. When the class as a whole fails to meet this test, repeat the activity. A reward system may also be useful. Encourage those students who are not stopping on signal to pay more attention because safety becomes an issue.

Demonstration

You or a selected student can provide a demonstration of the movement. Though teachers are sometimes hesitant to demonstrate movement, it is usually only recommended as a way to illustrate a concept for the students and is generally very simple. More often, having a student volunteer to demonstrate is more appropriate. Whether the purpose is to show a shape that is very open with arms and legs stretched apart or to demonstrate a way to gallop, hop, or skip or to show a creative way to melt from a high level to a low level, students love to solve movement problems. So why not let them? Remember, you are the director of the activity and your encouragement and watchful eyes are needed in that capacity. This should not discourage your active participation on occasion because children perceive you in a different way during such shared experiences. But in general, you should be in an alert and supportive mode that protects the students and the integrity of the activity.

Teacher-Centered and Student-Centered Approaches

In a teacher-centered approach, the teacher tells the students what to do. She tells them how and what to practice. The teacher may provide a clear demonstration followed by a clear explanation with appropriate cues. Finally, she provides feedback to the individual student or class so that they can improve during future practice attempts. The teacher-centered instructional approach is especially useful when teaching the specific steps of a structured dance. In chapter 6, the lessons Dances of the 1920s (lesson 60) and Universal Circle Dance (lesson 54) are examples of teacher-centered activities.

On the opposite end of the spectrum is the student-centered approach, in which the teacher asks guiding questions or presents a specific problem to be solved by the learners. For instance, the teacher may request that the students design a sequence of movements to a poem. The teacher may give cues, such as to use a variety of locomotor and nonlocomotor movements, but the specific movements are determined by the learner. Action Words (lesson 27, chapter 4), Curfew (lesson 47, chapter 5), and Room to Move (lesson 57, chapter 6) are examples of student-centered lessons.

In a teacher-centered approach, the teacher explains, and sometimes demonstrates, the movement.

Dance Vocabulary

Dance is a discipline composed of specific movement concepts, skills, and principles. The dance vocabulary included in this book is based on concepts and terminology from modern dance, motor development, and creative dance. It is our hope that the dance vocabulary will enable all teachers to identify and use the essential components of dance that promote clear connections with other curricular content.

Post the Vocabulary of Dance and Movement list in the dance class location (see pages 294–295). By posting these concepts, teachers and students alike will have ongoing access to the dance vocabulary. And as they share and practice this new language, they will gain confidence and competency in using dance to connect to other curricula—the interdisciplinary connection.

Process for Designing a MOVEnture

Dance is a language using the body and movement to express meaning. Moventure lessons show you ways to use the dance vocabulary to explore other curriculum. Learning the vocabulary of dance is similar to learning a second language. At first, one works through a two-step process, thinking in the native tongue (curriculum) and then struggling to translate it into the new language (dance). Eventually, a person begins to think in the language of dance, reducing the translation process to one step. *Interdisciplinary Learning Through Dance: 101 MOVEntures* gives you that experience and practice.

After implementing many of these Moventures, you will find that you are beginning to think of ways to design your own interdisciplinary moventures. After all, who is better able to determine the topics and connections that will best suit your students than you, the person who works with them daily?

First, select a curricular concept. Once selected, the teacher and students must gather information about that concept. For example, for The Water Cycle (lesson 74), students will need to explore the components of a stream and the processes of evaporation, condensation, and precipitation. Through the use of the movement concept chart (see table 2.1 as an example), clear and realistic connections to the curricular concept can be made.

Other examples of using a movement concept chart can be found in the following lessons: The Kelp Community (lesson 82), Microscopic World (lesson 83), and Save the Rainforest (lesson 80). From the initial connections on the chart, you can develop a complete lesson based on your specific observations.

Pay attention to the different methodologies used to teach the Moventure lessons. Beyond the use of the movement concept chart, you will see the use of improvisation as in Vowel Vamp (lesson 22) and Cliché Studies (lesson 32), narrative as in African Folk Tale (lesson 29) and A Native American Poem (lesson 61), and rhythmic structure as in Towers (lesson 18) and Jump, Everybody, Jump! (lesson 19) to develop interdisciplinary lessons.

Table 2.1 Connecting Science With Movement

Science Concept	Stream	Evaporation	Condensation	Precipitation
Space: place, levels, directions, pathways	General space, middle and low level	General space and self-space, low level to high level	Self-space, high level	General space, high to low level
Time: slow, medium, fast	Slow	Fast	Slow	Medium to fast
Force: energy, weight, flow	Smooth, light, free	Smooth, light, free	Smooth	Sharp
Body movement: locomotor, nonlocomotor, shapes	Stretching, bending, gliding	Floating, rising	Shapes	Bending, jumping to low level, pounding the floor

Summary

The key to success is a belief in the ability of the students to gain valuable knowledge and skills through the moventures. Every lesson will not be perfect, but each time you incorporate dance in a lesson, you will gain confidence and competence. Remember that the first time certain students try something new, especially in upper-elementary grades, they are often self-conscious and may hold back, make fun of it or the people trying it, and appear not to enjoy the activity. But students can get beyond their self-consciousness and discomfort through support from you and increased familiarity with the dance process. By using the lessons in this book, students have a hands-on, minds-on, bodies-on mode of celebrating their uniqueness. So prepare for an adventure that will take you and your students to a new level of enjoyment, creativity, understanding, and learning.

chapter 3

MOVEntures in Physical Education

During the school years, a student's only exposure to a structured movement experience may be physical education. Dance is the artistic partner to movement education, yet many students never experience it. By focusing on the similarities (movement concepts and skills) and presenting the creativity and artistry of composition and choreography, the lessons in this chapter provide both the classroom teacher and the physical education teacher with new experiences that are clearly aligned with the curricular goals of physical education.

Shake and Freeze

1

A LISTENING GAME TO WARM UP THE BODY.

GRADES: K TO 2   **LENGTH:** 10 TO 15 MINUTES

Materials

MOVEnture DVD (used as a warm-up for A Little Alliteration)
- A shaking percussion instrument (maraca, tambourine, or beaded gourd)

National Standards

Physical Education: 1

Dance: 1

Objectives

The students will be able to do the following:
- Move different body parts with shaking (vibratory) movement.
- Move when the shaking sound begins and stop moving (freeze) when the sound stops.

INTRODUCTION

Introduce the percussion instrument and ask what movement is required to cause its sound (shaking it). Let each child use one of the instruments to make the shaking sound. (If you have more than one instrument, this part of the lesson will go faster.)

THE MOVING ADVENTURE

1. Form a circle with the class. Tell the children the shaker instrument will now take control of their bodies and make each of their body parts shake. They may be sitting or standing to begin. Start simply by using just the fingers. As you shake the maraca, instruct the children to shake their fingers while they hear the sound. But when the maraca stops, they must also instantly stop, or *freeze* their movement in whatever shape in which it is caught. Repeat it two or three times until they are successful. Remind them to stay in their self-space.

2. Repeat the activity with other body parts: elbows, head, feet, arms, legs, hips, shoulders, knees, eyes (blinking). Or ask them for further suggestions. (Don't be surprised by suggestions for tongues or tails.) Remind them to shake only the body part requested.

3. Finally, ask the children to shake the whole body and freeze in response to the sound of the shaker. This can be done in an add-on fashion of starting with one body part and then letting it spread to other body parts, or jumping right in and shaking the whole body. ⚙ **Transforming**

ASSESSMENT

- Were you able to freeze when the shaker stopped?
- What was the hardest body part to shake?
- How did it feel to shake your body (silly, fun, relaxing, and so on)? Validate those responses, emphasizing that it is OK to move in ways that are funny.

Assessment Form

Movement Study Assessment form, for teacher use. Add these factors to the form: shaking single body part, freezing on time (listening).

Extensions

- See Silly Dance (lesson 2), page 13.
- Repeat the structure of this activity by adding music and requesting different movements in self-space. Students could melt, swing, reach, kick, and so on until the music is suddenly paused and they must freeze. The musical selection could be one of the general rhythms (tracks 10 and 41–43) on the accompanying CD.
- Repeat the structure of this activity by adding music and locomotor (traveling) movements. Students could skip, gallop, march, crawl, hop, or do any other locomotor movement through general space until the music is suddenly paused and they must freeze. See tracks 41–43 on the accompanying CD for appropriate selections of music.

Silly Dance

2

USING ISOLATIONS OF BODY PARTS.

GRADES: K TO 2   **LENGTH:** 10 TO 15 MINUTES

Materials

Moventure CD track 7
- Hand drum
- Audio playback system

National Standards

Physical Education: 1

Dance: 1

Objectives

The students will be able to do the following:

- Accurately demonstrate articulation of isolated body parts.
- Demonstrate kinesthetic awareness, concentration, and focus in performing movement skills.

INTRODUCTION

Ask students to find self-space, stand facing you, and be ready to listen for the name of a body part to move.

THE MOVING ADVENTURE

⚙ Body Thinking

1. Try really hard to move or isolate only the body part mentioned.

Face

- Begin with eyes: Look up, down, and to the side; open wide, close, blink fast.
- Nose: Wiggle it like a rabbit would.
- Mouth: Smile, frown, chew, kiss, blow a bubble-gum balloon, try fish lips.
- With your index finger, draw an imaginary line down the middle of your face. First scrunch your face toward the middle line and then open your face wide away from the line. Pat your cheeks.

Head

- Nod your head "yes," shake your head "no."

Shoulders

- Shrug your shoulders up as if to say, "I don't know," then bring shoulders down, then circle the shoulders.
- Shake shoulders forward and back like a washing machine.

Ribs

- Place fingers on ribs and play them like a piano.
- Move side to side, forward and back.

Head-head
Shoulder-shoulder
Rib-rib
Hip-hip
Knees-knees
Roll down-roll up
Arm-arm

Arms

- Sparkle fingers in all directions.
- Swing, do robot arms.

Hips

- Bump hips to right and left.
- Circle hips, but don't lose your balance.

Knees

- Put hands on knees, bend and straighten.
- Use your knees to jump on the count of 3 (bend to take off and land).

Feet

- Walk in place, run, kick, dance.

2. Put it all together and do the Silly Dance. Use the hand drum to accompany the movement. Start with the face, add the head, then shoulders, ribs, hips, knees, and feet and move everything! Freeze with a strong double drumbeat. Look at the all the interesting frozen statues. Check to see that they're frozen.

3. Isolation combination: Stand in a comfortable stance with feet shoulder-width apart.

Use the hand drum to keep time. Begin with head isolations and work through the list.

Counts 1-2	Drop head right, then left.	Counts 11-12	Drop upper body upside down.
Counts 3-4	Circle right shoulder, then left.		
Counts 5-6	Shift ribs right, then left.	Counts 13-14	Roll up back to center.
Counts 7-8	Press hips right, then left.	Counts 15-16	Circle both arms.
Counts 9-10	Bend right knee, then left knee.		

4. Add a simple pedestrian walk anywhere in the room for 16 counts. Students repeat the isolation combination in their new space, facing any direction.

ASSESSMENT

- Which body part was most difficult to isolate?
- Which was your favorite body part to isolate?
- Were you able to successfully perform the isolation combination by following the correct sequence of body part movements and staying with the beat?

Assessment Form

Participation Assessment form. Add these factors to the form: body-part isolations—head, shoulders, ribs, hips, knees, feet, arms.

Extensions

- Repeat the isolation combination starting on the left side of the body.
- Work with a partner to create a body-part dance.

Strong and Light

MOVING IN AND THROUGH SPACE
WITH GREATER AND LESSER FORCE.

GRADES: K TO 2 **LENGTH:** 30 MINUTES

Materials

MOVEnture CD track 6
- Audio playback system
- Chart with strong words—punch, slash, wring, and press
- Chart with light words—dab, flick, glide, and float
- Drum

National Standards

Physical Education: 2

Dance: 1, 2

Objective

Students will describe the properties of strong and light movements.

INTRODUCTION

Explore strong and light movements with the students. Some movements require a lot of force or a little force. We use strong movements when lifting weights, pushing a heavy cart, or pulling a heavy wagon. We use light movements when tiptoeing through the house or touching a baby. Ask students to make their muscles tight for strong movements. Then ask students to relax and soften their muscles for light movements.

THE MOVING ADVENTURE

1. Explore strong movement (movements that require a lot of force). In self-space, the students respond to words through movement as you read. Have the students look at the charts in the room. Read the strong words together, and in their self-space students perform their interpretation of the words. They can use various body parts (punching with the head, arms, legs; slashing with arms, legs, elbows; wringing hands, legs, head; and pressing whole body, legs only, and back).

2. Read the light words with the students; in their self-space they perform their interpretation of the words. Remind them that they need to use only a small amount of force to dab, flick, glide, and float. (You may think of more words to include on the list.)

3. In general space, the students practice different locomotor movements strongly and lightly. Use strong and light drumbeats throughout the activity. Students punch and kick when the drumbeats are loud; they float and glide when the drumbeats are soft.

4. Divide the room into two equal parts to represent "strong land" and "light land." Prompt students to move back and forth between the two sections, dancing with strong movements in strong land and with light movements in light land. Tell students to change their movement at the appropriate locations.

5. Use free dancing, also known as improvisation. Students pair up. The partners press hands together strongly, front to front, and then dance away lightly. They repeat with a new partner until music ends.

ASSESSMENT

- Ask students to describe strong and light movement.
- Ask students to name and describe the activities covered in the lesson.
- At the end of the moving adventure, have students perform a good-bye dance across the floor in groups of two as you call out a strong or light word.
- Create an assessment form to indicate each student's ability or inability to perform the concept.

Assessment Form

None.

Extensions

- Students explore what it means to be strong. They create a series of exercises designed to strengthen arms, legs, and abdominal muscles.
- Connect movement to explorations of variations in light and dark colors.
- Connect movement to explorations in variations in loud and soft sounds in music.

Sculpturing

CREATING LIVING SCULPTURES.

GRADES: K TO 2   **LENGTH:** 20 MINUTES

Materials

Hand drum

National Standards

Physical Education: 5

Dance: 3

Objectives

The students will be able to do the following:

- Use improvisation to discover, invent, and solve problems.
- Explore body design and use of the kinesthetic sense (motor memory).
- Work cooperatively with a classmate to achieve a goal.

INTRODUCTION

Ask students if they have used Play-Doh or clay to create a sculpture. They are the artists molding the clay, gently forming it into a sculpture of their own design. In this lesson students use their own bodies to design a living sculpture. ⚙️ **Analogizing**

THE MOVING ADVENTURE

1. Tell students to find a partner and a space in which to work. One student will be the artist and the other will be the clay. The artist will decide whether the sculpture will be standing, sitting, or lying down. The artist will carefully mold the partner, moving arms, legs, head, and even fingers into place. When the sculpture is complete, the artist will step back and take one last look, making sure there isn't anything to change.

2. Remind students who are the "clay" that they must hold the shape after being molded. Challenge students to remember their sculpture shapes. They close their eyes and think about the shape they're in. They must memorize where their arms, legs, head, and fingers are. Tell students to stand up and shake when you beat the drum. In this exercise students use their motor memory, or kinesthetic sense, to remember their shapes. Students then go back into their sculpture shapes exactly as they remember them. If artists should forget something, help them reshape the sculpture design. ⚙️ **Analogizing, Imaging**

3. Instruct students to take turns being the artist. They can make different statues using high (standing), middle (sitting), and low (lying down) levels. See if they can remember the sculpture shape using their kinesthetic sense each time.

ASSESSMENT

- What is your kinesthetic sense?
- Can you think of when you have used your motor memory (kinesthetic sense)? (Yes, in learning to jump rope or dribble a ball.) Your body remembers the movement and repeats it on command.
- Did your partner work gently with you as their clay?
- How did you do in remembering your sculpture shape?

Assessment Forms

- Participation Assessment form.
- Self-Assessment form (version appropriate for students' level). Add this factor to the form: use of kinesthetic sense (motor memory).

Extensions

- Design a three-dimensional sculpture using a rectangular piece of aluminum foil. Tear two slits about one-third down from the top of the foil, forming three sections. Gently crinkle and shape the center section into a head and the two side sections into arms. Tear a center slit one-third up from the bottom, and form the two sections into legs. Pinch in the center of the figure to form a waist. Continue to sculpt the body shape into your selected pose. When it's complete, staple the foil figure to a tag-board base.
- Explore sculpting a scene by working in small groups (three or four students). One group is the sculpting group and the other group is the clay. Each student in the group is sculpted into a shape that represents part of a scene. For example, a student is molded in the shape of a baseball pitcher, another shaped like a batter, and another as a catcher.

Mirroring

A LEADERSHIP AND FOLLOWSHIP GAME OF CONCENTRATION.

GRADES: K TO 2; GRADES 3 TO 5 CAN ADD THE VARIATIONS.
LENGTH: 20 TO 30 MINUTES

Materials

 MOVEnture CD track 1. Any background music that is adagio (slow, beautiful) works well.

- Audio playback system

National Standards

Physical Education: 1, 2, 5

Dance: 1, 2

Objectives

The students will be able to do the following:

- Understand that participation in physical activity provides opportunity for enjoyment and challenge.
- Demonstrate concentration and focus in performing movement skills.
- Demonstrate partner skills of leading and following.

INTRODUCTION

This activity is a favorite with all ages and is a quiet activity that can help students focus before taking a test. It can happen as students sit behind their desks, but it is much more fun when the desks are pushed aside or a large, unencumbered space is available, such as a carpeted multipurpose room or small gymnasium area.

Demonstrate the activity with one volunteer student first. Have the student face you directly. Instruct the class that you are a person looking into a mirror and that the volunteer student is your reflection. Therefore, that student must move in every way that you move but as a reflection (using the opposite side of the body, *symmetrical* movement). ⚙ **Observing, Empathizing**

Start with simple hand and arm movements. Progress to tilting side to side slowly or twisting or reaching and bending the body at the neck, waist, knees, and so on. Bring in ideas from everyday movement, such as drinking from a glass, throwing a ball, picking something up from the ground, and making facial expressions. Always do it in a sustained, smooth manner so that the volunteer student can anticipate your movement successfully. Correct the student quietly while moving if he uses the wrong side of the body to reflect you.

Ask the students who are watching to assess how well their classmate achieved moving slowly and exactly at the same time you did, as would a mirror's reflection. See if they noticed that if you moved too quickly, the student could not be as successful in moving exactly at the same time; or that if you turned your back to the student, he could no longer see you to know what you were doing; and other things they may have noticed and want to share.

THE MOVING ADVENTURE

1. Have all students in the class face you. Tell them that each one will pretend to be your reflection in the mirror. Repeat the Mirroring activity. Add the concepts of retreating from and approaching the mirror. Try traveling along the mirror to the right or left. Use high, medium,

and low levels. Repeat a movement a couple times, then challenge them by starting the same movement but changing how it finishes.

2. Discuss with the students what they experienced as your reflection.

3. Have each student partner with another student. Let them decide who will be the leader and who will be the follower the first time. Repeat the mirroring activity. Tell them that you want them to move so well together that you won't be able to know who the leader is. Therefore, leaders must take care of the follower and not make the follower look wrong; followers must concentrate hard on being good followers. Stop the activity by pausing the music and saying, "Freeze." Ask the students to hold their bodies still but to turn their heads to look around at the resulting sculpture garden as you point out the interesting shapes and relationships. Repeat the activity, letting them reverse roles with their partners.

ASSESSMENT

- Which did you prefer, leading or following? Why?
- Were you and your partner able to mirror well together?
- What was challenging about the activity? What was fun about the activity?

Assessment Form

Movement Study Assessment form, for teacher use. Add these factors to the form: leading (not giving lots of fast movement), following (moving exactly with leader), level of concentration.

Extensions

- Connect the concept of reflected shapes to the concept of symmetry. Symmetry is evident everywhere in nature and in human endeavors. To further explore this concept through movement, try the SASC (Sassy) Class, lesson 42, in chapter 5, MOVEntures in Mathematics.

- For grades 3 to 5 or second-graders who have achieved a high level of competency through practice, try these further variations:

  - Add a sound signal (a bell, wind chimes, or gong) to indicate to the partnerships that they should switch roles without stopping their movement or the music. To conclude the activity, fade the music so that partners gradually stop moving and slowly freeze.

  - Have half the partnerships mirror while the other half becomes an audience who will watch for who they think is leading each partnership's mirror movements. Switch the roles of performers and audience. Students could peer-assess by giving verbal comments after they observe partnerships' mirroring.

  - Have two leaders each lead half the class, pretending the mirror is the same surface (plane) for both, and then make sure the two leaders cross their paths, co-mingling the groups while trying to keep their own identity as a group. This is a fun challenge!

How Are You Feeling?

SAD, HAPPY, MAD, AND SCARED.

GRADES: K TO 2   **LENGTH:** 15 TO 20 MINUTES

Materials

MOVEnture CD track 2
- Audio playback system
- Sad, happy, mad, scared faces drawn on paper

National Standards

Physical Education: 5

Dance: 2, 3

Objectives

The students will be able to do the following:
- Use dance as a means of communication and self-expression.
- Interpret music with movement improvisation.

INTRODUCTION

Listen to a piece of music and ask the students to think about how that music makes them feel. Ask them to express four different emotions. After the students listen to the music, they will use movements that show how they feel.

THE MOVING ADVENTURE

1. Have students sit in self-space. Ask them how a piece of slow, sad-sounding music makes them feel. Have them look at a sad face drawn on a piece of paper and show you how their faces look when they feel sad. They can make their shoulders slump and add low energy to their movement when they move to the sad music.

2. When the energy of the music changes, ask students how their facial expressions change with this music. What movements best show happy feelings? Ask them to think of what makes them happy. Students do their happy dance with the happy music.

3. When the music changes again, ask students how they feel. Explain that it's a mad feeling, and sometimes we feel mad. Start with a mad face and add a strong energy to the movement, maybe stamping feet and jumping. Move throughout the classroom with a mad dance. Remind students to be mad in their self-space and not mad at someone else.

4. With the last piece of music (scary music), ask how students are feeling. Explain that everyone feels afraid at some time. Ask about what might scare them and how they look when they're scared. You might shake or try to hide. Tiptoe quietly as you sneak around the general space to the scared music.

5. Play all four pieces of music and have the students show you when their emotions change by the way that they move. 🎛 **Body Thinking**

ASSESSMENT

- Could you see the changes in emotion expressed?
- How did it feel to share your feelings with movements, not words?

Assessment Forms

- Participation Assessment form.
- Peer Assessment form.

Extensions

- Invite students to have a conversation with a partner expressing first mad and then sad. Ask them if they can think of a time when one person might be mad while the other is sad. Give an example—maybe their mother is angry that they have not cleaned their room. Her anger makes them sad. Or maybe they are angry with a friend for forgetting to call them to play. Their anger makes their friend sad.

- Play Brahms *Hungarian Dance #5 in G minor* and have students listen to the feelings expressed in the music. In groups of two, one will move angrily to the mad music while the other freezes in a sad shape. When the sad music plays, the mad person freezes and the sad person moves. In the middle of the piece, the music changes to happy and scared. Both partners will move happily and frightfully together. Students listen for the conversation between mad and sad to begin again. Then they trade feelings. If one was mad last time, that person tries the sad movement. And sad will change to mad. (This can be done in two groups rather than with partners.)

- Split the class into two groups and perform the partner conversations for each other.
  ⚙ **Transforming**

- When students respond emotionally to music and then express those feelings in another way, such as dance, they are transforming. Many artists purposefully find inspiration in transforming from one art to another. Ask students to create a drawing or painting that expresses one of the four emotions in the music. Talk about use of color and dynamics.

Diana's Walk

A DIRECTIONAL OBSTACLE COURSE.

GRADES: K TO 2   **LENGTH:** 20 MINUTES

Materials

- Poly spots (3)
- Hula hoop
- Carpet squares (3)
- Chairs
- Traffic cones
- Gates
- Silk flowers

National Standards

Physical Education: 2
Dance: 1

Objectives

The students will be able to do the following:

- Accurately demonstrate locomotor movements.
- Travel in different directions and at various levels.
- Observe and describe the action in a brief movement sequence.

INTRODUCTION

Create a story called Diana's Walk, an adventure with obstacles. Set up obstacles to represent each part of her walk. Look around the classroom or your equipment room and see what objects seem to fit. The items listed in "The Moving Adventure" section are examples of suggested objects.

THE MOVING ADVENTURE

1. Diana went for a walk. She went . . .

out the door:	traffic cones with gate closed
down the steps:	carpet squares
across the street:	poly spots
around a puddle:	blue hula hoop
over the rosebush:	silk flowers
through the playground:	large open-ended box
under the fence:	two chairs leaning together
	. . . and got home in time for dinner.

2. Demonstrate how to follow Diana's walk using directional cues.
   ✪ **Dimensional Thinking, Transforming**

- Open the gate and push out the door.
- Step across the carpet-square "steps." Change levels with each step (high, middle, low).
- Stand behind the poly spots, take three giant steps across the street. (Don't forget to look both ways before crossing.)

- Move around the hula hoop in a clockwise circular pathway around a puddle.
- Leap to a high level over the rosebush. Watch out for thorns!
- Crawl through the box through the playground.
- Slither carefully under the two chairs at a low level under the fence.
- Skip back to the start to get home in time for dinner.

3. Set up more than one obstacle course if your space and equipment can accommodate them. Strive to have as many students as possible moving at once.

4. Diana is being followed on her walk by a wolf that gets into trouble along the way. Ask students for ideas of what could happen to the wolf as he follows. Once the students have learned the course, have them follow Diana's walk in pairs. Give Diana a head start and signal the wolf to follow. You can add the wolf getting into trouble along the way. The wolf can pretend to bump into the door, fall down the stairs, dodge cars while she's going across the street, splash into the puddle, get pricked by rose thorns, roll with the playground box, and get stuck under the fence.

ASSESSMENT

- Where did Diana go on her walk?
- How did you move along Diana's walk?
- What happened when the wolf followed Diana on her walk?

Assessment Forms

- Participation Assessment form. Add this factor to the form: sequenced movements to follow the story line.
- Self-Assessment form (version appropriate for students' level).

Extensions

- This obstacle course can become a relay race. If you have more than one course set up, the groups can race against each other. Or you can have the wolf chase Diana when the students follow the course in pairs. Just be sure to give Diana enough of a head start to make it fair.

- Read *Rosie's Walk* by Pat Hutchins. Ask students to help set up a new obstacle course for Rosie. Try following Rosie's walk. Now, add the fox and follow Rosie's walk in pairs. You may want to explore the drama of the fox's getting into trouble along the way or make the course into a relay race.

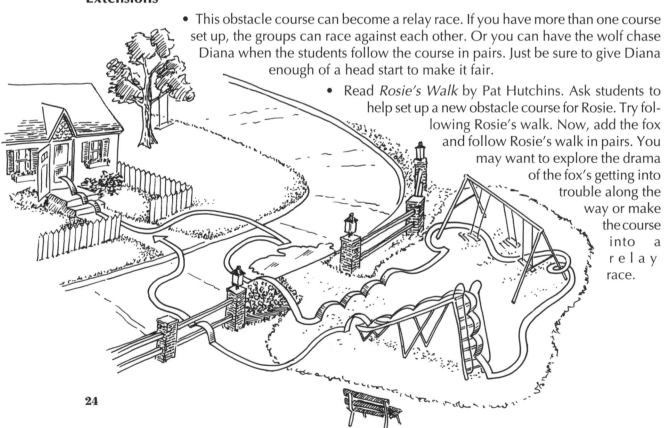

Flower Dance

AN INTERPRETIVE LESSON TO DEVELOP FLEXIBILITY AND ABDOMINAL STRENGTH.

GRADES: K TO 2   **LENGTH:** 20 MINUTES

Materials

MOVEnture CD track 3
- Audio playback system

National Standards

Physical Education: 1, 2, 5

Dance: 1, 2, 3

Objectives

The students will be able to do the following:

- Perform a teacher-directed dance sequence that requires abdominal strength and flexibility in the hamstrings and low back.
- Understand that nature can give us ideas for dances.
- Work cooperatively with peers to perform a group dance.

INTRODUCTION

This can be a warm-up or a cool-down activity.

Sit in a circle with the students, with toes pointing toward the center and legs together. This is called a toe pie. Have the students lie down on their backs and look up at the ceiling. Ask students what the group shape would look like to a bird flying over the group.   ⚙ **Imaging**

Explain that you think the group looks like a big flower, and each of you is a petal on the blossom. Many flowers close up at night, opening only in the light of day. So the group will dance that idea. Start by closing the flower.   ⚙ **Modeling**

THE MOVING ADVENTURE

1. Starting position: Students close the flower by folding their bodies over their legs (a pike position), keeping knees straight and toes pointed, reaching their hands long over their legs. This position requires flexibility when done correctly.

2. Instruct students to begin by slowly rolling down their backs onto the floor, which takes strength in the abdominal muscles. Arms should then rise up straight from the hips and over their heads to rest on the floor.

3. Each student raises the right leg into the air, pointing it with a straight knee toward the ceiling. Lower the leg. Repeat with the left leg.

4. Students then gently toss their legs over their heads (no longer keeping them pointed or straight) and then rock forward onto their feet into a squat. The squat position is with both hands and balls of the feet on the floor, knees between elbows. All students are now in a squat, facing into the circle.

5. From the squat position, each student picks a body part that slowly begins to reach toward the sky, such as an elbow, an ear, a hand, or a shoulder. As the body part reaches upward, their bodies grow until they are all standing in the circle.

6. Students create their own ways to twirl and melt down silently in their self-space at the edge of the circle, ending once again on their backs with their legs together and toes pointed toward the center, arms overhead on the floor.

7. All raise their arms off the floor, pointing their fingers toward their toes and curling their bodies up slowly (a sit-up), closing the flower and returning to the starting position. The sequence is now finished.

8. Now add music! The suggested selection on the MOVEnture CD is meant to create a mood for the dance. Students perform the dance in "felt time" rather than being guided by a specific rhythm in the music. This means that they try to do everything at the same time, staying together throughout the sequence of opening the flower, raising and lowering legs, growing, and closing the flower. When they have returned to starting position, fade the music manually. This lesson is a great way to increase children's sensitivity to others and to discipline one's own sense of timing to accommodate the group. ⚙ **Dimensional Thinking**

9. Share through the performance. Divide the class in half and have one group perform the Flower Dance while the other group observes. Elicit responses to questions such as "Did the students stay together?" and "What movements are your favorites to watch?"

ASSESSMENT

- Which of the movements was harder? What muscles do you think you needed to use to do those movements? (Here you can impart the names of the muscle groups as you guide them through reviewing the movement sequence.)

- Could you imagine what the whole flower looked like as it opened and closed? What other ideas for dancing could we borrow from nature? (Suggestions are animals, clouds, and water.)

Assessment Forms

- Movement Study Assessment form for teacher use and for student evaluation of the performance. Add these factors to the form: legs straight, pointed toes, abdominal strength, flexibility, working cooperatively.
- Self-Assessment form (version appropriate for students' level). Students can self-assess, covering the same performance objectives: legs straight, pointed toes, abdominal strength, flexibility, working cooperatively.

Extensions

- Examine blossoms from many kinds of common flower species. Observe their petal arrangements. Students could investigate whether the flowers close up at night, or they can work in small groups to arrange and interpret these blossoms using shape and levels.
- Have students draw, color, or paint their flowers.
- Related Moventure: Seed to Flower (lesson 72)

9 Over, Under, Around, and Through . . .Where Are You?

A LESSON IN SPACE EXPLORATION.

GRADES: K TO 2   **LENGTH:** 30 TO 40 MINUTES

Materials

MOVEnture CD track 6
- Audio playback system
- Scarves or newspapers

National Standards

Physical Education: 2

Dance: 1, 2

Objectives

The students will be able to do the following:
- Demonstrate the ability to define and maintain self-space.
- Demonstrate the ability to move safely in general space.
- Accurately demonstrate locomotor and nonlocomotor movements.

INTRODUCTION

Demonstrate options for selecting a self-space and making an appropriate choice. Take your scarf (newspaper) and place it close to a wall in the room. Stand behind the scarf and ask, "Is this a good choice for my self-space? No. I might bump into the wall, and I don't have enough space to move freely." Place the scarf in a space close to a student in the class and ask, "Is this a good choice for my self-space? No. I'm in Joey's space and we might bump into each other." Place the scarf next to a chair in the room and ask, "Is this a good choice for my self-space? Oh, dear, I would bump into the chair in this space." Finally, place the scarf in an open space and ask, "What about this space? Hooray! I found just the right space. Now, see if you can make a good choice for your self-space."

Each student takes a scarf (or newspaper) to a space, lays it flat on the floor, and stands behind it. (Fold the scarf or newspaper if space is limited.)

THE MOVING ADVENTURE

⚙ Body Thinking, Dimensional Thinking

1. Explore ways to travel over the scarf. Take a giant step over the scarf. Explain that if you take a giant step into the air it's called a leap. Have students show you a leap over the scarf. Ask who has another way to travel over the scarf. Point out individual students' ways of traveling over a scarf, such as jumping with two feet. Have all students jump over their scarves. Demonstrate a hop on one foot over the scarf.

2. Try moving under the scarf in various ways: Lift the scarf and slither under it. Do a log roll or a crawl while under the scarf. Make a shape while hiding under the scarf.

3. Stand close to the scarf and tiptoe around it. Remind students not to touch the scarf. Walk around forward, then try a backward walk. Ask what other choices they have for moving

around the scarf—a skip or a gallop, for example. Move at a low level and do a crab walk. Explain that the movements that travel are called locomotor movements.

4. Ask students to create a bridge shape over the scarf. Be careful not to touch the scarf. Have them look around to see all the different bridges over scarves. Everyone will make a bridge shape over the scarf when there is no music. When the music plays, explore ways to move over the scarf. Whenever the music stops, make a bridge over the scarf. Next time the music plays, move under the scarf. Once again, when the music stops, find a new bridge shape over the scarf. Finally, have students move around the scarf with a walk and listen for your directions to change their locomotor movements.

5. Explain to students that they have been moving in their self-space. Next, have them move through general space and share other people's scarves. They begin in a bridge shape over the scarf. When the music plays, they move over others' scarves scattered throughout the room. Tell them to watch out for others as they move. (You may want to designate a direction for everyone to move, such as clockwise.) When the music stops, they make a bridge shape alone, with a partner, or a small group over the nearest scarf. Continue exploration of general space using over, under, around, and a combination of all three.

ASSESSMENT

- Did you make a good choice for your self-space?
- Were you successful in traveling through general space without bumping into anyone?
- What kinds of locomotor movements did we use to travel through space?

Assessment Forms
- Movement Study Assessment form, for teacher use and for student evaluation of the performance.
- Peer Assessment form.

Extensions
- Create a movement phrase of over, under, around, and through to be repeated three times as a pattern. Select six students at a time to perform them for the class.
- Try moving with the scarf. Students pick up their own scarves and travel around the room clockwise with a walk and listen for your directions to change locomotor movement.
- Have students hold the scarves at chest level. They increase traveling speed to a jog or run and let go of the scarf. It's magic! As they travel, the air pressure against their chests holds the scarves in place.
- Toss and catch the scarf using different body parts. Try catching it with an elbow, knee, foot, back, or tummy. This can be useful as a warm-up for scarf juggling.

Who Can? I Can!

A TEACHER-CENTERED MOVEMENT POEM.

GRADES: K TO 2   **LENGTH:** 20 MINUTES

Materials

Hand drum or other percussion instruments, such as a bell, triangle, wood block, and tambourine

National Standards

Physical Education: 1, 2

Dance: 1, 2

Objectives

The students will be able to do the following:

- Perform locomotor and nonlocomotor skills in response to verbal cues.
- Form shapes at many levels.
- Explore the sensation of pride.

INTRODUCTION

Announce that you will read the "Who Can? I Can!" poem. Explain that it's made up of many questions that require answers. But the answers will not come from their voices. Their bodies can give the answers! (Proceed to read the poem.) Ask students to show you the answers with their bodies. Explain that there is one exception: The last line that reads, "I can, I can, me, me, me!" is a very proud statement. That part of the poem is the one time their voices and bodies get to answer together. Have them practice saying the line out loud, encouraging them to say it with pride and confidence.

THE MOVING ADVENTURE

1. The first time you explore this poem, let the students improvise in response. Have them start in self-space throughout the room. ⚙️ **Body Thinking**

Who Can? I Can!	Movements
Who can gallop?	Beat the drum at a galloping speed appropriate for this age group.
Who can skip?	Beat the drum at the same speed for the skip.
Who can twirl?	Ring a chime, finger cymbals, or a triangle as many times as you wish. Or scratch your fingernails on the drum but use no rhythm. Say the next line before the students get too dizzy.
Who can hoppity-hip-hip?	Hit a wood block.
Who can make a shape that is upside down?	Use a drum roll or tambourine. Wait for all to freeze in frozen shape
Who can make a shape that is like a tree?	Make soft drumming that decelerates. Wait for freeze.
Who can make a shape that is flat on the ground?	Pause after speaking, then as the last student finishes flat shape, say the final line.
Who can?	Students answer, "I can! I can! Me, me, me!"

by Diane Newman

2. Before repeating the movement adventure, spend time developing and memorizing the movements and shapes. Suggest more use of directions when traveling. (Ask if the students can gallop backward.) Or suggest different levels and sizes in their shapes (What kinds of trees are there? Little trees, pine trees, leafy tall trees, or trees that have fallen to the ground and become logs; all have different

shapes.) For the final line, encourage each student to create a very proud shape to finish on the last "Me!" using a variety of levels, gestures, and ideas to represent "I am proud of myself."

ASSESSMENT

- What locomotor (traveling) movements did you perform?
- What levels did you use to make shapes?
- What shape did you do at the end to show that you were proud of yourself?

Assessment Form

Movement Study Assessment form, for teacher use. Add these factors to the form: following directions, use of a variety of shapes, use of levels, originality.

Extensions

- Divide the class into two groups and have the students perform for each other, sharing comments.
- Have nonreading students write or draw a picture depicting a context in which they feel proud of themselves. Have readers write a brief essay on when they feel proud of themselves, such as in a specific incident or context. For example, "I felt proud of myself when I learned to ride my bike." "I feel proud when I help my grandmother do everyday things."

Do the Locomotion!

CREATING A DANCE WITH LOCOMOTOR MOVEMENTS.

GRADES: K TO 2   **LENGTH:** TWO 30-MINUTE SESSIONS

Materials

MOVEnture CD track 8 or 43
- Audio playback system
- Drum

National Standards

Physical Education: 1
Dance: 1, 3

Objectives

The students will be able to do the following:

- Identify the eight basic locomotor movements (walk, run, jump, hop, leap, slide, gallop, skip) when they are performed by peers.
- Create a dance with four different locomotor movements using ABA compositional form. In ABA form, A represents a movement phrase, B represents a different movement phrase, and A represents a return to the first movement phrase.

INTRODUCTION

Explain that when we travel across the room, we can travel on our feet in eight different ways. Ask students to tell you of ways to get from one side of the room to the other. Spend the next 30 minutes practicing the eight basic locomotor movements, then have the students create a dance using locomotor movements in a new combination.

THE MOVING ADVENTURE

1. Have the students walk through general space without bumping into anyone. Ask them to walk in the following ways: Walk low; walk high. Walk fast; walk slowly. Walk forward; walk backward. Walk proudly; walk sadly. Walk as if you are excited; walk as if you are afraid.

2. Have them hop on one foot five times, then switch to the other foot. Hop five times forward and five times backward. Hop five times fast and five times slowly.

3. Practice jumping. How is a jump different from a hop? The jump begins on two feet and ends on two feet. You bend your knees to prepare for a jump, take off into the air, and bend the knees when you land from your jump. Practice five times. Use your arms to help you. Swing the arms back when you bend and forward and up when you take off into the air. (Demonstrate the jumps.)

4. Divide the students in various ways and have them run. Have everyone wearing white run through general space. Remind them to stop on the signal. Then everyone wearing glasses should run through general space. Now everyone wearing yellow should run through general space.

5. A leap is a long run. A leap takes off on one foot and lands on the other foot. Imagine leaping over a large rock. Run and leap to this rhythm—run, run, leap; run, run, leap. Beat a drum with a short, short, long pattern (quarter note, quarter note, half note).

    run   run   leap   run   run   leap

    —   —   —   —   —   —

6. Skip, gallop, slide. Perform locomotor movements that are combinations of the simple locomotor movements. First, a skip—a combination of a walk and a hop. Next, perform a gallop—a combination of a walk and a leap. And finally, a slide—a combination of a walk and a leap moving sideways. Skip in a circular pathway and a straight pathway—knees high! Skip to the rhythm of the drum. Play an uneven drum beat: long, short, long, short, long, short, long.

1	and	2	and	3	and	4
step	hop	step	hop	step	hop	step

— – — – — – —

Have the students gallop in general space. Remind them to keep the same foot in front at all times. Now lead with the other foot. Remember to move in a forward direction. Then have everyone face you. Extend your arms at shoulder height and slide across the room. Remember to move sideways. Have both feet in the air, and bend your knees when you land and take off.

7. Creating the dance. Put several of the locomotor movements together to make a dance. Walk, hop, and skip. Perform each four times to the rhythm of the drum. Walk, 2, 3, 4, hop, 2, 3, 4, skip and 2 and 3 and 4 and. Now speed it up. Now slow it down.

Ask students to create their own ABA dance. Use the walk, hop, skip as the A section; select three different locomotor movements as the B section; then return to the walk, hop, and skip as the final A section. Give students three minutes to practice. Instruct students to add a beginning and ending shape to the ABA pattern together. Make a strong shape on a middle level to begin, and a strong shape on a low level to end. Then students all perform together. Instruct them to assume a strong shape, then begin. Hold ending shape until everyone else in the class is finished. Repeat two more times. ✿ **Forming Patterns**

8. Share through performance. Have half of the class perform while the other half observes like good audience members. Add background music. After each performance, question the students about the names of the locomotor movements.

ASSESSMENT

- Name the eight basic locomotor movements. Have one student at a time demonstrate a locomotor movement. The students raise their hands to provide answers to the question of what locomotor movement is being demonstrated.
- Have each student describe his or her ABA dance in locomotor terms to a partner. ✿ **Recognizing Patterns**

Assessment Form

Movement Study Assessment form, for teacher use.

Extension

Use the canon choreographic form as a locomotor movement dance. In a canon—like the song "Row, Row, Row Your Boat"—the locomotor movement phrases occur at different times with different individuals or groups.

12

Ahh! Relaxation

LEARNING STRATEGIES FOR RELAXATION.

GRADES: 3 TO 5   **LENGTH:** 20 TO 30 MINUTES

Materials

MOVEnture CD track 1 and 4
- Audio playback system

National Standards

Physical Education: 2

Dance: 6

Objectives

The students will be able to do the following:

- Perform a breathing exercise.
- Perform progressive relaxation.
- Perform a meditation activity.

INTRODUCTION

Explain that when we are tense, our muscles are tight, and we have trouble relaxing. Tell students that they will experience three ways to relax their bodies and minds.

THE MOVING ADVENTURE

⚙ Body Thinking

Students are in self-space, lying on their backs. Use the following prompts to guide your students in the relaxation exercises:

1. Breathing exercises: Concentrate on your breathing. Breathe in through your nose, and breathe out through your mouth, as if blowing through a straw. Let your belly expand as you breathe in and contract as you breathe out (demonstrate).

2. Progressive relaxation:
   - Tighten the muscles in your feet. Tight, tight, tight, now release and let go.
   - Tighten the muscles in your legs. Tight, tight, tight, now release and let go.
   - Take a deep, cleansing breath.
   - Tighten the muscles in your belly and buttocks. Tight, tight, tight, now release and let go.

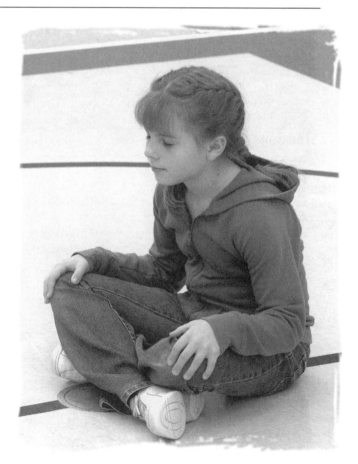

- Tighten the muscles in your hands and arms. Make a fist! Now release and let go.
- Tighten the muscles in your chest. Now release and let go.
- Bring your shoulders up by your ears and tighten. Now release and let go.
- Take another deep, cleansing breath.
- Now make a face. Frown, scrunch your nose, and hold that look! Now release and let go.
- Now tighten the muscles in your whole body. Tight, tight, tight, now release and let go.
- Repeat.

3. Meditation: Students sit in a crossed-leg position on the floor. Meditation is a strategy to help us quiet and focus our minds. Now every time you breathe out, think the word *one.* Inhale, expand your abdomen, and exhale, thinking the word *one.* Repeat. Your mind will begin to drift to other things. As soon as you are aware, just come easily back to the word *one.* Practice for 30 seconds. Now one minute.

ASSESSMENT

- How do you feel after relaxing today?
- Describe three types of relaxation activities.
- Create an assessment form to help you record your observations for the students' ability to contract and release muscles.

Assessment Form

None.

Extensions

✿ Imaging

- Students explore the use of imagery for relaxation.
- Students create an imagery script for themselves. For example, "Imagine your favorite place using all of your senses."

13

Energy Study

EXPLORING PERSONAL ENERGY THROUGH A GAME OF SELF-CONTROL.

GRADES: K TO 2; 3 TO 5
LENGTH: 15 MINUTES FOR K TO 2; 10 MINUTES FOR 3 TO 5

Materials
Drum

National Standards
Physical Education: 2, 5
Dance: 1, 3

Objectives

The students will be able to do the following:

- Describe personal energy and how muscles feel in different energy states.
- Control the force of their movements and actions.

INTRODUCTION

This is a good activity to use as an energy builder after lunch or on sluggish mornings or rainy days.

Explore personal energy with the students. Talk about examples of high-energy days—getting up in the morning and just feeling great. Maybe a good night's sleep, a good breakfast, or a birthday makes them excited and full of energy. Ask students to show you how they would sit if today were their birthday. (Students sit straighter and prouder; their facial expressions are brighter.) Now what if the opposite is true? Staying up too late, skipping breakfast, or feeling sick or sad can affect their energy levels. Ask them to show you how they would sit then. ⚙ **Body Thinking**

Play with these opposites. Have students make a shape so full of energy that they have to stand up and reach for the sun because the energy is so strong! Instruct them to reach with all of their personal energy. Tell them to freeze in that shape and notice how hard all their muscles are working.

Ask the students what happens to their bodies if they have absolutely no energy at all—not even enough to sit up. (Students should finally arrive at the solution that the body would be completely on the floor as if sleeping. Head, shoulders, elbows, and knees should not be raised off the floor because that requires too much energy.) Now tell them to be completely still in this shape and feel as relaxed as possible. Ask them what it feels like in their muscles when they are relaxed and have very little energy.

You are now ready to play a game using these two opposite shapes and two opposite states of personal energy: strong and relaxed.

THE MOVING ADVENTURE

1. In self-space, the students begin in the low-energy shape, lying on the floor. Say, "Going up." Begin counting slowly to 5 (this can be accompanied by five beats on a drum). The students gradually gain energy and rise from the floor so that by the fifth count, they are reaching toward the sun with all their energy. Even the counting can gain energy—give the voice more excitement and increase the pitch as you get to five.

2. Reverse the process, signaling by saying, "Going down." Count to 5 while losing energy in the voice as well as the body so that students return to the floor, ending in a relaxed position.

Adjectives such as *melting* assist the students in feeling the loss of energy. Students should arrive at the floor on time and should stay very still. ⚙ **Imaging**

3. Practice the activity again to increase students' familiarity with the rules and encourage stronger performance.

4. When satisfied with their accomplishment, tell them that they did it so well and easily that you have to make the game harder to challenge them. Ask them to subtract one count. Now they must gain and lose energy in 4 counts. (They love this.) Repeat the exercise with 4 counts. Continue to count down as students become successful at each level. Count down 3, 2, and finally 1! Encourage them to express the 1 as clearly as any of the other numbers, rocketing up to the high-energy shape and melting (not jumping to the floor) to the low energy (losing energy as if fainting). Remind them that how they lie on the floor is their own choice of position and that some shapes may be more helpful in rising quickly or melting to the floor on time.

ASSESSMENT

- What is personal energy? (The amount of energy a person uses to accomplish a task.)
- How did your muscles feel at high energy? (Tense, quivery, powerful.) At low energy? (Relaxed, soft, vulnerable.)
- How did you solve the problem of rising and falling when the time to do it got shorter?

Assessment Form

Movement Study Assessment form, for teacher use and for student evaluation of the performance. Have students travel across the floor in groups of two as you call out, "High energy!" or "Low energy!" Use the form to indicate each student's ability or inability to perform the concept.

Extensions

You can add challenge to the lesson in other ways:

- Repeat the entire game, requesting that the students use their bodies in more interesting ways as they gain and lose energy. Twist on the way up, slither on the way down, and so on.
- For a study in dynamics, students can move sharply (percussively) on each count when rising and move smoothly (sustained) when descending. Or rise smoothly and descend sharply.
- Repeat the activity, growing and melting in a different amount of time: 6 counts, 10 counts!
- Compliment the students on their success at controlling their energy. Remind them that just as they made choices for themselves during the dance lesson, they make all kinds of choices each day about how to act. Engage them in discussion, or have them write about matching the appropriate amount of energy to a given situation. Discuss personal responsibility—that people are accountable for their actions and that sometimes people *react* before they purposefully choose how they *should* act.
- Have fun connecting to the real-world context of the appropriate selection of energy and phenomena: food for personal energy, sun's heat to dry clothes on the line, wind-up toys, electrical energy for appliances, and so on.

14

Senses Aware!

SENSORY PERCEPTIONS THROUGH MOVEMENT.

GRADES: 3 TO 5   **LENGTH:** TWO 20-MINUTE SESSIONS

Materials

- Open classroom space
- Blindfolds for half the class
- Class journals

National Standards

Physical Education: 5

Dance: 1

Objectives

The students will be able to do the following:

- Learn how to express themselves and communicate with others.
- Demonstrate movement using changes in space and energy.
- Understand the contribution of the five senses in perception and interpretation of themselves in the environment.
- Build an awareness of disabilities.

INTRODUCTION

⚙ Observing, Transforming

Each of our five senses makes us aware of our world in a unique way. When we lose one of our senses, the remaining four senses become more intense. Ask students to imagine how their lives would change if they lost their sense of sight (blind) or hearing (deaf).

THE MOVING ADVENTURE

Session 1: Blindfold Walk

1. Partners (one blindfolded, one with hands on a partner's shoulders) walk around the classroom, building, or outdoors. The blindfolded partner should focus on her sense of touch, hearing, and smell. The blindfolded partner must trust her partner to guide her safely. Keep the first blind adventure short by moving around the classroom so that each partner understands the safety concerns and the students have an opportunity to reflect on what their senses perceived.

2. What were the textures, sounds, and smells that were most intense? Students might remember the texture of a wall, the

sound of the lights humming, the smell of lunch being prepared. Ask students if they can create a shape or movement representing the wall texture. It was a bumpy surface, so they should make a bumpy shape. The sound of the lights was a vibration, so they would move with a vibratory or shaking movement. The smell of lunch made them hungry, so can they find a "hungry shape" (rubbing the tummy or reaching out for food)? Tie these shapes and movements together with a simple walking pathway from the blindfold walk. Ask students to record in their journals their sensory experience.

Session 2: Quick Draw

Partners stand, one with the back turned to the other. The back represents a canvas or sketchpad. Partner 1 uses a finger to draw a simple pathway line on partner 2's back. Partner 2 must feel the pathway (touch) and then travel through space following the same pathway. He may interpret the pathway with what he thinks is an appropriate locomotor movement. For example, if partner 1 draws with a dotted line, partner 2 may choose to jump or hop along that line. Ask them to draw their pathway lines in their journals. You can choose to have them draw their pathways before or after they travel. Partners can respond to the pathway performed by looking for the lines they drew and appreciating the movement interpretation.

ASSESSMENT

- What sense did we lose in these two experiences?
- What senses became more intense, and how did you use them?
- How was your partner helpful in guiding you through the experiences?
- Have your students reflect on their experiences in their journal.

Assessment Forms

- Participation Assessment form.
- Self-assessment form (version appropriate for students' level).

Extensions

- Invite students to perform their blind walk experience using the three shapes or movements along a designated pathway for their partners. Partners respond to the performance by interpreting what they observed.
- Discuss disabilities and what makes each of us unique. Reflect on how a person might adapt her lifestyle or her environment to accommodate a disability.

Seven Jumps

A DANISH FOLK DANCE.

GRADES: 3 TO 5 **LENGTH:** TWO 30-MINUTE SESSIONS

Materials

 MOVEnture CD track 5
- Audio playback system

National Standards

Physical Education: 1
Social Studies: 1, 3
Dance: 1

Objectives

The students will be able to do the following:
- Perform the Danish folk dance Seven Jumps.
- Execute good balance and control.

INTRODUCTION

Explain that students will perform the Danish folk dance called Seven Jumps. The dance is from the country of Denmark. This is in the continent of Europe. (Show map if possible.) The dance was originally done by men as an elimination dance. If they lost their balance during the holds, they would be "out." Explain that you and the students will all do the dance together and that there will be no elimination, but you do expect all of them to keep their relationship in the circle as they move around it. Give the example of the way a merry-go-round moves: The horses don't get closer together just because the merry-go-round is going around. Tell students to focus on having good balance during the holds.

THE MOVING ADVENTURE

⚙ Forming Patterns

Part I

Students should hold hands in a circle formation.

Beats	Movement Description
1-7	Step-hop seven times clockwise beginning with the left foot.
8	Jump on both feet.
9-16	Step-hop seven times counterclockwise beginning with the right foot. Release hands in preparation for next part.

Part II

Place hands on hips.

Sustained chord 1	Raise right knee.
Next chord	Place right foot back on floor.
Last sustained chord	Wait.

Repeat Part I

Part III

Place hands on hips. Repeat movements for sustained chord 1 and add on:

Sustained chord 2	Raise left knee.
Next chord	Place left foot back on floor.
Last sustained chord	Wait

Repeat Part I
Part IV

Place hands on hips. Repeat movements for sustained chords 1 and 2 and add on:

Sustained chord 3	Kneel on right knee.
Next chord	Stand back up.
Last sustained chord	Wait.

Repeat Part I
Part V

Place hands on hips. Repeat movements for sustained chords 1, 2, and 3 and add on:

Sustained chord 4	Kneel on left knee.
Next chord	Stand back up.
Last sustained chord	Wait.

Repeat Part I
Part VI

Place hands on hips. Repeat movements for sustained chords 1, 2, 3, and 4 and add on:

Sustained chord 5	Place right elbow on floor.
Next chord	Stand back up.
Last sustained chord	Wait.

Repeat Part I
Part VII

Place hands on hips. Repeat movements for sustained chords 1, 2, 3, 4, and 5 and add on:

Sustained chord 6	Place left elbow on the floor.
Next chord	Stand back up.
Last sustained chord	Wait.

Repeat Part I
Part VIII

Place hands on hips. Repeat movements for sustained chords 1, 2, 3, 4, 5, and 6 and add on:

Sustained chord 7	Touch forehead to the floor.
Next chord	Stand back up.
Last sustained chord	Wait.

Ending: repeat Part I

ASSESSMENT

How did you keep your body under control while you were dancing?

Assessment Form

Self-Assessment form. Do this lesson more than once using the self-assessment tool to document progress.

Extension

Draw a picture of the type of apparel that might be worn by people from Denmark performing this folk dance.

16

Straight, Curved, Zigzag, Dot!

A LESSON ON PATHWAYS.

GRADES: 3 TO 5   **LENGTH:** 20 TO 30 MINUTES

Materials

 MOVEnture CD track 41, other music selection with a walking rhythm, or other percussion artists such as Brent Lewis or Mickey Hart

- Audio playback system

National Standards

Physical Education: 1, 2

Visual Arts: 3

Dance: 1, 2

Objectives

The students will be able to do the following:

- Perform the three basic pathways while traveling through general space: straight, curved, and zigzag.
- Perform a variety of locomotor movements.

INTRODUCTION

This lesson can be used as a warm-up or as a full lesson on exploration of pathways. Pathways can be readily connected to map making, positional concepts, and visual arts (which share the same vocabulary for the shapes of lines).

Introduce the subject of pathways. Tell the students to imagine a girl walking in a gymnasium. There are three basic pathways that she can take as she travels through the general space: She can walk in a *straight line,* she can walk in a *curvy* path, or she can *zigzag* as she travels. No matter how she travels, her pathway will be made up of a combination of these three pathways. Explore these pathways together.

THE MOVING ADVENTURE

1. Have the students pretend to brush paint on their feet in a color they choose. Instruct them to walk about the room, making imaginary footprints on the floor as they travel. Ask them to make only straight-line footprints with only sharp corners whenever they change directions. (This can be done in silence, or you can introduce music that has a nice walking rhythm.) Remind them that they can move forward, sideways, or backward as long as they make only straight-line paths with sharp corners. ☼ **Imaging**

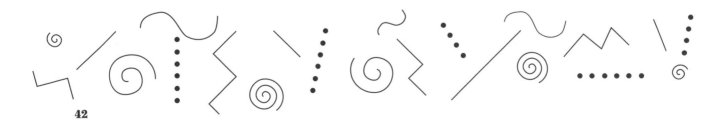

2. Repeat the exercise, putting a new color of paint on their feet and walking in only curvy pathways.

3. Repeat for a new color and zigzag the paths.

4. Now have students *jump* one of the three pathways, the result of which will be a pattern of dots on the floor. (Remember that a jump is from two feet to two feet.) Students can perform just one of the pathways, or they can quickly change from one pathway to another to create a "polka-dot" effect. (This is similar to the technique of pointillism in visual arts. Pointillism is a technique of painting in which a lot of tiny dots are combined to form a picture.)

5. Now explore these pathways again, but instruct the students to pretend paint is on parts of their bodies other than their feet. How would they make colored pathways on the floor with their elbows? Their knees? Their tailbones? Belly buttons? Making dots with these is very interesting! ⚙ **Imaging, Dimensional Thinking**

ASSESSMENT

- What are the three basic pathways we can use to travel through space?
- What locomotor movements did you use to travel along your pathways?

Assessment Form

Movement Study Assessment form, for teacher use. Add these factors to the form: straight, curved, and zigzag pathways. As students travel across the floor in groups of two, call out different types of pathways, recording their ability to perform the tasks correctly.

Extensions

- Repeat the activity, allowing the students to use any kind of locomotor (traveling) movements as long as they are true to the design of the path. Add instrumental percussion music (no lyrics) as background. To assess, use the Movement Study Assessment form to indicate each student's ability to travel the different kinds of pathways using a variety of locomotor movements.

- To increase their familiarity with pathways as well as connect to visual arts, instruct the students to draw each of the three pathways on paper with a crayon as follows: First, have them draw a single straight line on the paper. Where that line stops, start the next single line but make it curvy this time, allowing it to change directions. Next, connect a zigzag line to the curvy line. And finally, have them make two or more dots in the vicinity of where the zigzag line finishes. Encourage them to use the whole paper and not to confine the drawing as a small design in the middle of the page. The final drawing should be one continuous line that starts out straight, gets curvy and then zigzaggy, but ends with an array of dots. Now instruct the students to pretend the design they have just drawn is a map. Encourage them to use different locomotor movements to travel the straight line, the curved line, the zigzag line, and the dots as one connected sequence. Create a strong starting shape and a clear ending shape. ⚙ **Transforming**

- Perform the "maps" in smaller groups for the rest of the class.

- Related Moventure: Expedition (lesson 58).

17

Express Yourself!

SELF-EXPRESSION THROUGH MOVEMENT QUALITIES.

GRADES: 3 TO 5 **LENGTH:** FOUR 30-MINUTE SESSIONS
(TWO FOR MOVEMENT ADVENTURE, ONE FOR CREATING,
ONE FOR PERFORMING AND SHARING)

Materials

MOVEnture CD track 14
• Audio playback system

National Standards

Physical Education Standard: 2

Theater: 2

Dance: 3

Objectives

The students will be able to do the following:

- Perform movement qualities (percussive, sustained, swinging, vibratory, and suspended and collapsed).
- Express various emotions through movement.

INTRODUCTION

Explain that the qualities of movement will be helpers to the students as they express themselves through movement. The movement qualities are sustained, percussive, swinging, vibratory, and suspended and collapsed.

THE MOVING ADVENTURE

Qualities of Movement

- Sustained movement has no distinct beginning or ending; it is smooth. Instruct students to move a finger in a sustained manner. Then move an arm, now the whole body. Move through general space in a sustained manner. The movement does not have to be slow, just never ending.
- Percussive movement has a distinct beginning and ending; it is sharp movement with sudden and dynamic changes in the speed and rhythm. Tell students to start with a finger, then the arms. Then add the whole body as they move percussively through the general space.
- The swinging body part begins with the release of the swinging part into gravity, then the lift and suspension on the other side of the arc and the drop back into the pull of gravity again. Tell students to swing the head side to side. Swing arms side to side and forward and back. Swing while walking in general space.
- Vibratory movement occurs when the body or part of the body moves in very short, percussive movements—shaking like a jackhammer. Tell students to move arms, legs, head, and whole body in a vibratory manner.
- Suspended and collapsed movement work together. Suspend high and collapse low. Start with the finger only, then the arms. Suspend and collapse the upper body. Suspend and collapse the whole body to the ground.

Sustained

Pairing Emotions With Movement Qualities

Connect a feeling with a movement quality. (Use appropriate music or sounds.) Guide students through the following explorations:

- Happiness expressed with swinging movements
- Anger expressed with percussive movements
- Excitement expressed with percussive movements
- Contentment expressed with sustained movements
- Sadness expressed with sustained movements
- Fear expressed with vibratory movements
- Nervousness expressed with vibratory movements
- Anticipation and disappointment expressed with suspended and collapsed movements

Imaging and Transforming

⚙️ **Imaging, Transforming**

- Instruct students to lie down in self-space. Tell them to fill their minds with an experience of when they were very happy. Ask them to think about all of the details: See the people or place very clearly; hear the sounds of the place; feel the texture of the place and time. Have students move through general space expressing the happiness they felt at that time. Have them include movement qualities and locomotor and nonlocomotor movements.

- Students again lie down in self-space. Tell them to fill their minds with an experience of when they were very sad. Ask them to think about all of the details: See the people or place very clearly; hear the sounds of the place; feel the texture of the place and time. Students then move through general space expressing the sadness they felt at that time. Have them include movement qualities and locomotor and nonlocomotor movements.

- Students lie down in self-space. They fill their minds with an experience of when they were very angry. They think about all of the details: See the people or place very clearly; hear the sounds of the place; feel the texture of the place and time. Students move through general space expressing the anger they felt at that time. They include movement qualities and locomotor and nonlocomotor movements.

- Students lie down in self-space. They fill their minds with an experience of when they were very afraid. They think about all of the details: See the people or place very clearly; hear the sounds of the place; feel the texture of the place and time. They move through general space expressing the fear they felt at that time. They include movement qualities and locomotor and nonlocomotor movements.

- Students lie down in self-space. They fill their minds with an experience of when they were excited with anticipation of something, then became disappointed when it did not happen.

They think about all of the details: See the people or place very clearly; hear the sounds of the place; feel the texture of the place and time. They move through general space expressing the anticipation and disappointment they felt at that time. They include movement qualities and locomotor and nonlocomotor movements.

- Come to an ending and have the students lie back down on the floor.

Create a Dance

- Have students create a dance about one of their experiences. They express the emotions they experienced through movement. Use the shape, move, shape choreographic form (see description in Vocabulary of Dance and Movement, p. 295).
- Remind them to start with a beginning shape and end with an ending shape. Then begin the dance.
- Tell students to hold their ending shapes until everyone in the class is finished.

Share and Guess

Each student shares his or her dance with one other person in class. The partner guesses the emotions included in the dance. They discuss the qualities of movement used in the self-expression dance.

ASSESSMENT

Demonstrate and name the qualities of movement.

Assessment Form

Partner Assessment of Movement Qualities. As a final assessment, invite each of the partners to evaluate the other partner's ability to perform each of the movement qualities.

Extension

- Ask students to write a paragraph or draw a picture about one of the emotions they expressed through movement.
- Related lessons: How Are You Feeling?, lesson 6; The Art of Silence, lesson 31; The Animal Tale, lesson 92.

Towers

SHARING WEIGHT (MASS) THROUGH CANTILEVER SHAPES.

GRADES: 3 TO 5   **LENGTH:** TWO 20- TO 25-MINUTE SESSIONS

Materials

MOVEnture CD track 6
- Audio playback system
- Drum

National Standards

Physical Education: 2, 5
Dance: 1, 2

Objectives

The students will be able to do the following:
- Define and describe a cantilever shape.
- Perform cantilever shapes.
- Sequence movement patterns to rhythm.

INTRODUCTION

This activity would be a good beginning-of-the-year activity for building trust and a sense of cohesion within the classroom. It is also a good warm-up for other movement activities.

This Moventure requires students to work with a partner. The partners must find a balance together by pushing or pulling. The lesson is called Towers because it begins with every partnership standing facing each other, hands pressed together overhead. The distance between the partners should be farther between their feet than their shoulders. They lean into the palms of each other's hands to find a common balance. This shape resembles a tower. (Pick a volunteer to demonstrate the shape with you, as shown in the accompanying photo.)

With your volunteer, create a tower shape with your bodies while balanced together. Explain that if your partner takes her hands away, you will fall forward. So in this shape you are pushing or leaning to find a common balance. Ask students to think about what happens if they grab wrists with their partner and pull away from each other. If they both keep their feet flat on the floor and pull their hips backward, they can lower themselves to almost sitting on the ground and not lose their balance. And they can rise up again just as successfully. (Demonstrate with partner.)

Sharing your weight through pushing or pulling to find a common balance like this is called a cantilever shape. Tell students to find a partner and try these two cantilevers, one pushing at high level and one pulling at low level. Point out the element of trust required between partners to work together to succeed—a serious purpose that must be remembered even when having fun together.

THE MOVING ADVENTURE

Session 1: Rhythmic Study

1. This dance is a rhythmic study using 32 counts, or four 8-beat sequences. Partnerships start by finding self-space together in the room. The starting shape is the tower cantilever, the one leaning together at a high level. Each student should lift one heel from the floor.

2. Give students a steady 8-beat rhythm, the same speed as the music on the CD, by drumming, clapping, or counting out loud. On each beat, the students must drop one heel and lift the other.

3. Instruct students to grab wrists and practice the pulling cantilever shape, lowering and rising back to the tower shape. When all have worked it out, give them 4 even counts to lower and 4 counts to rise. Practice all 16 counts from the beginning.

4. Partnerships now decide to designate one partner to be an "A" and one partner to be a "B." The A partner freezes into a shape that has lots of empty spaces (negative space), which the B partner can go over, under, around, and through for the next 16 counts. A hand, head, or foot can explore small spaces, and the whole body can explore wide spaces, such as by standing with wide legs and having the partner crawl through underneath. Students should return to the tower shape by the 16th count. ⚙ **Dimensional Thinking**

5. Students repeat the dance from the beginning, reversing roles during the A and B sections.

Session 2: Now Add the Music

The rhythm and phrasing will be the same as your drumming and counting. Initially you will have to help the students count the 16 beats during the A and B sections because they are busy having fun exploring the negative space and often lose track of time. When the students are more proficient at this activity, tell them that you will no longer count out loud or signal them that the 16th beat is coming; you will expect them to count on their own.

ASSESSMENT

- Who can define a cantilever shape in words? Who can demonstrate the two that were used in this dance?
- What was challenging about the dance Towers? Were you able to count the A and B sections on your own? Did you get back to your partner on time?
- Can you relate what you learned from this lesson to anything else in your life?

Assessment Forms

- Movement Study Assessment form, for teacher use and for student evaluation of the performance. Add these factors to the form: cantilevers, return on time, partner skills (taking turns, level of cooperation).
- Peer Assessment form.

Extensions

- As proficiency improves, you can vary the dance by allowing students to explore many of the nearby frozen shapes during the A and B sections, as long as students return to their own partner by the 16th count.
- Have the students experiment with different cantilever shapes, using a variety of connections to find a common balance: grasping elbows and pulling, leaning back to back, pulling with a handshake. Remember, cantilever shapes must include pushing or pulling, a type of force. If a student holds another student off the floor completely on her own and can find a balance, this is not a cantilever. In dance terms this is called a lift. Cantilevers require mutual sharing of force as well as weight. This is the test of a cantilever: If they let go of their connection, do they both start to fall? If no, then it is not a cantilever.
- Try three-person cantilevers.
- The use of cantilevers is an integral part of architecture. The flying buttress, as shown by the Notre Dame Cathedral in Paris and other gothic churches, allowed for extremely high ceilings without a multitude of columns to hold them up. Churches became much more open in their interior spatial design. Pictures of these buildings demonstrate how the high-level tower shape imitates this openness when it begins to pull back for the sitting-behind-heels shape. As the hips begin to pull back to sit, a wider space is created at the top of the shape and the ceiling of the building widens. The hips are the flying buttress.

19

Jump, Everybody, Jump!

JUMPING PATTERNS.

GRADES: 3 TO 5   **LENGTH:** 20 MINUTES

Materials

MOVEnture DVD

MOVEnture CD track 7

• Audio playback system

National Standards

Physical Education: 4

Dance: 1, 6

Objectives

The students will be able to do the following:

• Perform aerobic activity for cardiovascular conditioning and endurance.

• Accurately demonstrate a jump and jump variations.

• Perform a choreographed rhythmic movement sequence with accuracy.

INTRODUCTION

A jump requires taking off from two feet and landing on two feet. Talk to your students about when a jump happens in sports and recreation, such as jumping for height or for distance. Jumping is an impact movement that offers excellent conditioning and, in repeating the jump pattern that follows, students can develop aerobic endurance.

THE MOVING ADVENTURE

1. Working in self-space, facing front, students start with feet together, parallel first position (feet next to each other with toes facing forward).

2. Have students try a jump in parallel first position.

3. Remind students to bend their knees at the start of their jump (to push off) and at the landing, absorbing the impact by rolling through their feet, from the balls of the feet to heels when landing.

4. When performing a tuck jump, pull knees into chest in the air; in a pike jump legs extend straight in front while in the air. ⚙ **Body Thinking**

Counts	Movement Description
1-4	Jump four times in parallel first.
5-8	Repeat four jumps in second position (feet shoulder-width apart).
1-4	Jump together, apart, together, apart.
& 5	Jump, cross feet together in the air, land in parallel second.
6	Hold.
& 7	Jump, cross feet together in the air, land in parallel second.
8	Jump to parallel first.
1-3	Jump three times with feet together (parallel first).
& 4	Jump by lifting the right knee and then the left knee "over the brook" to the right.

& 5	Tuck jump and hit your knees.
& 6	Pike jump (straight legs forward), stretch hands to toes while in the air.
7	Jump with feet in parallel first.
&	Jump with feet shoulder-width apart.
8	Jump feet wider than shoulder-width apart.

Return to parallel first and repeat the pattern.

5. Remember to allow time for the students to fully stretch their legs and cool down before and after jumping.

ASSESSMENT

- Did you bring your heels to the floor and bend your knees on the landing of each jump?
- How many times could you repeat the jump pattern?
- Did you perform the 16-count pattern with accuracy?
- What movement in the jump pattern did you find most difficult?
- Which movement was easiest for you?

Assessment Forms

- Participation Assessment form, for teacher use. Add these factors to the form: jump technique, pattern performance, aerobic endurance.
- Self-assessment form (version appropriate for students' level).

Extensions

- Create your own jump pattern. Invite students to explore jump variations and build their own sequence of movements using counts. ✿ Pattern Forming
- The following are suggested jump variations:
  - Do jump turns in place: quarter, half, three quarters, and full.
  - Do contrasting jumps: forward and back, light and heavy, big and little.
  - Change the speed, height, or force of jumps.
  - Alternate one foot forward and one foot backward.
  - Jump from a crouched position.
  - Jump over a spot on the floor or something or someone.
  - Jump forward, backward, side to side.
- Teach your jump pattern to a partner. Have students combine their patterns with a partner's pattern and perform them together.

20

Bouncing Buddies

BALL-HANDLING SEQUENCES.

GRADES: 3 TO 5   **LENGTH:** 30 TO 45 MINUTES

Materials

MOVEnture CD track 8
- Audio playback system
- Playground balls or basketballs

National Standards

Physical Education: 1

Dance: 1, 2

Objectives

The students will be able to do the following:

- Demonstrate proficiency in ball-handling skills.
- Demonstrate accuracy in moving to a musical beat.
- Demonstrate kinesthetic awareness and concentration in performance.

INTRODUCTION

Review ball-handling skills appropriate for the students' developmental level. Select a favorite song and perform the skills to the rhythmic phrasing of the melody. The students will have fun adding ball-handling skills of their own like the Harlem Globetrotters do. Set the sequence of ball-handling skills to the melody and practice, practice, practice. ⚙ **Body Thinking**

THE MOVING ADVENTURE

Introduce the following skills:

- Bending-knee bounce
- Tossing ball from right hand to left hand
- Tossing and catching overhead
- Slow bouncing in place
- Turning in place and setting the ball on the floor (or preparing to pass)
- Bounce-passing to partner
- Dribbling in place at different levels (one knee down or standing)
- Traveling dribble
- Pivoting
- Manipulating ball around legs
- Lunging and reaching or faking a pass right and then left
- Lifting the ball overhead and spinning in place

Students can repeat any of these skills throughout the song to complement the melody. Tempo can vary depending on the skill being performed and the students' ability. Students can perform these skills solo, with a partner, or in a group (circle or line formations).

ASSESSMENT

- What is the sequence of skills performed?
- How did it feel performing ball-handling skills to a rhythm?
- Was there a skill that was especially difficult for you to maintain control of the ball?

Assessment Form

Self-Assessment form (version appropriate for students' level).

Extensions

- Select an assortment of music with a recognizable beat to accompany dribbling drills. Musical accompaniment adds to the enjoyment and motivation for developing ball-handling skills.
- Younger students can explore the rhythm and motion of dribbling using an imaginary ball (air ball).

21 Rockin' to the Oldies

AN AEROBIC WORKOUT.

GRADES: 3 TO 5   **LENGTH:** 20 TO 30 MINUTES

Materials

- A Child's Celebration of Dance Music and Best of Rock 'n Roll of the 50s (see References and Resources)
- Audio playback system

National Standards

Physical Education: 4

Music: 7

Dance: 1, 6

Objectives

The students will be able to do the following:

- Explain how regular aerobic exercise contributes to healthful living.
- Demonstrate accuracy in moving to a musical beat and responding to changes in tempo.
- Accurately demonstrate locomotor and nonlocomotor movements.

INTRODUCTION

A certain intensity and duration of exercise are required for conditioning the muscles and cardiorespiratory system, leading to physical fitness. Keep in mind that good conditioning exercise is not overly strenuous. The aerobic exercise session appropriate for each student is dependent on the student's level of conditioning. Students should do continuous aerobic exercise for a minimum of 15 minutes to attain a well-conditioned heart rate. Remind students to keep their feet moving during the 15- to 20-minute session and follow the movement phrases you demonstrate. After the students have practiced the phrases, you can invite a student or two to lead the class. ⚙ **Body Thinking**

THE MOVING ADVENTURE

1. Aerobic dance uses basic step patterns to complement the selected recorded music. The following musical selections have a 1950s theme and total close to 15 minutes of continuous movement.
2. Before you begin, introduce the steps to be performed in the movement phrases and have students find self-space scattered throughout the general space.

Duke of Earl

Introduction

- Seated butterfly position: Soles of feet are together.
- Extended: Legs are extended in front.
- Straddle: Legs are open to sides.
- Round back: Drop head toward toes.
- Flat back: Reach arms forward with straight back.
- Isolations: Move one body part at a time.

- Lateral stretch: With arm overhead, do a side stretch while facing front of room.
- Runner's stretch: Front knee is bent, back leg is straight (lunge stretch).

Movements

Counts 1-8	Sit in butterfly position, round over, and tap floor for 8 counts.
Counts 1-8	Reach with flat back and click fingers for 8 counts.
Counts 1-8	Extend legs in front, round over, point toes, and tap floor for 8 counts.
Counts 1-8	Reach with flat back and flexed feet and click fingers for 8 counts.
Counts 1-8	Open legs to straddle, round over, point toes, and tap floor for 8 counts.
Counts 1-8	Reach with flat back and flexed feet and click fingers for 8 counts.
Counts 1-8	Twist toward right leg, round over, point toes, and tap floor for 8 counts.
Counts 1-8	Reach with flat back toward the right leg and flexed feet and click fingers for 8 counts.
Counts 1-8	Twist toward left leg, round over, and tap floor for 8 counts.
Counts 1-8	Reach with flat back and flexed feet and click fingers for 8 counts.

Repeat round-back and flat-back stretch in butterfly position, extended, straddle center, and right and left.

Counts 1-12	Stand.
Counts 1-8	Do head isolations side to side.
Counts 1-8	Do shoulder isolations up and down.
Counts 1-16	Do lateral stretch right and left (8 counts each).
Counts 1-8	Do open-arm stretch.
Counts 1-32	Do slow runner's stretch right, left, right, left (8 counts each).

Rockin' Robin

Introduction

- Step kick, step kick, run, run, run, clap. (See description in verse.)
- Pony step: Step down on right, up left, down right. Curve left arm overhead, curve right arm under.
- Slide, step together.
- Cross elbow to knee.
- Do the "bird"—flap wings, perch, peck.

Verse

Counts 1-2	Step right, kick left.
Counts 3-4	Step left, kick right.
Counts 5-6	Step right, kick left.
Counts 7-8	Step left, kick right.
Counts 1-4	Run in place right, left, right, clap.
Counts 5-8	Run in place left, right, left, clap.

Repeat two 8-count sequences.

Refrain

Counts 1-4	Pony step right.
Counts 5-8	"Rockin'"—Pony step left.
Counts 1-4	"Robin"—Pony step right.
Counts 5-8	Pony step left.
Counts 1-16	Flap wings—do the "bird."

Repeat verse and refrain sequences.

Counts 1-4	Slide right, feet together right, clap.
Counts 5-8	Slide left, feet together left, clap.
Counts 1-4	Right elbow to left knee, left elbow to right knee.
Counts 5-8	Right elbow to left knee, left elbow to right knee.

Repeat.

Counts 1-4	Slide right, feet together right, clap.
Counts 5-8	Slide left, feet together left, clap.
Counts 1-4	Right elbow to left knee, left elbow to right knee.
Counts 5-8	Right elbow to left knee, left elbow to right knee.

Verse

Counts 1-2	Step right, kick left.
Counts 3-4	Step left, kick right.
Counts 5-6	Step right, kick left.
Counts 7-8	Step left, kick right.
Counts 1-4	Run in place right, left, right, clap.
Counts 5-8	Run in place left, right, left, clap.

Repeat two 8-count sequences.

Refrain

Counts 1-4	Pony step right.
Counts 5-8	"Rockin'"—Pony step left.
Counts 1-4	"Robin"—Pony step right.
Counts 5-8	Pony step left.
Counts 1-16	Flap wings—do the "bird."

Repeat verse and refrain sequences three times to the end.

At the Hop

Introduction: Hold for 8 counts.

Verse

Counts 1-2	Step right, extend left heel, feet together, arms push up.
Counts 3-4	Step left, extend right heel, feet together.
Counts 5-6	Step right, extend left heel, feet together.
Counts 7-8	Step left, extend right heel, feet together.
Counts 1-8	Repeat with arms press forward.
Counts 1-8	Repeat with arms push down.

Refrain

Counts 1-4	Run forward, clap.
Counts 5-8	"Let's go"—Run backward, clap.
Counts 1-8	"to the hop"—Knees up right, left, right, left.
Counts 1-4	Run forward, clap.
Counts 5-8	Run backward, clap.
Counts 1-8	Knees up right, left, right, left.
Counts 1-8	Dig step right, dig step left, rock step (back right, forward left).
Counts 1-8	Dig step right, dig step left, rock step (back right, forward left).

Repeat verse and refrain sequences.

Counts 1-24	Free dance.

Verse

Repeat theme step in 8 counts: arms push up, press forward, push side, push down.
Continue moving feet in 4 counts.

Counts 1-4	Arms push up.
Counts 5-8	Arms press forward.
Counts 1-4	Arms push side.
Counts 5-8	Arms push down.

Continue moving feet.

Counts 1-2	Arms push up.
Counts 3-4	Arms press forward.
Counts 5-6	Arms push side.
Counts 7-8	Arms push down.

Repeat in 2 counts.

Counts 1-16	End in free dance.

Yakety Yak

Introduction

- Lunge with arm reach.
- Do grapevine step.
- Run in a circle, shoulder press.

Movements

Counts 1-4	Lunge, extending right leg back, reaching right arm forward.
Counts 5-8	Lunge, extending left leg back, reaching left arm forward.
Counts 1-4	Do grapevine right.
Counts 5-8	Do grapevine left.
Counts 1-8	Run in a clockwise circle (around self-space).
Counts 1-2	Press right shoulder toward left knee, hands on knees.
Counts 3-4	Press left shoulder toward right knee.
Counts 5-6	Press right shoulder toward left knee.
Counts 7-8	Press left shoulder toward right knee.

Finish with a reach!

Ask students to walk three times around the space and take a heart rate. Repeat the "Duke of Earl" stretch to complete the cool-down.

ASSESSMENT

- How did your breathing and heartbeat change as your aerobic workout progressed?
- Did you find the workout easier after two or three days of conditioning?
- What sports provide you with aerobic conditioning?
- Was it difficult to find your pulse?
- Develop a conditioning chart to help you and your students track progress.

Assessment Form

Participation Assessment form.

Extensions

- The target heart rate zone provides a means for regulating exercise performance. Demonstrate finding a pulse. Ask students to find the pulse immediately after the exercise and count for 6 seconds. Multiply by 10 to obtain the count for a minute. They quickly learn that all they need to do is add a 0 to their number to get their pulse rate. Provide students with an appropriate target zone. The maximum heart rate (MHR) formula is 220 minus age in years, multiplied by 60% to 80%. For example, the target heart rate zone for a 7-year-old child (second grader) is calculated to be 128 to 170 beats per minute, or 12.8 to 17 beats every 6 seconds.
- Discuss what activities are aerobic and why. Suggest participation in an aerobic activity three times a week for at least 30 minutes as homework. Ask students to record their exercise activity for two weeks and share it with the class.

chapter 4

MOVEntures
in Language Arts

Besides the obvious use of dance as a tool for acting out or conveying a story, dance can reinforce the glorious love of words. Lesson plans that provide engaging opportunities to explore subjects such as grammar and punctuation, which often seem boring to students, become moments of anticipated pleasure. Teaching vowels to kindergarteners by reciting and marching the familiar chant "A, E, I, O, U, and sometimes Y!" sets up a repetitive, rhythmic pattern for both the body and the brain to practice and remember. Consequently, whether you're teaching alliteration or creative writing, the iambic pentameter or the stringent form of haiku, dance becomes the glue that helps make concepts stick.

The beauty of words in song, story, and everyday conversations can lift us from the ordinary to the extraordinary. Children love to be read to, and adults love to read to them, inspiring their imaginations to believe the possibilities ahead of them are limitless. The power of words, coupled with the power of dance, is a unique aesthetic. The popularity of musical theater, opera, and contemporary dance are evidence of this aesthetic.

22

Vowel Vamp

MOVING TO LEARN VOWELS.

GRADES: K TO 2   **LENGTH:** 15 MINUTES

Materials
Hand drum

National Standards
Language Arts: 5, 6
Music: 1
Dance: 1, 2

Objectives
The students will be able to do the following:
- Recite the vowels of the alphabet.
- Move and freeze with a rhythmic chant (use timing).
- Perform a variety of locomotor (traveling) steps.

INTRODUCTION

Explain which letters of the alphabet are vowels. Then have the students rehearse the following chant: A, E, I, O, U, and sometimes Y! Accompany them with 8 beats on the drum so that they voice the chant rhythmically as follows:

> Beat 1: A
>
> Beat 2: E
>
> Beat 3: I
>
> Beat 4: O
>
> Beat 5: U
>
> Beat 6: and sometimes
>
> Beat 7: Y!
>
> Beat 8: Silent

Repeat many times.

THE MOVING ADVENTURE

1. Ask the students to make the shape of the letter Y with just their fingers, then their arms, then their whole body. They will have lots of ideas once they get started. Students may stand with their feet together and their arms open, or they might lie on the floor with their arms by their sides and their legs open. Encourage them to use these high and low levels as well as medium levels in creating their shapes. Upside-down Ys are also acceptable. ⚙️ **Recognizing Patterns**

2. The students now travel while chanting. Start with marching. As they step on each beat, they chant, "A, E, I, O, U, and sometimes Y!" almost as if they are stamping the letter into the floor with their feet. As they move and say the letter Y, they must freeze in one of their Y shapes (fingers, hands, arms, body). When the chant begins again, encourage them to freeze at the end in a different Y shape.

3. After practicing with simple marching, the students can move on to galloping, skipping, hopping, or rolling as they chant, as long as they freeze in a Y shape when they say Y. They may have suggestions for other ways to travel as well (such as slither, crawl, ooze, jet).

ASSESSMENT

- What did you like about this dance?
- Was it hard? Why? What was easy?
- What kinds of traveling steps did we perform?
- After covering other subject areas or activities, revisit the vowels later in the school day. Ask students to raise their hand if they can recite the vowels of the alphabet. Choose a student to recite it. This concept should be fresh in their memories, and most will remember correctly. Repeat the exercise another day. Then wait a couple days before asking someone to recite the chant. Retention of this concept will still be excellent a few days—even weeks, months, and years—after they learn it.

Assessment Form

Movement Study Assessment form, for teacher use. Add these factors to the form: Y shapes, levels, freeze on time, locomotor movements.

Extensions

- Use the letter Y as a starting point for a drawing. Have the children draw one on paper. Ask what else a Y looks like. (Students might suggest a fork, a vase, or a part of a tree.) What if you turn the Y upside down or sideways? Now what does it look like? Encourage the students to transform the Y into one of these suggestions as they color and draw around the Y. ⚙ Recognizing Patterns

- Use this activity as a warm-up for other alphabet activities.

23

Alphabet Soup

A LESSON OF STRAIGHT AND CURVED LINES.

GRADES: K TO 2   **LENGTH:** 30 MINUTES

Materials

MOVEnture CD track 9
- Audio playback system
- Letter squares (letter squares can be purchased from classroom and physical education suppliers)
- Hand drum

National Standards

Language Arts: 1

Dance: 1, 2, 7

Objectives

The students will be able to do the following:
- Demonstrate straight and curved shapes using various body parts.
- Create letters using straight and curved shapes with the whole body.
- Understand that there are different solutions for creating letters by using the body.

INTRODUCTION

Ask students to join in a warm-up of body parts using straight- and curved-line designs. Ask students to make a straight-line shape with their fingers. Point out specific examples of students' designs so that others can get ideas. For example, one child might have his fingers pointing toward each other, whereas another child has her fingers pointing toward the ceiling. Ask students to try making a curved-line shape or circle shape with their fingers. Again, point out specific students' designs to other students: One child might have all her fingers forming a circle while another child makes two circles in the shape of glasses. Ask students to make a straight-line shape with their arms. Suggested shapes are one arm up and one down or both arms behind the back, as long as they're straight. Tell students to change that shape to a curved-line design. Point out specific examples of shapes that students make, such as the shape of the sun overhead. Students continue creating straight- and curved-line shapes, first using the legs and then the whole body. Tell students to look closely at the curved-line design of their legs. What do the points in their bent knees make the shape look like? (A diamond.) What different levels can they use to make whole-body shapes? ⚙ **Body Thinking**

THE MOVING ADVENTURE

1. Write three letters on the board, such as A, B, and C. Start with all uppercase letters and choose letters that have straight and curved lines. Ask students how they can make a shape that looks like the letter A. Point out specific examples of shapes that students are making: One might make an A while lying down; three others might make an A as a group. Notice all the different ways they can make the letter A by using straight lines.

2. Dancing noodles: Arrange students in a large circle representing a soup pot. They should each stand on the edge of the pot in a stiff, straight-line shape, like an uncooked spaghetti noodle. Ask them what happens to a noodle when it goes into a pot of boiling water. (It begins to soften and get wiggly.) Explain that when you place them in the pot, they should start moving

around the pot, first stiff and straight, then slowly softening and adding curved lines. Tell them to watch out for other noodles as they cook. When the music stops, they should freeze into the shape of the letter A. Remind them that there are many ways to become the letter A. Tell them you're looking for straight lines. Go around the circle and gently tap each "noodle" to enter the pot. They love being wiggly noodles. Compliment the students on the variety of A shapes they've designed, and start them cooking again with the music. Tell them to freeze into the shape of the letter B this time, and explain that you're looking for a straight line with two curved lines.

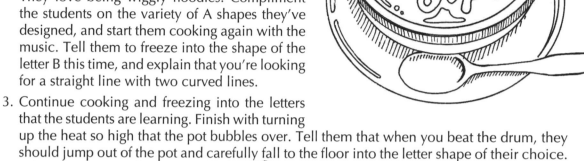

3. Continue cooking and freezing into the letters that the students are learning. Finish with turning up the heat so high that the pot bubbles over. Tell them that when you beat the drum, they should jump out of the pot and carefully fall to the floor into the letter shape of their choice. What a mess! Noodles everywhere! ✿ **Transforming**

ASSESSMENT

- Which letters are easy to make with your body?
- Which letters are most difficult to make with your body?
- Did some of you make a letter shape with a partner?
- Did anyone make a letter shape in a small group?

Assessment Form

Participation Assessment form. Add these factors to the form: straight-line and curved-line shapes into letter formation.

Extensions

- Put students in groups of three or four and assign each group a word to spell with their bodies.
- Try working with a large group to create a complete sentence.
- Make an "A is for . . ." chart using all the letters of the alphabet or just the letters from your current lesson. Think of movement as you generate your ideas. Here are some possibilities:

A is for Angry Alligator.	D is for Diving Dolphin.
B is for Buzzing Bee.	E is for Exercising Eagerly.
C is for Crawling Cat.	F is for Funny Faces.

- Ideally, picture cues for each letter would be helpful for nonreaders to follow. Otherwise, you can read the chart to cue the students' movement. Use a soft signal (finger cymbal or triangle) to suggest moving on to the next letter. Remind students to maintain their self-space as they move like a diving dolphin or buzzing bee through the general space.
- Explore movement interpretations to *The Marcel Marceau Alphabet Book* by George Mendoza or *Chicka Chicka Boom Boom* by Bill Martin Jr. and John Archambault. Ask your librarian to suggest other children's alphabet books.

24 High, Low, Stop, and Go

A LESSON OF RHYMING ANTONYMS (OPPOSITES).

GRADES: K TO 2 **LENGTH:** TWO 15- TO 25-MINUTE SESSIONS

Materials

- Antonym word list or a picture list
- Balloons or beanbags (if use Extension activity)

National Standards

Language Arts: 5
Physical Education: 1
Dance: 1, 2, 7

Objectives

The students will be able to do the following:

- Demonstrate an awareness of words that have opposite meanings.
- Create movements to represent a word and its antonym.

INTRODUCTION

Ask students to make a list of words (or collect pictures) and their opposite meanings. The name for the opposite word is antonym. Ask students to look at their lists (or read aloud) and identify any words that rhyme. For example, *low* and *go* are rhyming words. Here are other possibilities of rhyming antonyms:

Mom, dad: happy, sad

Hot, cold: young, old

Dirty, clean: nice, mean

Peace, war: rich, poor

THE MOVING ADVENTURE

Session 1

Ask students to do a movement that describes the first word on the list. Have just the girls move for *mom* and just the boys move for *dad.* The next rhyming antonym starts with *happy.* Have students show you a happy dance. The opposite is sad. How would the sad movement look? Continue through the list and explore movement ideas for each. Rhyming and antonyms are two different concepts and may need additional explanation. **⚙ Body Thinking**

Session 2

Instruct students to find a partner. One of the partners will do the first movement and the other will follow with the antonym movement. Have them perform four sets of rhyming antonyms.

1. You can add a partner hand clap for the syllables of *rhy* (clap right hand across to partner) and *ming* (clap left hand across to partner).
2. For *an-to-nyms* (or *op-po-sites),* pat thighs three times. **⚙ Forming Patterns**
3. Perform four more rhyming antonyms and repeat the partner hand clap. You have created a pattern of verse, chorus, verse, chorus. Add a melody and you have a song.

ASSESSMENT

- Was it difficult to think of the antonym quickly?
- For which words was it easy to find movement?
- For which words was it difficult to find movement?

Assessment Form

Participation Assessment form.

Extensions

- Have students determine four new rhyming antonyms, adding another verse with movement. The following are some suggestions:

    ground, sky: hello, goodbye

    fast, slow: stop, go

    curly, straight: early, late

    up, down: smile, frown

- Join two or three partners to make a small group. Pass out a balloon or beanbag to each group. One member of the group says a word and taps the balloon or tosses the beanbag into the air. Another member of the group goes for the balloon or beanbag, says the antonym, and taps or tosses it to a new member of the group. The member selects a new word, the balloon or beanbag goes into the air, and the next person says the antonym as he receives the balloon or beanbag. The balloon or beanbag stays in play as long as the students have ideas of antonyms.

A Little Alliteration

PLAYING WITH THE SOUNDS OF LETTERS.

GRADES: K TO 2   LENGTH: 20 MINUTES

Materials

DVD MOVEnture DVD
* Samples of alliteration in famous poetry or prose (optional)

National Standards

Language Arts: 2

Dance: 1, 2

Objectives

The students will be able to do the following:

* Recognize and create alliterative phrases or sentences.
* Demonstrate confidence in improvisation.

INTRODUCTION

Whether students are early learners or experienced with writing sentences, alliteration is an engaging tool and a poetic way of expressing ideas. Explain to students what alliteration is: using the same sound to start many words in the same sentence. Offer examples in poetry or prose and have them pick out the sound that is repetitively used.

THE MOVING ADVENTURE

The following sentences are examples of alliteration that also inspire movement. Use them as an improvisational study. Tell the students that you will read the first sentence aloud while they quietly listen. But when you read it a second time, the students must interpret the *meaning* of the sentence through movement; their bodies will talk the sentence along with you. Teach them that this is called improvisation—to immediately create a solution to a problem, to think on their feet. ⚙ **Playing**

The Letter L

* The lazy lizard laughed himself off the log and into the lake.
* Little lilies love the light.
* Lips look like lumpy lines.

The Letter B

* The butter bubbled and boiled out of the pot.
* The boy blew the balloon bigger, and bigger, and bigger, and *boom!*
* You better be backward!

The Letter R

- The ring-tailed raccoon rolled out of his root bed and reached for a star.
- My round rainbow rubbed the sky with its red smile.
- The rusty rocket rattled as it roamed.
- Rectangles roll roughly.

The Letter S

- Silly spaghetti slithered off the supper plate.
- Several soldiers started saluting.
- Some days seem sad.
- Squares stand strong.
- Soft snow melts silently.

ASSESSMENT

- What is alliteration?
- What is improvisation?
- Do you remember any of the movements or shapes you performed? Would anyone like to share how you danced your favorite alliterative sentence?

Assessment Form

Participation Assessment form. Add this factor to the form: confidence in improvising.

Extensions

- Have students use other letters to make up their own sentences. If appropriate, interpret these sentences through movement.
- Students make up alliterative phrases or sentences that they think would be fun to interpret through dance.
- Students draw and color their favorite alliterative sentence that they danced. Play soft music in the background as they create.
- Write out the sentences and have students circle the letters or sounds that create the alliteration in each one. Or use completely different alliterative sentences that they have not danced or heard previously, scoring their responses on whether they can pick out the alliterative sound.

26 Silly Syllable Dance

DANCING OUR NAMES.

GRADES: K TO 2 **LENGTH OF LESSON:** 20 MINUTES

Materials
Musical instruments: drums, woodblocks, rhythm sticks

National Standards
Language Arts: 3
Dance: 1, 3

Objectives
The students will be able to do the following:
- Verbally articulate syllables of names.
- Create a movement sequence to accompany names.

INTRODUCTION

Ask the students what a syllable is. (It is a word or part of a word pronounced with a single sound of the voice.) Explain that they will learn to recognize syllables by dancing them and moving to the syllables in their names.

THE MOVING ADVENTURE

Children are seated on the floor in a circular formation.

1. One at a time, each student states his or her first name.
2. The rest of the students repeat the names while clapping the rhythm of the syllables.
   ⚙ **Recognizing Patterns**
3. Repeat names with musical instruments (half of class plays while half says names). Students move into a scattered formation in self-space.
4. Direct students to use different movements for the different syllables. Remind students to make movements distinct.
5. Expand the individual ideas into a name dance. Ask the students to each create three different ways of expressing the syllabification of their name. These should vary in level, shape, pathway, or direction. Connect the three ideas together, and each student will have a short name dance with three parts. Students could recite their names as they dance, adding different pitches of the voice for each part. ⚙ **Forming Patterns**
6. Divide students into partners. One partner plays rhythm instruments as the other partner performs the Silly Syllable dance.

ASSESSMENT:

- What is a syllable?
- How many syllables are in your name? How many syllables are in your neighbor's name?

Assessment Form

Peer Assessment form.

Extension

Create a trio name dance. Choreograph a dance using syllables from the names of all three dancers. Perform first names in a canon (one after the other) and perform the last names in unison.

27

Action Words

ACTION WORDS EQUAL MOVEMENT WORDS.

GRADES: K TO 2   **LENGTH:** 45 MINUTES

Materials

- Chart paper and easel or blackboard/dry erase board with action words
- Papers with lists of action words for each student

National Standards

Language Arts: 6

Dance: 1, 2

Objectives

The students will be able to do the following:

- Identify verbs.
- Select five words from a given list.
- Choreograph a dance based on action words.

INTRODUCTION

Ask students what action words are (words that express an action). Ask for a few examples of action words (jump, run, swing, twist). Explain that they will choreograph a dance based on action words.

THE MOVING ADVENTURE

Show students the chart with the action words. Invite them to select an action word from each column. Have students get in scattered formation in general space. Repeat the selected action words, in this example: *stretch, skip, twirl, fall,* and *open.*

1. Have students perform each action.
2. Use the elements of dance and movement to invite them to make variations for each action. For example, stretch on various levels; skip in straight and curved pathways; twirl high, twirl low; fall slowly, fall quickly; open one body part; open at a high level. Focus on smooth transitions between the movements. ⚙️ **Forming Patterns**
3. Students will select five action words from their sheets.
4. Students explore five action words through movement. (Focus on the movement concepts to expand movement.)
5. Students select a beginning and ending shape to make their action word dance.
6. On signal, students begin action word dance together. They each hold the final shape until everyone in the class is finished. (Add music to accompany dances.)
7. Students dance for a partner who attempts to guess the action words.

ASSESSMENT

- Tell me what you discovered about action words.
- What made the choreography interesting?

Assessment Forms

- Action Word Worksheet.
- Action Word Chart.

Extension

Create an action word dance in the choreographic form of theme and variation (a movement phrase with several variations on the original theme).

28

Joey's Adventure

A DANCE STORY ABOUT A FROG.

GRADES: K TO 2 **LENGTH:** 30 MINUTES

Materials
None.

National Standards
Language Arts: 6
Science: 6
Dance: 3

Objective
The students will enact the story "Joey's Adventure" through creative dance.

INTRODUCTION

In the dance story, a young frog who lives at the edge of a pond decides to explore the middle, but the big fish he encounters there gives him quite a scare. Open the session with comments about frogs and their habitats, focusing on all sensory details. Focus on how they look, how they move, the environment, and any other details. Tell the story to the children and discuss the plot by having students tell you the action in the beginning, the middle, and the end. Describe the characters in terms of feelings, appearance, and action. ⚙ **Recognizing Patterns**

THE MOVING ADVENTURE

1. See the sidebar "Dance Story: Joey's Adventure" for the dance story script and movements.
2. Students find their self-space.
3. Use the Vocabulary of Dance and Movement (p. 294) to help students explore movement for the characters and the environment of the story.
4. Narrate the dance story with students providing character dialogue and movements.
   ⚙ **Transforming**

ASSESSMENT

- Was the story clear?
- Why is it important to listen to our parents?
- What can we change about the dance to make the story clearer and more interesting?

Assessment Form
Movement Study Assessment form, for teacher use.

Extensions
- Redance the story, switching parts.
- Consider changing or adding on to the story.
- Students circle pictures that describe what happens at the beginning, middle, and end of story.

Dance Story: Joey's Adventure

by Lynnette Overby

Characters

Water, reeds, fish, lily pads	8 to 10 students
Joey the Frog	1 student
Mother and father frog	2 students
Snapper (Joey's friend)	1 student
Big Fish	2 students

Dance Story

Narrator: This is the story of Joey the Frog. Joey lived by the edge of a large pond with his mother and father. One day Joey decided he would go to the middle of the pond. So, he asked his friend to go with him. *(Joey moves from edge of space toward center.)* His friend's name was Snapper. Snapper was a fish.

Snapper: I can't go with you, Joey. I have to go to school. *(Snapper moves around edge of entire space.)*

Joey: Well, I'll go by myself.

Narrator: So, he swam and swam. He swam toward the middle of the pond. The longer he swam, the deeper he swam. He swam toward the middle of the pond. Joey was so busy looking at the plants and snails. He did not know how far he had gone. *(Joey swims using floating movements toward center of space.)* Suddenly, Joey came face to face with Big Fish. *(Enter Big Fish: two students in the shape of a fish.)*

Joey: Oh, hello, Big Fish. How are you?

Narrator: Big bubbles came from the Big Fish.

Big Fish: Bulp! Bulp! Bulp! I'm hungry!

Joey: What time is it?

Big Fish: Lunch time.

Joey: *(Looks around.)* There are a lot of plants and snails nearby.

(continued)

(continued)

Big Fish: I don't want any plants. I don't want any snails. I want . . . *you!*

Joey: Oh no!

Narrator: Joey turned and swam as fast as he could. He swam away from the middle of the pond. The faster he swam, the faster Big Fish swam. Now they swam from the middle of the pond. Joey swam up and he swam down, down, and down to the bottom of the pond. He saw lots of sand and stones. Joey began to flip sand back into the eyes of Big Fish. Then, by chance, one of Joey's webbed feet clutched a large stone. The stone went hurling back. Big Fish had his mouth open. In went the stone. Right into the jaws of Big Fish. He sank to the bottom. He wrestled to get free of the stone. Joey swam. Away he went. He swam and swam and swam. He even swam past his friend Snapper. He did not stop until he reached the edge of the pond. He popped his little head above the water where he saw his mother and father.

Mother: Joey, Joey, where have you been? We searched everywhere but could not find you.

Father: Where were you?

Joey: A place I did not have permission to go . . . the middle of the pond.

Narrator: The end.

From *Interdisciplinary Learning Through Dance: 101 MOVEntures,* by Lynnette Overby, Beth Post, and Diane Newman. 2005. Champaign, IL: Human Kinetics.

African Folktale

29

A SPIDER IN TROUBLE.

GRADES: K TO 2   **LENGTH:** 30 TO 45 MINUTES

Materials

MOVEnture CD track 10
- Audio playback system
- *Anansi the Spider: A Tale From the Ashanti,* by Gerald McDermott (see References and Resources, p. 299, for full citation)

National Standards

Language Arts: 6

Social Studies: 1, 9

Dance: 1, 2, 5

Objectives

The students will be able to do the following:

- Demonstrate kinesthetic awareness and concentration in performing movement skills.
- Follow a story line through movement, creating a sequence with a beginning, middle, and end.
- Perform movement phrases to interpret characters.
- Demonstrate the ability to move to the beat.

INTRODUCTION

Read McDermott's *Anansi the Spider* to your students. Identify Anansi's six sons and discuss Anansi's encounter with the fish and the falcon. The book actually contains two stories. The first adventure is Anansi "falling into trouble" and his sons coming to the rescue. The second folktale explores the legend of the moon. This lesson involves reading and moving through the first adventure only.

THE MOVING ADVENTURE

1. Introduce African music and point to where Africa is located on a world map or globe. The book shows the country of Ghana as the location in which the Anansi folktale was passed along from generation to generation.
2. Students practice moving to the beat. They begin by clapping the beat, then they can try marching to the beat. Have students design a spider walk for the story. They lift elbows and knees and move to the beat.   ⚙ **Body Thinking**

3. Begin reading. Have students use a signature movement for each son as he is introduced. Feel free to design your own or invite the students to create a movement phrase for each son.

Character	Suggested Movements
Anansi	Move in self-space with your spider walk.
See Trouble	Ask students how they might move as See Trouble. Suggest a lookout shape to the right for 4 counts and to the left for 4 counts, and lunge center with lookout for 4 counts. ⚙ **Empathizing**
Road Builder	Build a road by pounding hands to the right for 4 counts, pounding on the left side for 4 counts, and finishing with a hand gesture in the center to smooth out the road.
River Drinker	Take a scoop with your arms to gather the water, open your mouth, and wiggle as you gulp the water. Use 4 counts for each movement.
Game Skinner	Try doing four hand-chopping motions and then jump four times to show Anansi escaping from inside the fish.
Stone Thrower	Reach back to prepare (4 counts) and throw. The power of the throw takes you into a spin (throw and spin 4 counts).
Cushion	Swing arms back and overhead (4 counts). Round over and bounce knees (4 counts).

4. Students repeat the signature movement phrases each time a character enters the story. Follow the story line with the movement of See Trouble, Road Builder, River Drinker, and Game Skinner.

5. Repeat the spider walk as Anansi goes "far from home . . ."

6. Add a falling movement as Anansi "fell into trouble . . ."

7. Then create a movement or pose for "inside fish."

8. Repeat the spider walk for "More trouble . . ."

9. Lift onto tiptoes or jump for "It was Falcon . . ."

10. Follow the story line with the movements of Stone Thrower and Cushion.

11. Finish with a celebration dance for "They were very happy . . ."

ASSESSMENT

- Was it difficult to move to the beat?
- Who are the six sons of Anansi? Who is your favorite son?
- What happened to Anansi when he "fell into trouble"?
- What happened when "more trouble came"?
- Can anyone find the country of Ghana on the map? What is the name of the continent?

Assessment Forms

- Movement Study Assessment form, for teacher use and for student evaluation of the performance. Add these factors to the form: moving to the beat, performing story sequence, staying in character, and working cooperatively.
- Self-Assessment (version appropriate for students' level).

Extensions

- Make an elastic spider web to be attached to hooks and hung in the room. Spread out the web and allow the students to determine a pathway through the web. They should try not to touch the web as they move through or they might get "stuck" in the web.
- Prepare a stage performance:
  - Assign the role of Anansi and divide students into groups representing each son.
  - Game Skinner, Stone Thrower, and Cushion groups can also play the part of the fish moving inside a large lycra bag.
  - See Trouble, Road Builder, and River Drinker groups can play the part of the Falcon wearing wings under a sheer curtain.
  - Dancers wait in the wings (off stage) for their entrance cues. They enter to center stage, perform their movement phrase, and exit. They must listen closely to the story as it is read to know when to enter and exit.
  - Add the African music accompaniment and perform.
  - Related lesson: A Spider's Life, lesson 91.

30 Boom, Zip, Hiccup, Drip

ONOMATOPOEIA IN ACTION.

GRADES: 3 TO 5 **LENGTH:** TWO 15- TO 25-MINUTE SESSIONS

Materials

- Onomatopoeia cards (see sidebar for a list you can use to help you create these cards)
- Hand drum or triangle (for signals)

National Standards

Language Arts: 2

Dance: 1, 2, 7

Objectives

The students will be able to do the following:

- Identify onomatopoeia and interpret sounds through movement.
- Work cooperatively in groups to compose a movement phrase.

INTRODUCTION

Onomatopoeia, or words which suggest sounds, provide a unique motivation for movement through their sound texture. Each sound suggests a different dynamic energy. Your students will enjoy creating a movement interpretation to boom, zip, hiccup, or drip (to name a few). Begin by introducing your favorite onomatopoeia. Ask students to find self-space and improvise a movement to the sound. They may use a single body part or their whole body. Be sure to compliment the students on the imaginative solutions they have demonstrated. Explore another example of onomatopoeia representing a different texture and movement quality. ✿
Observing, Transforming

THE MOVING ADVENTURE

Session 1

Ask the students to form a large circle. Pass out an onomatopoeia card to each student. Ask students to take a minute to create a movement for their sound. When everyone is ready, go around the circle and have everyone share what they have created. Students should be prepared to perform their movement when it's their turn. Tell them that if they are uncertain the first time around, they can say, "pass" and you'll catch them the next time.

Session 2

1. Have the students work in small groups. Shuffle the onomatopoeia cards and deal them out to each group (one card for each group member). As a group, students will create a movement phrase using the onomatopoeia cards they've been dealt. They must put the sounds into an order. The group composition may be composed of individuals within a group moving to the sounds or the whole group moving together in unison.

2. Each group should perform their onomatopoeia compositions for the class. After dancing it with sound words, they dance it again in silence. Ask students to identify the onomatopoeia by watching the movement without the sound.

Suggested Onomatopoeia Cards

Boom	Crash	Zoom	Clang	Ding
Splash	Zing	Crack	Honk	Slurp
Hum	Hiccup	Whir	Beep	Buzz
Tick	Snap	Whoosh	Munch	Crackle
Plop	Glug	Pop	Vroom	Crunch
Sigh	Sniffle	Drip	Jingle	Bang
Swish	Pow	Tinkle	Sizzle	Ping

ASSESSMENT

- What are onomatopoeia?
- Was it difficult to create a movement for your sound? What words were easy?
- Did your group work cooperatively in creating their onomatopoeia composition?
- Ask students to list onomatopoeia words.

Assessment Forms

- Participation Assessment form.
- Peer Assessment form.
- Group Evaluation form.

Extensions

- Invite the students to think of their own onomatopoeia and write them on cards.
- Connect onomatopoeia to creating group machines. Each group will use sounds to accompany the mechanisms of a real machine or an imaginary machine. Remind students that each movement is important to the function of the machine. Think of the relationship between each part.
- Share an example of onomatopoeia in literature. The students will enjoy reading onomatopoeia in context. Follow with a creative writing experience structured to include three to five sounds in a brief composition.

31

The Art of Silence

COMMUNICATION THROUGH PANTOMIME.

GRADES: 3 TO 5   **LENGTH:** TWO 45-MINUTE SESSIONS
(OR FOUR 20-MINUTE SESSIONS)

Materials

- Feelings chart
- Situation cards

National Standards

Language Arts: 8

Theater: 2

Dance: 1, 2

Objectives

The students will be able to do the following:

- Understand the importance of body language in self-expression.
- Demonstrate mime techniques as a means of communication.
- Sequence scenes into a dramatic study with a beginning, middle, and end.

INTRODUCTION

Pantomime challenges students to communicate without sound. Students develop an appreciation for self-expression innate in us all through our kinesthetic sense.

Introduce your students to pantomime by sharing the work of famous mimes Charlie Chaplin and Marcel Marceau. Charlie Chaplin was a well-known actor of silent movies in the 1920s. French professional mime Marcel Marceau has been acclaimed as the world's greatest mime. Show your students some sample video footage of the work of Charlie Chaplin and Marcel Marceau. (Check your local video store or library.)

THE MOVING ADVENTURE

These pantomime exercises invite your students to use gestures and body movements to communicate feelings, characters, and situations. Take the time with each exercise to become aware of the details essential to making the feeling, character, or situation believable. You and your students need to visualize the exercise first, focus, and learn to stay in character throughout the exercise. The following are explorations that you can use with your students. ⚙ **Body Thinking**

1. Hands

"Let's begin by using our hands in a different way. Your hands offer a wonderful means for self-expression. Sit up tall and place your hands in your lap. Listen and follow as we warm up our hands together. Imagine your hands are . . ." ⚙ **Empathizing**

strong or weak	mother's hands	holding a baby
the wings of a bird	father's hands	playing cards
climbing a rope	putting on jewelry	a fan
directing traffic	a snake	picking a flower
your grandpa's hands	a dog burying a bone	writing a letter

2. Feelings

Create or find a chart of facial expressions representing a variety of feelings. "We use our facial expressions to demonstrate the many different feelings we experience throughout the day. Take a minute to warm up your facial muscles before we explore our facial expressions. Open your eyes wide, close them tight, blink them fast, and try looking in different directions. Wiggle your nose, sniff, and take a deep breath. Smile a big toothy grin, frown, open wide, make fish lips. Now wiggle your whole face and finish by patting your cheeks. We're ready to show our feelings. Let's look at the feelings chart for some ideas. How would your face show you're feeling angry? What do your eyes look like? What happens to your mouth? Now how would your face change to show fear?" ⚙ Empathizing

3. Imaginary Box

Ask the students to sit in a circle. Each student should create a mental picture of a box and its contents. Demonstrate for them a sample box, gesturing the size and shape of the sides, top, and bottom. Then open the box in a manner appropriate to its contents. For example, for a cereal box you would unfold the top, rip open the inside wrap, and pour the cereal into a bowl. "Visualize the box you have in mind and think about how you can present it to the class realistically. When it's your turn, begin by showing us the dimensions, size, and weight of the box. Open the box in the appropriate manner, and you may take something out of the box. We will need to see the detail to determine what kind of box you are sharing. Class, remember to wait to guess the box until you have seen the entire mime demonstration."

4. Situation Scenes

Once the students have become comfortable with pantomime, you can take their dramatic skills into any scene and explore acting it out. Write some situation scenes on cards. Until your students have the confidence to perform individually, design scenes that are appropriate for groups. Have them get into small groups. Pass a card to each group and give them time to develop their scene. Start with a tableau (frozen shape) representing their scene. A tableau is like a photograph. We can see what people are doing but no one is moving. The students will then need to determine the parts and plan a beginning, middle, and end to the scene. You can keep the scenes a secret and ask the class to guess what each group has performed. Your scene cards may represent everyday activities or follow a theme or piece of literature they're currently studying.

Situation Scenes

Emergency room	Road construction	At the beach
Baseball game	On a picnic	Beauty parlor
Firefighters	Classroom	Assembly line
At the circus	Grocery shopping	Riding the bus

ASSESSMENT

- Were the mime gestures realistic and believable?
- Was it difficult to concentrate and stay in character?
- Did your group work together cooperatively in creating your situation scene?
- Did your scene have a clear beginning, middle, and end?

Assessment Forms

- Movement Study Assessment form, for student evaluation of the performance.
- Participation Assessment form.
- Peer Assessment form.
- Group Evaluation form.

Extensions

- Portray a feeling by creating a frozen body shape (tableau). Try a variety of feelings from the feelings chart. Think about details for a realistic body shape.
- Discuss situations in which you might see some of the feelings explored in your individual tableaus. Now bring together three or four students reacting to each other, establishing relationships in group tableau, such as someone hurt on the playground with a teacher and a concerned friend assisting. This activity could be an excellent tool for conflict resolution.
- Related lesson on emotions: Express Yourself!, lesson 17.
- Related lesson on tableaus: We the People, lesson 59.

Cliché Studies

32

HAVING FUN WITH TRITE REMARKS.

GRADES: 3 TO 5   **LENGTH:** 20 TO 30 MINUTES

Materials
The following list of clichés, plus a few extra copies to hand out to small groups:

National Standards
Language Arts: 6

Dance: 1, 2, 3

Suggested Clichés

When push comes to shove	Out on a limb
Touch and go	Not a leg to stand on
Walk on the wild side	Out of the loop
Turn one's back	Tip-top shape
In full swing	By leaps and bounds
Over the hill	Down and out
Fall head over heels	Over the top
In the long run	In good hands
Hitting below the belt	Up in arms
Making ends meet	Go for broke
My way or the highway	

Objectives
The students will be able to do the following:
- Define and identify a cliché.
- Interpret a cliché through shape and movement.
- Work in a small group to develop a movement study.

INTRODUCTION

Ask students if they know what a cliché is: an idea or expression that has been so overused that it has lost its originality and impact. Sometimes we get tired of hearing these phrases in our language, but these sayings are often full of movement. Proceed to read a couple of the cliché phrases listed previously. Put them in full sentences to give them context, helping students recognize that they may have heard these expressions before.

THE MOVING ADVENTURE

1. Use the clichés first as an improvisational study. Read one aloud while the students listen. Then repeat the same cliché and instruct them to interpret it literally through movement or shape and to keep their invention to no more than 20 seconds long. Repeat with each phrase listed. Feel free to add other clichés to the list. ⚙️ **Playing, Transforming**

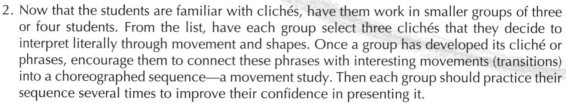

2. Now that the students are familiar with clichés, have them work in smaller groups of three or four students. From the list, have each group select three clichés that they decide to interpret literally through movement and shapes. Once a group has developed its cliché or phrases, encourage them to connect these phrases with interesting movements (transitions) into a choreographed sequence—a movement study. Then each group should practice their sequence several times to improve their confidence in presenting it.

3. Each group should silently perform its cliché movement study for the rest of the class. When finished, students will have fun trying to identify what clichés were being performed.

ASSESSMENT

- Who can tell me what a cliché is?

- Encourage responses about what they enjoyed, both in terms of interpreting the clichés in their groups and in terms of the things they appreciated when they watched others perform.

- Ask the students if they can think of other clichés in contemporary language. Do any of them readily lend themselves to be interpreted through movement?

- Have the students write in their portfolios the clichés they interpreted.

Assessment Forms

- Movement Study Assessment form, for teacher use and for student evaluation of the performance. Add these factors to the form: originality, cooperation, transitions, and confidence.

- Self-Assessment form (version appropriate for students' level).

- Group Evaluation Form.

Extensions

- Have students develop other clichés not listed here.

- Have groups rechoreograph their movement study using the implied meaning of each cliché, in contrast to the literal interpretation of the words.

Dancing Dreams

DANCING THE POEMS OF LANGSTON HUGHES.

GRADES: 3 TO 5   **LENGTH:** 30 MINUTES

Materials

MOVEnture DVD
MOVEnture CD track 11

- Audio playback system
- Copy of poem "Dreams Deferred" by Langston Hughes
- Copy of poem "Dream Variation" by Langston Hughes

National Standards

Language Arts: 6
Dance: 1, 3

Objectives

The students will be able to do the following:

- Interpret two poems by Langston Hughes through creative dance: "Dreams Deferred" and "Dream Variation."
- Articulate meanings of desires that seem unobtainable.

INTRODUCTION

The two poems that students will dance are by a famous African American poet named Langston Hughes. Hughes lived during a time when many Americans believed that African Americans should not have the same opportunities as White Americans. Langston Hughes used his poetry as an artistic medium for the expression of his feelings about the plight of the African American.

THE MOVING ADVENTURE

1. Have students listen to the words, discuss the meanings, suggest movements, and then explore movements to the words.
2. The poem should be written on one side of the chalkboard; students give suggestions for movement that can be written on the other side.

"Dreams Deferred" by Langston Hughes

Line of Poem	Suggested Movements
What happens to a dream deferred?	Begin in a reaching shape. Stretching, searching
Does it dry up like a raisin in the sun?	Shrinking movement
Or fester like a sore and then run?	Running in a circular pathway
Does it stink like rotten meat?	Striking, kicking movements in self-space
Or crust and sugar over like a syrupy sweet?	Move into groups of four
Maybe it just sags like a heavy load.	All four dancers collapse in a pile

Or, does it explode!

Jumps and leap turns
End in a reaching shape

"Dream Variation" by Langston Hughes

Line of Poem	Suggested Movements
To fling my arms wide	Two wide shapes
In some place of the sun	
To whirl and to dance	Turning in self-space
Till the white day is done.	
Then rest at cool evening	Low-level resting shape
Beneath a tall tree	
While night comes on gently,	Smooth movements in general space
Dark like me—	
That is my dream!	Tall, strong shape
	(Divide class into two groups.)
To fling my arms wide	Group 1 turns in self-space
In the face of the sun,	
Dance! Whirl! Whirl!	Group 2 turns in self-space
Till the quick day is done.	
Rest at pale evening . . .	All dancers at low-level resting shape
A tall, slim tree . . .	
Night coming tenderly	Smooth movements in general space
Black like me.	Asymmetrical shape

ASSESSMENT

- Tell me how the poems make you feel.
- How did the movement help us to express the words and feelings of the poem?

Assessment Form

Movement Study Assessment form, for teacher use.

Extension

- Select another poem by Langston Hughes. With a partner, connect the stanzas of the poem to movement.
- Create a dance to the poem.
- Students write a short paper about what it means to want something that seems unobtainable.

34

Haiku Dances

READING, WRITING, AND DANCING POETRY.

GRADES: 3 TO 5 **LENGTH:** TWO 30-MINUTE SESSIONS

Materials

MOVEnture CD track 12
- Audio playback system
- A collection of haikus that inspire movement, printed on a page, one sheet per group

National Standards

Language Arts: 2, 6
Dance: 1, 2, 7

Objectives

The students will be able to do the following:

- Recognize the haiku form of Japanese poetry.
- Interpret a haiku poem through dance using shapes and movement.
- Write a haiku poem.

INTRODUCTION

During the first session, explain that haiku poetry is a Japanese form of poetry that has a simple structure, which is 3 lines, 17 syllables. The first line is usually 5 syllables, the second is 7 syllables, and the final line is again 5 syllables. The haiku was developed for the Japanese language, not English. So a suggestion is to use a structure of short, long, short or to use 3 to 5 syllables, 5 to 7 syllables, and 3 to 5 syllables for the respective lines. Haikus frequently use nature for their point of inspiration and often lead the reader down an imagistic path, only to offer a twist in the final line. This creates drama and is a unique part of the charm of haikus.

THE MOVING ADVENTURE

1. The haikus that follow were selected because they imply motion and movement. Read one aloud. Ask the children to picture it in their minds. Read it aloud again and have them interpret it through movement and shapes as you read. Repeat the activity with other haikus. Refer to Cliché Studies (lesson 32) for another example of an introduction to improvisation. ⚙ **Imaging**

Haiku Samples by Robert J. Rentschler

Snow blankets the beds
but look! crazy crocuses
raise their yellow heads.

Cool morning rain brings
out bright umbrella blossoms
first flowers of spring.

And look! What's going by
tissue tumbling in the wind
small white butterfly?

Such a moving sight
to see the moon in motion
hurrying the night.

The driven snow fills
crevices and corners clings
to the window sills.

Kites are flying high
kaleidoscope-confetti
scattered on the sky.

Reprinted, by permission, from R. Rentschler, 1980, *Michigan: Four seasons.* Robert Rentschler, The Marble Collective, East Lansing, Michigan. Reprinted by permission.

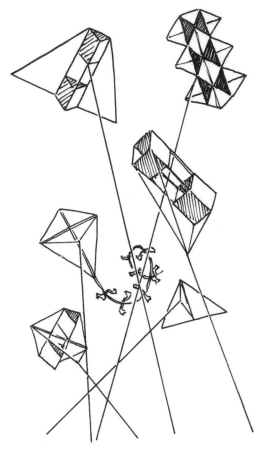

Kites are flying high.

2. Have the students work in duets or trios. Give them a sheet of the haiku collection and have them select one or two to interpret through dance. They should decide whether they will say the poem aloud while they dance, or say it first and then dance it. Encourage them to use different levels and vary the energy to make their haikus interesting, even though the poems are simple and short. If they do not have enough time to finish, they can pick up where they left off at session 2. ⚙ Synthesizing

3. During session 2, have each group perform their haiku dances for the rest of the class. After they dance it with words, they dance it again in silence. Students can give positive comments to one another when each group finishes performing.

ASSESSMENT

- What culture developed the haiku form?
- What is that form?
- What dance ideas were used to express the poetry? (Looking for dance vocabulary here: levels, shapes, soft movement, strong movement, directions, facial expressions.)
- Have each student write three additional haikus. Use photographs of natural objects or living things as a starting point for inspiration.
- Have them record in their journals the haikus they interpreted and perhaps describe what movements and shapes they used to dance them.

Assessment Forms

- Movement Study Assessment form, for teacher use and for student evaluation of the performance. Add these factors to the form: haiku-appropriate form, use of language, originality.
- Self-Assessment form (version appropriate for students' level).
- Group Evaluation Form.

Extensions

- Ask the students to dance one of their own written haikus. Or have them trade a haiku with another person and dance each other's poem.
- For upper-elementary students who are ready for more challenges, have students write a haiku in response to watching another student dance his or her own haiku in silence. Compare the two haikus—the one performed by the student in silence with the haiku written in response to observing.
- Perform the haiku dances and poems for a parent event, school function, or another class.
- Related lesson: Imaginative Thinking Tools, lesson 38.

35

Too Much TV

DANCING TO SHEL SILVERSTEIN'S "JIMMY JET AND HIS TV SET."

GRADES: 3 TO 5   **LENGTH:** 30 TO 45 MINUTES

Materials

MOVEnture CD track 13
- Audio playback system
- The book *Where The Sidewalk Ends* by Shel Silverstein
- Drum or triangle for signal

National Standards

Language Arts: 6

Dance: 1, 2

Objectives

The students will be able to do the following:

- Demonstrate an understanding of focus using directions and body parts.
- Sequence the movement study to include a beginning, middle, and end.
- Use kinesthetic sense (motor memory) to create and recall shapes and sequence.

INTRODUCTION

Celebrate Reading Month (March) by reading "Jimmy Jet and His TV Set" to your class. Jimmy Jet is a little boy who watched so much TV that he turned into a TV set. Remind students to turn off the TV and pick up a book, or else they may turn into a Jimmy Jet.

THE MOVING ADVENTURE

1. Explain that when the TV is on, your focus turns to the TV screen. It's difficult to look away. Play around with focus. Have them focus forward on the TV, turn away, look backward, try not to look at the TV, and look right and then left and finally down. Repeat forward, back, right, left, and down. They can try to turn, reach away, and escape from the control of the TV, but the power of the TV is too strong.

2. Have them settle into a TV-watching shape. It can be at any level. They can use an imaginary sofa or chair. Ask them to think about their shape and remember where their arms, legs, and torso are. Ask them what kind of facial expression they would have. This is shape 1. Then have everyone stand up and shake. See if they can return to their first shape. Then they create a second shape, a TV-watching shape, different from the first. Ask them to use the kinesthetic sense (motor memory) to remember it. And, finally, they make a third TV-watching shape. ⚙ **Body Thinking, Empathizing**

3. As the TV takes control of the students, they begin being pulled toward the TV by a body part. Start with an elbow. Tell them to try to resist as the force of the TV pulls the elbow. Then try a foot. They fight it, but then the focus changes to the nose. They reach their noses toward the TV until they are overcome and collapse gently to the floor.

4. Students then become a Jimmy Jet and must turn into a TV set. Using the MOVEnture CD, tell them to take 32 counts to make a TV shape alone, with a partner, or with a small group. They must move like a machine or robot using percussive movements for the 32-count transition and finish in a shape that looks like a TV.

5. Split the class and perform the Too Much TV dance with minimal cues in two groups.

ASSESSMENT

- What were the four parts of the Too Much TV dance?
- How did we use focus in this dance?
- Could you perform the whole sequence—beginning, middle, and end?
- Vocabulary review:
  - focus—Dancer's directional look or pull of body parts; it draws the audience's attention in.
  - kinesthetic sense—Motor memory.
  - percussive—Sharp, robotic movement.

Assessment Forms

- Movement Study Assessment form, for teacher use and for student evaluation of the performance. Add these factors to the form: performing poem sequence and staying in character.
- Peer Assessment form.

Extensions

- The Too Much TV dance can be done to counts (4 to 6 counts for each movement) with music or felt time with drum or triangle cues.
- Discuss TV watching versus reading. Ask students to share educational shows they have seen on TV. Also, invite students to recommend good books to read.

36

Dance Me a Story

A DANCE BASED ON THE BOOK EARTHDANCE BY JOANNE RYDER.

GRADES: 3 TO 5   **LENGTH:** TWO 30- TO 45-MINUTE SESSIONS

Materials

MOVEnture CD track 14
- Audio playback system
- The book *Earthdance* by Joanne Ryder
- Drum or triangle to signal transitions
- Blue, green, yellow scarves (optional)

National Standards

Language Arts: 6

Visual Arts: 1

Dance: 1, 2

Objectives

The students will be able to do the following:
- Work cooperatively with a partner and in small groups.
- Use kinesthetic sense (motor memory) to create and recall choreography.
- Follow the story sequence from beginning to end.

INTRODUCTION

The images presented in this wonderful story lend themselves to many interpretations. Joanne Ryder has shared a perspective of our world that invites a celebration of movement. Take your time exploring each page. Engage your students in creating movement individually, with a partner, or in groups. Take liberty with the structure of the story, and work to capture the essence in a manner that works best for you and your students. The story is full of imagery and movement possibilities.

THE MOVING ADVENTURE

Here is one interpretation you might explore. Begin in a double-circle formation, facing outward. ⚙ **Body Thinking, Transforming**

Earthdance by Joanne Ryder	Suggested Movements
Imagine you are standing tall in an empty space.	Stand in self-space, reach tall.
Stretch your arms out wide and slowly spin around.	Extend arms to the side, slowly spin in self-space.
You are growing so large, so tall no one can see all of you now.	Students stand in front of a partner (inside or outside circle).
Imagine you are dancing in space, even larger than the moon.	Back student leaps out of circle.
Blue flowing seas, dark green woods and deserts of golden sand.	Three groups (blue, green, and gold); using scarves each interprets the element of nature as a group (seas, forest, desert).
Proud roar of icebergs cracking.	Each group makes an iceberg shape (designing a group shape by filing in the empty or "negative" space around each other) and "cracks" with a percussive movement when the drum beats.
Waterfalls tumbling.	In a line, become a waterfall.
Your whisper is a breeze murmuring through the reeds.	One dancer represents the whisper and moves through the "reeds" of the group.
A tiny wave lapping land.	At low level, make a small wave motion.
Wiggle your shoulders and mountains tremble and quake.	Make a group mountain and shake.
You are streaked with roads . . .	Partner cars begin driving through general space.
. . . and bridges.	Make a partner bridge or an over-and-under shape.
Cars and ships carry people from one place to another, all places on you.	Move while supporting your partner on piggyback or as a wheelbarrow.
Children run and run.	All dancers run in a clockwise circle.
Imagine them leaping and dancing with you as you spin.	Dancers leap, free dance, and spin.
You are where people meet . . . their voices humming as you twirl.	Shake hands with someone.

Turn your face to the bright sun, and cities wake up, yawning to morning.	Face back of the room; stretch in yawning shape.
Behind you, cities in darkness turn on their lights, go to sleep, and dream.	At low level, place hands as a pillow.
You are shelter for people who may never meet but share one thing—you are their home.	Large group forms over-and-under shape for shelter.
May they hear your whispers, feel your strength under their feet, and treasure you.	Find a balancing or listening shape and then a hugging movement in self-space.
For you are home, You are precious Earth.	Finish raising joined hands in a large circle, facing outward.

Text from EARTHDANCE by Joanne Ryder, © 1996 by Joanne Ryder. Reprinted by permission of Henry Holt and Company. LLC.

To interpret the entire book in one class is ambitious. It may be useful to take two class periods or be selective about what excerpts to include when presenting. The students will need sufficient rehearsal to learn the story cues and how to transition from one line to the next. With limited time, just open the book and explore the images that jump off the pages. ⚙️ **Imaging**

ASSESSMENT

- Did your partner and group work cooperatively?
- Were the words of the story and our movement ideas easy to follow?
- What part was most difficult to perform?

Assessment Forms

- Movement Study Assessment form, for teacher use and for student evaluation of the performance. Add this factor to the form: memorizing sequenced movements to follow the story line.
- Self-Assessment form (version appropriate for students' level).

Extensions

- Take some time to create an "Earth" with your students through visual arts. You may include landforms, bodies of water, roads, bridges, and cityscapes using tempura or watercolor paints. Mount it onto poster board and use it as a prop. Design a front side as the Earth and the reverse side as the seas, forest, or desert with the use of blue, green, or gold. Look for and develop connections to lessons in geography.

- Using *Earthdance* as inspiration, have your class create a mural of people on Earth in costume by using simple construction-paper shapes.

- Have students reconstruct the story by drawing a picture or creating an Earth portfolio.

37

Slush Mouth

ARTICULATE AND INARTICULATE SPEECH.

GRADES: 3 TO 5   **LENGTH:** 30 TO 45 MINUTES FOR ONE SESSION, OR TWO 20-MINUTE SESSIONS

Materials

Tape recorder to record students' speeches

National Standards

Language Arts: 8
Dance: 1, 2, 3, 5

Objectives

The students will be able to do the following:

- Identify verbal speech, both articulate and inarticulate (slush mouth), and describe the characteristics of each.
- Create and memorize a composition of six movement phrases.
- Be able to perform their compositions at different speeds and levels of energy.

INTRODUCTION

After studying the six phrases in The Moving Adventure, you begin this lesson by reciting the phrases to the students as *inarticulately* as possible, slurring the words into something approaching gibberish. They will laugh at the absurdity of their teacher speaking in such an unintelligible manner! Ask them, "What did I say? Can anyone tell me what I was saying?" It will be interesting to hear their responses!

Now recite the same six phrases to the students, speaking *very articulately*. Ask them, "What did I say? Who can repeat some of the phrases they heard me speak?" Together they will remember most of the phrases. Ask them, "Which way that I spoke, the first way or the second, was easier to understand? Which way do you think I was more successful communicating with you?"

THE MOVING ADVENTURE

1. Start with the students in a scattered formation, each one standing in a simple shape of feet together, arms by sides, and facing any direction. Instruct them to interpret the following phrases through movement and shapes:

   Brush your ear to the floor

   Lift your heel to the ceiling

   Bring your nose to your knee

   Torso twist

   Jump, fall

   Belly-button perch

2. To help students get started, use this simple process:

   - Create each phrase in an add-on fashion, working from the first phrase to the final phrase.

   - Develop each phrase by trying different movement possibilities and then selecting the most interesting way as the final choice. Make sure there is a pause at the completion of each phrase.

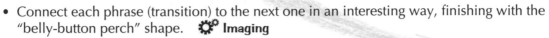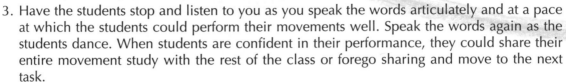

- Connect each phrase (transition) to the next one in an interesting way, finishing with the "belly-button perch" shape. ⚙ **Imaging**

3. Have the students stop and listen to you as you speak the words articulately and at a pace at which the students could perform their movements well. Speak the words again as the students dance. When students are confident in their performance, they could share their entire movement study with the rest of the class or forego sharing and move to the next task.

4. As the students sit to listen to you, speak the words of the study as *slowly* as you can, drawing out the individual words to do so. Tell the students, "Now, it's your turn. I'd like you to perform your memorized movement study in slow motion. Do it as slowly as you can and still perform the movements safely. I will not speak the words since you no longer need them to know what you are doing." The students will enjoy this challenge. After they do the slow-motion movement, reflect together on what was easy or hard, fun or challenging. ⚙ **Dimensional Thinking**

5. Now do the opposite. Speak the words as *fast* as you can as they listen; then have them dance as *fast* as they can, as in a fast-forward on a videotape. Challenge the students to include the pauses at the end of each phrase, even if they last only a microsecond.

6. For the final interpretation of this task, speak the words in a slurred manner, blending consonants into vowels, with no pauses between phrases, and (best of all) with a prevailing attitude of acting cool or hip. This lack of articulation has been described as slush-mouth English. (Most of us have experienced this phenomenon when trying to understand certain messages on phone answering machines. Sometimes it's hard to tell if a person is even speaking English.) Instruct the students to dance their compositions in a slush-mouth style, blending everything together, sloppy in execution, no pauses (run-on sentences), all with a nonchalant, cool attitude.

7. You can pause this lesson for sharing through performance (see explanation on p. 6 in chapter 2) at any of the variations listed, and then the class as a whole can move to the next task. Or you can do the activity and all its variations in a streamlined format, going from developing the compositions to using slush mouth in one lesson. Go in the direction that seems to keep pace with the students' interest.

ASSESSMENT

- What do we mean by the term *slush mouth*? What do we mean by *articulate speech*?
- When you danced your compositions, which required more effort: fast, slow, or slush mouth?
- Which was the most interesting to watch? Which was funniest?

Assessment Forms

- Comprehensive Assessment form, for teacher use. Add these factors to the form: performance of fast movement, performance of slow movement, confidence, originality.
- Self-Assessment form (version appropriate for students' level).
- Peer Assessment form to generate discussion or written responses.

Extensions

- Have the students read text, poetry, or essays in very articulate and very slush-mouth style. Record them on audiotape for playback.
- Have students write an essay about the importance of articulation in communication.

Imaginative Thinking Tools 38

OBSERVING, ABSTRACTING, FORMING PATTERNS, AND TRANSFORMING IN POETRY AND DANCE.

GRADES: 3 TO 5 **LENGTH:** 90 MINUTES

Materials

- Photographs of nature (such as animals and plants)
- A variety of objects (one per student)
- Paper and pencil for each student

National Standards

Language Arts: 2, 6

Dance: 7

Objective

The students will use the imaginative thinking tools developed by Robert and Michele Root-Bernstein to develop skills in poetry and dance.

INTRODUCTION

Explain to students that they will use abstracting skills in their writing and dancing. Ask them how observing can help them to become better writers and dancers. (They will experience more, which will provide them with more material for writing and dancing.) Then ask them whether they know what it means to abstract something. (It means to focus on the bare essentials, the essence, of something.)

Pass around an orange. Ask students to use all of their senses as they observe the orange. Ask students to say one important observation about the orange. (Encourage them to use all of their senses to observe the orange, not just the visual aspects of the orange.)

THE MOVING ADVENTURE

Stage 1: Observing

1. Instruct the students to observe a photograph. They must use all of their senses to imagine themselves in the setting of the photograph (sight, hearing, touch, smell, taste).

2. Instruct the students to write down everything they thought about on a piece of paper. It will look like a web of information.

3. Have students leave their papers and find their self-space.

4. Instruct the students to dance their observations. They will explore all their observations with the body, beginning with the imitation of real shapes and movements. Students

elaborate these observations in self-space using space, time, force, and body elements. ⚙ **Observing**

Stage 2: Abstracting

1. Have students sit down with paper and pencil.

2. Instruct the students to choose two qualities from the list of observations. These observations are the most important experiences of the photograph. The students record the abstracted observation in one or two sentences.

3. Instruct the students to explore these qualities further by using visual, kinesthetic, and emotional associations of the object. Have them write down these qualities and associations.

4. Instruct students to find their self-space and prepare to dance.

5. Have the students choose one movement observation. They will dance the qualities and use the elements of dance to elaborate on these qualities (space, time, force, and body elements). Focus first on the use of space: levels, directions, and pathways (freeze). Next have them focus on the element of force: energy, smooth and sharp, flow, bound and free, weight, strong and light. ⚙ **Abstracting**

Stage 3: Pattern Forming

1. Have students sit down with paper and pencil.

2. Describe the haiku form to the students.

3. First line is 3 to 5 words; second line is 5 to 7 words; and third line is 3 to 5 words.

4. Ask students to create a haiku from their abstracted qualities.

5. Instruct students to move into their self-space and again prepare to dance.

6. Describe the dancing haiku.

   • First phrase is 3 to 5 movements.

   • Second phrase is 5 to 7 movements.

   • Third phrase is 3 to 5 movements.

7. Have students create a dance haiku based on the abstracted movement qualities.

8. Use the following teaching cues: "Use the elements of dance to refine your choreography; use personal and general space; vary your use of time and force; use both locomotor and nonlocomotor movements. Now practice the first short phrase. Ready, begin." (Allow one minute.) "Practice this phrase twice more. Now review the second long phrase. Ready, begin." (Allow two minutes.) "Practice the phrase twice more. Now review the third short phrase. Ready, begin." (Allow one minute.) "Practice the phrase twice more. Now you will perform the complete dance. Begin and end your dance with a frozen shape." ⚙ **Forming Patterns**

Stage 4: Transforming

1. Divide students into partners.
2. One partner watches the other partner dance the haiku and then writes a haiku based on this observation. ⚙ **Transforming**

ASSESSMENT

- Describe observing, abstracting, pattern forming, and transforming.
- Did moving enhance the observations you expressed in writing?
- Does writing affect how you move?
- Do the two combined give you more to say about your photograph?
- Does patterning your words and movements change your expression?
- How easy was it for you to transform your partner's dance into a written haiku?

Assessment Form

Movement Study Assessment form, for teacher use.

Extensions

- Students create a visual art work based on abstraction of the photograph.
- Students dance the visual art abstraction.
- Students write a monologue based on abstraction of the photograph.
- Students create a portfolio of observations, abstractions, patterns, and transformations found in pictures and other media.
- Related lesson: Haiku Dances, lesson 34.

This lesson was developed in association with the John F. Kennedy Center for the Performing Arts, Washington, D.C.

chapter 5

MOVEntures in Mathematics

Children enjoy the intrigue of numbers, though some feel early on that they will never master the mystery. Consequently, they think they don't like math. But numbers can be fun for children regardless of their level of aptitude or achievement.

Mathematics has been called the universal language. Dance is considered a universal language as well. Through the body's ability to form shapes, create action, define space, and express feelings, the language of dance communicates energies of the mind and spirit. Dance at its most basic construct sets up patterns, a concept fundamental to the understanding of mathematics. But dance and mathematics also share fibers in a much richer fabric. The math lessons in this chapter illustrate these interdisciplinary connections. Basic arithme-

tic skills, spatial concepts and orientation, shaping and shape relationships, X–Y coordinates, symmetry and asymmetry, and fractions are all taught through dance with the more complex concepts of probability, continuity, and complexity interwoven.

The creative act of choreography strengthens students' ability to explore variability and change in diverse contexts, investigations, and problems. The student choreographer must coordinate *time* (music and its rhythmic pattern) and *space* (how dancers enter and exit, orient themselves in the space) with the *order* of the sequences of movement and then *organize* it all into a coherent expression of an idea. This is the stuff of multidimensional thinking, the kind that satisfies, engages, and inspires. This is the awesome experience of active learning.

Shape, Shape, Shape

39

LEARNING SHAPES THROUGH THE BODY.

GRADES: K TO 2   **LENGTH:** 30 MINUTES

Materials

MOVEnture CD track 15
- Audio playback system
- Hand drum

National Standards

Mathematics: 5

Dance: 1, 2, 3

Objectives

The students will be able to do the following:

- Form repeatable shapes with their bodies alone and with a partner.
- Move through general space.
- Match another student's shape.

INTRODUCTION

Ask the students to look around the room and notice all the shapes. Some are straight, some are round, and others are angular. Students will explore a variety of shapes with their bodies.

THE MOVING ADVENTURE

1. For the warm-up, students find self-space. They make a straight shape with their bodies. Ask them to change levels with their straight shape. Ask them to make a different straight shape. Then ask them to make a round shape with their bodies and then make three different round shapes with their bodies. Then they make a shape with angles (triangle, square, or rectangle) and make three different angle shapes on different levels.   ⚙ **Body Thinking**

2. Play a game called 16 Count. Students pair with partners and get in scattered formation. Each partnership makes a round shape together. While one partner holds the shape, the other partner leaves, travels through space, and returns on the 16th count and makes the original

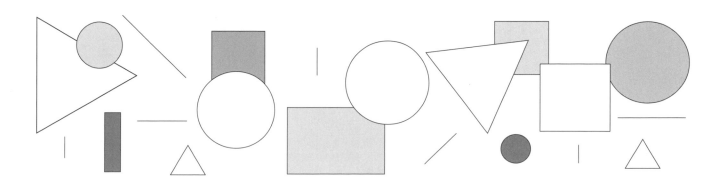

round shape with the partner. Count to 16 as the students do the exercise. Then each partnership makes a straight shape together, and the other partner travels through space using 8 counts this time. Repeat with various cadences, speeds, and counts. Change the shapes, and emphasize traveling through the space before returning for the original shape.

3. Play a movement game called Musical Match My Shape. For this game, have half of the class stand by you. The other half will make a shape in their space. When the music begins, the students who are not making shapes will enter the space and dance around the shapes. When the music stops, they must match a classmate's shape exactly. The music will begin again, and the students who first made the shapes become the dancers. The game continues with several changes. This activity works best with a demonstration. ⚙ **Empathizing**

4. For the Shape, Shape, Shape dance, partners choreograph a shape dance with at least three different connected shapes, three different locomotor movements, and movement on three levels. ⚙ **Forming patterns**

ASSESSMENT

• Describe the shapes you made alone and with a partner in terms of location, direction, level, and shape.

• For homework, students may observe and draw pictures of objects in their homes that are round, triangular, square, or rectangular.

Assessment Forms

• Movement Study Assessment form, for teacher use.

• Participation Assessment form.

Extension

In groups, students create a list of three-dimensional shapes and choreograph a shape dance with the following components: three shapes, three locomotor movements, and three levels.

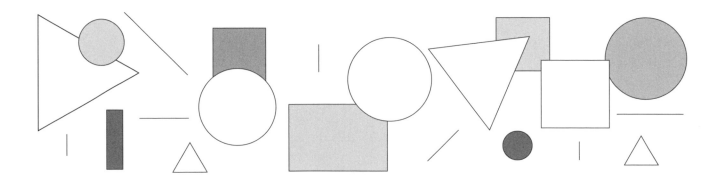

Rope Dances

MAKING LINES AND SHAPES WITH ROPES.

GRADES: K TO 2   **LENGTH:** 30 MINUTES

40

Materials
- Hand drum
- Jump rope for each student

National Standards
Mathematics: 5
Dance: 1, 2, 3

Objectives
The students will be able to do the following:
- Form shapes with the ropes.
- Move beside, in, out, and over the ropes.
- Create a dance with ropes.

INTRODUCTION

Students will use ropes to help them remember shapes and directional concepts. They will also make a dance.

THE MOVING ADVENTURE

Students find self-space and jump with their ropes to warm up. (Some children will be able to jump rope. Others may have to practice jumping without the rope.)

Rope Activity 1

Have students stretch their ropes on the ground and walk beside the ropes in a straight line. Then they jump and hop as they move up and down the rope.

Rope Activity 2

Each student makes a rope into a circle and then walks around the rope. Then they slide around the rope.

Rope Activity 3

Each student leaves the rope in a circle and moves through general space, jumping in and out of all of the circles in the room.

Rope Activity 4

Students use the rope in the rope dance. Use a signal for each part of the dance, and call out the following cues:

Place your rope in a straight line on the floor.

Make yourself into a straight shape.

Now jump over your rope four times.

103

Now make your rope into a round shape.

Now slide around your rope.

Move through general space jumping in and out of the ropes.

Return to your rope and make a round shape inside your rope.

ASSESSMENT

- Describe the shapes and locomotor movements you performed.
- For homework, each student will create his or her own rope dance to share. They must include at least two different shapes and two locomotor movements.

Assessment Forms

Participation Assessment form.

Extensions

- Students use the rope to make letters.
- Students draw three shapes on paper. Connect the shapes with straight, curved, and zigzag lines (pathways). Transform the drawing to the movement space and dance the movement map by making a round or straight shape with the body and rope and then jumping with the rope on the connecting line (pathway) to the next shape.

Beanbag Boom!

41

A LESSON ON GROUPINGS.

GRADES: K TO 2   **LENGTH:** 15 TO 20 MINUTES

Materials

 MOVEnture CD track 16 or other lively instrumental music (without lyrics)

- Audio playback system
- Hand drum or other instrument to strike
- Small beanbags, one per student

National Standards

Math: 1

Physical Education: 2

Dance: 1

Objectives

The students will be able to do the following:

- Demonstrate the ability to form groups and work cooperatively.
- Perform the eight basic locomotor movements.
- Create group shapes at low, medium, and high levels.
- Perform one-to-one matching between their bodies and rhythm.

INTRODUCTION

This lesson helps students to explore the concept of grouping through the use of a prop—a beanbag. It also teaches students the eight basic locomotor movements that humans do on their feet: walking, hopping, galloping, sliding, skipping, leaping, running, and jumping.

Seat the children in a circle and ask for two volunteers. Give them each a beanbag. Ask them to go into the center of the circle and make a frozen shape together in which they are each touching their beanbag to the other student's body. Encourage them to touch the beanbag to a shoulder, an elbow, the top of the head, a knee, and so on. Advise that the beanbag should touch the other student's body clearly, but *gently*. Repeat with three students making the touching shape, and again with four students.

Now ask for a volunteer student to demonstrate one of the eight basic locomotor movements. Have all students briefly practice. Repeat with each one of the locomotor movements.

Gather the students back to you, standing or sitting. Teach them the structure of the dance: 1) you will play music; 2) when the music stops, you will strike the drum twice for groups of two to form, three times for groups of three to form, four times for groups of four to perform, and so on; and 3) upon hearing the number of drumbeats, they must quickly form and freeze in those groupings.

THE MOVING ADVENTURE

1. Students each receive a beanbag and spread out to find their own self-space in the room.
2. Start the music. As the music plays, children travel through space using one of the eight basic locomotor movements: walking, hopping, galloping, sliding, skipping, leaping, running, or jumping.

3. When the music pauses (or if you pause it manually), immediately drum 2 beats clearly in the silence. Students respond by quickly gathering into groups of two and touching their beanbags to their partners' bodies with high-, medium-, or low-level shapes. Count the number of groups of two out loud with the children.
⚙ Recognizing Patterns, Forming Patterns

4. If there is an odd number of students in class, the one student who has no partner announces, "Beanbag Boom!" All students toss their beanbags straight up into the air and let them fall with a smack on the ground.

5. After students pick up their beanbags, repeat the exercise choosing a different locomotor movement and perform three drumbeats, indicating groupings of three should gather. Again, count out loud with the children the number of groups of three that are in the room. If there are "leftover" students, they announce, "Beanbag Boom!" If, after counting out loud the number of groups, no students are left over, start the music again without the "Beanbag Boom!"

6. Repeat the exercise as many times as you wish, using same or different groupings to practice forming groups. If you use the grouping number that would be for the whole class, such as 25, then all children should make a huge group shape together, touching beanbags to one another.

ASSESSMENT

- What numbers did we use for gathering into groups?
- What kinds of movement did we use to travel through the general space?
- What levels did we use to make shapes?
- Were you easily able to find someone to touch with your beanbag when it was time?

Assessment Forms

- Movement Study Assessment form, for teacher use. Add these factors to the form: locomotor movements, levels.
- Self-Assessment form (version appropriate for students' level).

Extensions

- You may also suggest additional locomotor movements, such as crawling, rolling, slithering, or interpreting animal movements, even though they are not one of the eight basic locomotor movements.
- Have the students balance the beanbag on a body part as they travel: the back of the hand, on a shoulder, on the back.
- For further challenge, give each student two beanbags and work with even numbers, or give some students two beanbags and others just one.
- Repeat the activity with older students, emphasizing the inverse relationship of size of group to number of groups (10 groups of 2, but 2 groups of 10).
- Related Moventure: 1-3-5, 2-4-6 (lesson 45).

42

SASC (Sassy) Class

SYMMETRICAL, ASYMMETRICAL, SIMPLE, AND COMPLEX SHAPES.

GRADES: K TO 2   **LENGTH:** THREE 20-MINUTE SESSIONS

Materials

- A simple melodic musical instrument such as a glockenspiel, finger cymbals, gong, or triangle
- Pictures of objects or the objects themselves that have the characteristics of symmetry, asymmetry, simple, and complex shapes

National Standards

Math: 5

Dance: 1, 2, 3

Objectives

The students will be able to do the following:

- Describe or define four types of shapes in mathematical terms: symmetrical, asymmetrical, simple, and complex.
- Sequence four shapes into a memorized phrase.
- Demonstrate knowledge and use of levels in creating dance shapes.

INTRODUCTION

NOTE: This lesson assumes three dimensions because we are using the three-dimensional human body to represent shapes in space.

Show symmetrical objects such as bookends, a face, or a paper snowflake. Ask students to notice how, when you draw a line down the center of the object, each side mirrors the other. In other words, the object is the same on both sides. An object that is the same on both sides of a line drawn through it is *symmetrical*. (Have the students say the word *symmetrical* with you.) After discussion, have the students think of other things that are symmetrical. This eventually will lead them to recognize that animals, including humans, are symmetrical. ⚙ **Recognizing Patterns**

Now show the students pictures or objects that are asymmetrical. A fork and a spoon are symmetrical, but what about a knife? It is almost symmetrical, but just a little difference on one side makes it not symmetrical. Many things are almost symmetrical, almost identical on both sides, but even just one clear difference means they cannot be called symmetrical objects. The name for things that are different on each side is *asymmetrical.* Ask students to suggest objects that are asymmetrical, a much more common type of shape than symmetrical.

THE MOVING ADVENTURE

1. For the first session, ask the students to find self-space in the room. Instruct them to create a symmetrical shape at a low level. Repeat this assignment two or three times, creating new shapes using a different base of support such as sitting, lying on back or front, or suspended off the floor.
2. Repeat the activity at medium level and then at high level.
3. Now have the students create a shape at each level and memorize it. Perhaps start with low: Instruct them to create a shape and memorize every position of every body part. Do it again

at medium level, and then at high. The shapes are now in a sequence, a phrase or "sentence" that each student can repeat.

4. For the Symmetry Dance, add the aesthetic component of music. Have the students all start in neutral, which is standing upright, feet together and body proud, hands by sides. Inform the students that you will make three ringing sounds on the musical instrument. When they hear them, they should gently move into the low symmetrical shape they memorized. When you repeat the rings, they should transition into their medium symmetrical, and then they should do the same for the high symmetrical shape. Encourage them to find interesting ways to transition: melt, twirl, shake, explode, ooze, and slither.

5. To address *asymmetry,* repeat the activity in number 4 with asymmetrical shapes, from the observation of pictures and exploration at each level through to the development of a full phrase—an Asymmetry Dance. To demonstrate the fragility of symmetry, you can have the students repeat their symmetry phrase, changing only one thing on each of the shapes—an arm, a leg, or the turn of the head—to make it become asymmetrical. But certainly having them create all new shapes in which each side of the body has the freedom to do something different is exciting to them after the great attention required for making a shape symmetrical.

6. For the second session, repeat the activity from observing pictures, drawings, and objects through to a finished, memorized phrase with *simple* and *complex* shapes. In dance, we define simple as a shape that is easy to copy. In three-dimensional math, it is defined as a shape in which no lines cross. Complex is defined in dance as a shape that is difficult to copy, with lots of details (such as varying shapes of fingers, facial expression, and eye focus); an example is the shape of a pretzel. In three-dimensional math, complex is defined as a shape in which at least one line crosses another. Create a Simple and Complex Dance using the same structure as the Symmetry Dance.

7. During these sessions, students can perform any of the finished phrases in small groups for the rest of the class (share through performance). This gives you an opportunity to assess progress and comprehension. Always encourage positive feedback from the observers to the performers so that students get a sense of what is working well for them without fear of harsh criticism from their peers. When sufficient trust in the process has been built, students can offer suggestions for improvement.

8. For the third session, develop a more complex phrase: symmetrical, asymmetrical, simple, and complex. Or do the shapes in a different order, letting the students choose the order as long as all four shapes are included. Encourage changes of level, direction, and energy.

ASSESSMENT

- What are the four types of shapes that we explored?
- Can these shapes be more than one type at the same time?
- Did you use levels in your dance? Which ones did you use or see others perform?
- What did you find challenging about this dance activity?
- Use math concepts: Hold up a series of pictures of objects and have students write down each object's characteristics of shape.

Symmetry

Asymmetry

Assessment Forms

- Movement Study Assessment form, for teacher use and for student evaluation of the performance. Add these factors to the form: use of levels, accuracy of SASC shape, memory skills.
- Self-Assessment form (version appropriate for students' level).

Extensions

- Have the students work with a partner to develop SASC shapes.
- Ask the students to make a list of everyday objects for each of the SASC shapes.
- Bring in objects and have students list all the different characteristics they can identify about each, using all their senses—color, smell, texture, size, and certainly shape. (This exercise incorporates aspects of the scientific method.)
- Connect to visual arts by having the students draw, paint, or sculpt SASC shapes.
- This lesson is also useful in investigative science (in which objects must be observed and described in detail) and in visual arts (in the study of line and shape).

43 Thinches and Toe Rulers

USING THE BODY AS A REFERENCE FOR MEASUREMENT.

GRADES: K TO 2   **LENGTH:** 30 TO 40 MINUTES

Materials

String (optional)

National Standards

Math: 4

Dance: 1

Objectives

The students will be able to do the following:

- Define a unit of measurement and describe how it is useful; define a *standard* unit of measurement and give examples.
- Identify directions, levels, and speeds of traveling through space.

INTRODUCTION

Though most appropriate for second grade, this lesson can be tailored to introduce even the youngest students to the satisfaction of knowing how to measure. Inform students that throughout history, people have used different units, or standards, to measure things. For example, we use the inch, foot, and meter to measure distances; the pint, liter, or gallon to measure volume; the pound, kilogram, or ton to measure weight or mass; and the minute, month, and year to measure time. Many of today's units of measurement have an interesting history. For instance, the "foot" we use, which is the length of a standard ruler of 12 inches, was established by a certain king's actual foot size.

But there were units of measurement used by ancient peoples that are no longer used today. Consider the period in history when Noah built his ark. One unit of measurement that was used at that time was a cubit. (Ask students if they know what a cubit is or how long it is.) A cubit is the distance from a person's elbow to the tip of the middle finger. On an adult, it usually averaged from 17 to 21 inches. Using part of the body to measure things makes sense, because you always carry that body part with you. Explain that students will invent their own unit of measurement that uses a part of the body, and they will call it a *body unit of measurement,* or BUM for short. They can give those units whatever name they like. For instance, maybe someone wants to measure the edge of a desk. He could decide to use the length of his thumb as his unit of measurement and call it . . . a *thumbinch.* He could even shorten that word into *thinch.* ("My desk is 17 thinches long," one could say.) Or, if someone used her big toe as the unit of measurement, maybe she'd call it a *toeruler.* Of course, depending on the BUM they decide to use, students may find that their bodies have to move in some unusual ways to actually measure something. And some BUMs will allow them to measure faster or slower than other BUMs. Advise students to pay attention to how they have to move for the following activity.   ⚙ **Body Thinking**

THE MOVING ADVENTURE

1. Students should begin in self-space in a scattered formation.
2. Have each student measure the length of his or her leg, from the knee to the ankle, in thinches. Remind them to notice how they have to use their bodies to do the measuring.

3. Have each student measure the length of the sole of his or her foot in toerulers. Using a big toe to measure the other foot gets the legs and body in some odd shapes!

4. Have students toss out other suggestions for a body unit of measurement (such as backbone length, shin length, shoulder width, hand span). Experiment with measuring large, medium, and small things.

5. Tell the students that they will work in pairs or in small groups to measure the length and width of the room. Students should agree on a BUM for their group that each will use to measure. Encourage them to measure as accurately as possible. Partners can help the marking off of each measure and help record data for the student who is moving. For a group that chose something very small for a BUM, like a pinky finger, it may seem daunting to measure a large room. It's a good place to introduce the concept of conversion. Suggest converting to another object as a tool for measurement. For instance, cut a length of string equal to 10 times the length of the BUM—in this case, the pinky finger. Then use the string to measure the room dimensions. Or convert the small BUM to a larger BUM, such as a stride. How many pinkies in a stride? Then stride the distance.

6. Make sure the students give their BUM a name.

7. Have the students in each group compare their measurements for the same distances. Compare with the results of the whole class.

8. Students will find that even within their group using the same BUM, results will vary significantly. Introduce the concept of a *standard* unit of measurement, one that is constant and widely accepted, such as an inch, or a pound, or a liter. Tools for measurement, such as rulers and scales, are based on these standards. ⚙ **Abstracting**

ASSESSMENT

- What is a unit of measurement? What is a standard unit of measurement?

- What did you find out when you compared the results using the same body unit of measurement from one person to another in your group?

- What do we use today as tools for measurement? (Rulers, yardsticks, scales, thermometers.) If everyone measured the length of the room with a yardstick, how would our results compare?

- When measuring the length and width of the room, did you have to travel at high, medium, or low level? At what speed were you able to travel? What direction did your body face while you measured? Up? Down? Backward?

Assessment Forms
- Participation Assessment form.
- Group Evaluation form.

Extensions

- This is a great tool to use for developing powers of estimation. Have students estimate distances using a BUM with which they've had a lot of experience, such as estimating the height of the same room with the BUM they used to measure the length and width.

- Have them estimate the distance of things they cannot measure, like the distance across a river or the height of a building. They can be given a range in which to estimate, for example, 1) same as the length of a classroom; 2) two classrooms long; 3) more than three classrooms long. Go beyond linear measurement to estimating how long it would take to do a certain job or estimating the weight of an object.

- Have the students convert the BUM they used into accepted standard units such as inches and feet or centimeter and meters.

- Give the students drawings of various shapes on 8.5- by 11-inch paper and have them measure the perimeter of the shapes using a ruler. For shapes with curves, or closed shapes, offer them string with which to problem-solve.

- Read *How Big Is a Foot?* by R. Myller.

44

Changes

RECOGNIZING AND FORMING PATTERNS.

GRADES: K TO 2   **LENGTH:** 30 MINUTES

Materials

MOVEnture CD track 34
- Audio playback system
- Hand drum

National Standards
Math: 1
Dance: 2

Objectives
The students will be able to do the following:
- Form patterns of movement.
- Describe patterns of movement.

INTRODUCTION

This lesson is about creating or discovering new ways to organize locomotor patterns. A pattern must repeat. During this lesson students will form new patterns and describe or recognize new patterns made by classmates.

MOVING ADVENTURE

1. Forming Patterns: Changes 1 (basic locomotor movements: walk, run, jump, hop, leap, gallop, slide, skip). Choose one locomotor movement and have the students explore doing that locomotor movement in any direction, changing direction when they want. Then repeat the pattern (use a drum or a hand clap to keep a steady beat for the class). Have the students explore changing directions with other locomotor movements

2. Changes 2. Choose a different locomotor movement, and have the students move 8 counts in one direction and 8 counts in a new direction. Continue keeping the steady beat and having the children explore changing direction on the first beat of every 8 counts. Repeat the activity, changing direction every 4 beats, every 2 beats, and on each beat. Explore with different locomotor movements.

3. Changes 3. Choose one locomotor movement. Using the time sequence 8, 8, 4, 4, 2, 2, 1, 1, have the students change direction on the first beat of every number. (This can be done 8 right, 8 left, 4 right, 4 left, and so on). Repeat the pattern.

4. Changes 4. Have each student choose three different locomotor movements and three numbers (three skips, two walks, five gallops). Have each student choose three different directions to match the locomotor and number sequence. Have them practice doing their change-of-direction dance. ⚙ **Forming Patterns**

5. Pattern Recognition: Students are divided into partners. One student performs while the other student tries to guess the number sequence the performing partner created. ⚙ **Pattern Recognition**

ASSESSMENT

How did you make your pattern interesting?

Assessment Forms

Peer Assessment: Change of Direction Dance. One partner uses the assessment form to determine the other partner's ability to use movement to create a pattern.

Extension

Students learn the grapevine step. This is a series of side steps in which one foot crosses alternately in front of and in back of the other foot. The grapevine is a step used in many folk dances.

45

1-3-5, 2-4-6

ODD VERSUS EVEN RELATIONSHIPS.

GRADES: 3 TO 5   **LENGTH:** TWO 20- TO 30-MINUTE SESSIONS

Materials

MOVEnture CD track 18
- Audio playback system
- Hand drum

National Standards

Mathematics: 2
Dance: 1
Music: 6

Objectives

The students will be able to do the following:

- Classify numbers as even or odd.
- Recall even and odd movement phrases.
- Recognize and interpret the beat of the music through movement.
- Identify and perform nonlocomotor movement.

INTRODUCTION

Count together from 1 to 10. Count again and clap on the odd counts, 1, 3, 5, 7, 9. Repeat and clap on the even counts, 2, 4, 6, 8, 10. Continue to explore odd and even counts by using a stomp, alternating shoulders, or nodding the head to represent the accent.   ⚙ **Recognizing Patterns**

THE MOVING ADVENTURE

Session 1

1. Invite the students to find a partner and stand shoulder to shoulder.
2. Begin counting together to 10 at a steady tempo. Assign each partner as odd or even counts. Count again and alternate stepping in place on the odd or even count.
3. Switch assigned counts and alternate stepping in place on the odd or even count.
4. Finish by stepping together (in unison) for another 10 counts. It's important to step at a steady tempo and focus on coordinating steps with your partner.
5. Combine partners to form groups of four or six and try to perform the odd- and even-count steps as small groups.
6. Count together to 10 first. Count again, and half the group steps on the odd count, the other half steps on the even. Reverse roles and repeat.
7. Step together for 10 counts to finish. Practice saying the counts aloud, and then try it with only a vocal count on the first 10 (to establish the tempo).   ⚙ **Transforming, Body Thinking**

Session 2

1. Refer to the list of nonlocomotor movements in the Vocabulary of Dance and Movement list (p. 294), and select a movement to be performed in self-space for 1 count, a movement for 3 counts, a movement for 5 counts, and a movement for 7 counts. For example, an odd-count movement phrase could be push (1), jump (3), spin (5), punch (7).

2. Next, select a movement to be performed in 2 counts, then separate movements for 4, 6, and 8 counts. For example, the even-count phrase could be kick (2), sway (4), bounce (6), and balance (8).

3. Write the phrase on the board or have a sign for each movement to cue the students.

4. Keep a slow, steady beat on the hand drum. Ask students to move to the beat with the odd-count phrase: push (1), jump (3), spin (5), punch (7).

5. Have the students count aloud for the first few performances. They should try to count internally as they perform the movements.

6. Continue the steady beat as the students perform the even-count phrase: kick (2), sway (4), bounce (6), balance (8).

7. Ask half the students to clap the steady beat while the other half perform the odd or even count phrase.

ASSESSMENT

- What was challenging about moving with a partner to the odd or even counts?
- What was challenging about moving with a group?
- Did you maintain a steady tempo as you moved?
- Was it difficult to remember the order of movements of each phrase?

Assessment Forms

- Movement Study Assessment form, for teacher use and for student evaluation of the performance. Add these factors to the form: odd and even counts, step in place with partner, step in place with small group, odd-count movement phrase, and even-count movement phrase.
- Self-Assessment form (version appropriate for students' level).

Extensions

- Introduce the music (count 4 beats to a measure). Challenge the students to perform the odd- and even-count phrases to the music.
- Create your own dance with a beginning, middle, and end, sequencing movements based on the even and odd theme.
- Related lesson: Beanbag Boom!, lesson 41.

Fractions Sounding Off

46

EXPLORING SOUND WAVE AND PITCH.

GRADES: 3 TO 5   **LENGTH:** 15 TO 20 MINUTES

Materials

- Four glasses of water: one-quarter, one-half, three-quarters, and completely full
- Four musical instruments of varying pitches or a pitch pipe (optional)

National Standards

Mathematics: 2

Science: 9

Music: 1, 2

Dance: 1

Objectives

The students will be able to do the following:

- Demonstrate shapes at low, middle, and high levels.
- Develop an understanding of the basic concepts of fractions.
- Recognize and sing independently on pitch.
- Identify frequency through sound waves.

INTRODUCTION

Place four glasses in a row, and fill each with water to a different level (quarter full, half full, three-quarters full, completely full). Ask students to tell you which glass will make the highest sound. Tap each glass gently with a spoon. The full glass makes the lowest sound. The more space for the sound waves to move through, the less frequency there is and the lower the pitch. The pitch is determined by the frequency of vibration in the sound waves. Create a visual aid to represent the relationship between fractions, sound waves, and pitch by using pictures of glasses of water and pictures of instruments and sound waves. ⚙️ **Observing**

THE MOVING ADVENTURE

1. Stand four students in a row. The quarter-full student sits. The half-full student kneels. The three-quarters-full student stands with knees bent. The final student stretches to a "full" shape.

2. Ask students to predict the pitch of instruments of different sizes (such as piccolo, flute, trumpet, and tuba). Play four instruments with four levels of pitch (if available), or invite the students to make sounds with vocal pitch at four varied levels.

3. When the lowest sound is made (tuba), the glass is full, so all students should take a stretched, "full" shape. Sitting down represents the quarter-full, or highest, sound (piccolo). Continue to move through the demonstration of fractions by using sound pitch and body levels. ⚙ **Body Thinking**

ASSESSMENT

- What is pitch?
- How did we use fractions and levels to demonstrate a change in pitch?
- How did this exercise demonstrate the relationship among fractions, sound waves, and pitch?
- Did you immediately recognize the change in pitch as it was played?
- Label pictures of glasses with the appropriate fractions.
- Draw sound-wave frequency for each glass of water.

Assessment Forms

Movement Study Assessment form, for teacher use. Add these factors to the form: a demonstration of low, middle, and high levels.

Extensions

- Invite the students to make large shapes for the low sounds and small shapes for the high sounds so that they explore size instead of level.
- Create a short musical composition using the four levels of pitch (quarter, half, three quarters, and full). Interpret the composition using shapes at the four different levels.

Curfew

47

VARIABLES AND CONSTANTS, X-Y COORDINATES.

GRADES: 3 TO 5   **LENGTH:** 30 TO 40 MINUTES

Materials

- The "space" factor: a gymnasium or large, empty activity room is preferable, but a classroom with all desks and chairs moved aside can work, although it's less safe
- The "time" factor: a drum or other handheld instrument to keep a steady beat

National Standards

Math: 5

Physical Education: 2

Dance: 1, 2, 3

Objectives

The students will be able to do the following:

- Conceptualize and describe the location of a single spot as the intersection of two directions.
- Travel through general space in a given amount of time without touching another student.
- Manipulate variables of the game by suggesting ideas.

INTRODUCTION

Ask students if they know what a curfew is. (It's the time on the clock when parents say children must be *home.*) So if children are out playing or visiting a friend in the neighborhood, they know that they must get home by the curfew or they might be grounded.

Pretend that the room is the neighborhood in which the students all live. That means each person needs to pick a spot in the room to represent his or her home. To do that, it might be helpful to create a map. In math we identify one direction as the X coordinate. The direction perpendicular, or at a right angle, to X is the Y coordinate. So the wall with the clock on it will be the X, and the wall at a right angle to X will be the Y. (In geography these directions are defined as latitude and longitude.) ⚙ Dimensional Thinking

Ask students to go out into the space and choose a spot to stand in that is not too close to the walls or furniture or to another person.

- Before they begin, don't give students too much information on how to be successful; let them discover that information as they experience it and then follow up the discovery with a bit of discussion.
- Because the students are playing a game, they do not necessarily get upset with their failures, nor do they always see it as work or learning. Yet they are working very hard mentally and physically. With the positive connections you make to the curriculum and to the broader context of their ability to make choices, they come to appreciate that they are learning, and it's fun.

THE MOVING ADVENTURE

1. Instruct each student to memorize the exact spot of his or her self-space in the room. This is home. Students will use "landmarks" such as electrical outlets, doorknobs, lines on the walls or floor, and wall posters to help them memorize their spot. This is a great time to help the

119

Y   X

students realize that pinpointing their space *as the intersection of both X and Y coordinates* (or latitude and longitude) will best locate the exact spot of their home. Introduce appropriate math vocabulary so that they are able to say, "I am across from the doorknob on this wall *and* across from the drinking fountain on the wall that is at a right angle [or perpendicular, or at 90 degrees] to it." Some students might try to solve the problem by counting the number of squares of floor tile from a wall to locate their home. However, this method will not be consistently successful because at times they will be moving at too great a speed to count the squares and still be home in time. ⚙ **Abstracting**

2. Teach them the starting signal: Beat the drum four times, saying, "One, two, ready, go." Tell the students that today the curfew is 10 o'clock. This will be represented by 10 beats on the drum. (After giving the starting signal, beat the 10 counts at a steady, moderate speed so that they know how long they will have to travel and return home.)

3. As with any game, there are rules. Rules are usually for safety and fair play. The major rule of Curfew deals with the concept of self-space.

   • Rule 1: No one can touch another person or any object at any time; each person is responsible for keeping to his or her own self-space.

   • Rule 2: No talking while moving. If questions arise, they know to raise their hands. Dance emphasizes communicating nonverbally.

4. Each student starts by standing in his or her home. Instruct the students that they may travel around their neighborhood in any direction as long as they are back in their home exactly at 10 o'clock—no earlier, no later. Remind them that they cannot touch others during their journey.

5. To start simply, tell them that the first time they journey through the neighborhood, they may *only walk;* they can use no other way of moving. Give the starting signal and drum 10 counts, counting out loud together with them as they travel through the general space. On the 10th count, everyone should be back in their home, at their intersection of their X and Y. Have them notice whether they were successful; ask if everyone understands the rules: Walk for 10 counts, and don't touch anyone else at any time. (If they mention that counting out loud violates rule 2, tell them that it is not considered talking. They are using their voices as a rhythm instrument to keep the beat with the drum.) Repeat the activity with walking again so that those who were not successful the first time can succeed now. This will assure you that they all understand the game. Eventually, ask them to stop counting out loud as they travel. You might still need to support the counting vocally if they lose track, but they must try to be increasingly self-reliant.

6. When the students get home on the 10th count, they must freeze in a shape. (Strike the drum especially hard on that count or give a quick double drumbeat.) Repeat the exercise, and have them freeze on the 10th count in a medium-level shape. Practice with a high shape and then a low shape. Ask students to look at all the different shapes people made at the level—everyone may be different, but everyone is correct.

7. Play with the variables. You now have exposed the students to the entire structure of variables: how to start, how to travel, how long to travel, and how to stop. They have practiced the two rules *(do not touch* and *no talking while moving).* You may have them sit out one round of the game if they are home late or touch others or talk while moving. In other words, they are "grounded." While sitting out, they observe others and watch to let you know if anyone is late or touches another student while moving.

8. Now you can make the game more challenging by playing with the variables:

   • To change the *speed* of travel (which affects how *far* they travel), offer different ways of traveling each time you repeat the game: hop, crawl, roll, skip, gallop, slither, twirl, scoot, jet. Ask the students for suggestions, too. Remind them that there are as many ways to crawl or slither as there are people in the room. Movement does not always have to go forward; humans can skip sideways or backward or in circles. They can twirl at a high level, or at a medium level, or on their tailbones at a low level. Encourage originality in their responses.

   • Each time they repeat the game, have a student suggest at what level they must all freeze on the *ending count* of 10. Fun suggestions include traveling at a high level (jumping) but freezing in a low shape when they get home, or rolling to travel but freezing in a high shape.

   • It is not advisable to change the *time variable,* or number of counts, for quite a while because students need a constant in order to work through the other variables. (At some point, stop the students from counting the 10 counts out loud so that they have to do it for themselves silently.) Eventually, they will become more proficient at juggling the variables (concentration and thought-organization skills) and will be able to change the three factors (how to travel, how long, and ending-count shape) and still experience success.

ASSESSMENT

Evaluate the students in an ongoing way throughout the lesson. Use questions such as the following:

- Were we all successful at getting home at curfew? Why or why not?
- How can we be more successful at getting home on time? (Guide the students into the correct answers by asking them to look for empty spaces so that they don't have to worry about running into anyone else and starting to head home around 5 o'clock.)
- How has math helped us to learn to locate our home?

Assessment Forms

- Movement Study Assessment form, for teacher use. Add these factors to the form: listening, moving in general space, levels, appropriate use of time.
- Self-Assessment form (version appropriate for students' level). Add these factors to the form: questions about getting home on time, traveling without touching, remembering the variables.

Extensions

- Construct a master drawing of the room in which Curfew is being played. Include the basic landmarks such as the clock, the blackboard, the windows, and the flag. Identify the X wall and the Y wall. Then have each student put a mark (a dot or circle in a distinctive color) where each student thinks his or her home is on the master drawing.
- Using a globe, point out the location of the students' school. Identify this home point with the numerical latitudinal and longitudinal expression, the concepts of X and Y (the "doorknob" and "drinking fountain") on a global scale.

Ready, Set, Geometry

48

STRETCHING SHAPES.

GRADES: 3 TO 5   **LENGTH:** 20 TO 30 MINUTES

Materials

- Large elastic bands
- Examples of geometric shapes
- Musical accompaniment or hand drum

National Standards

Mathematics: 5

Dance: 1, 2, 7

Objectives

The students will be able to do the following:

- Work cooperatively to create group shapes.
- Understand and demonstrate the vertices and line segments of geometric shapes.

INTRODUCTION

Introduce the vertices (points where the sides meet) and line segments that represent a square, triangle, and rectangle. Display examples of these basic shapes. Add a pentagon, hexagon, and octagon, and display the examples. Don't forget to review circle and oval.

THE MOVING ADVENTURE

1. Divide students into groups of eight or more. Give each group an elastic band.
2. Lay the band on the floor. Have everyone step inside and pull the band up behind their lower backs.
3. Gently stretch the band as a group into a circle shape to begin.
4. Create a sequence of five geometric shapes. Arrange the examples on the board.
5. Call out the next shape, triangle. Each group moves into a triangular shape by a slow count of 8. They must decide who will represent the three points and how to form the three lines. ⚙ **Modeling**
6. Call out the next shape, pentagon. Transition to a five-point and five-line pentagonal shape, again by a slow count of 8. Teamwork is necessary for working efficiently and for success-fully forming the vertices and line segments on time. If necessary, one student may step into the middle, away from the shape. Students will need to discuss the formation as it is created. The goal is to memorize the shapes and perform them in silence. ⚙ **Forming Patterns**
7. Students continue to structure two additional shapes of their choice using the 8-count transi-tion.
8. Remind students to think about who represents the vertices and line segments for each shape so that they can easily construct them.
9. Have the students perform the shape sequence with music, counting the 8s in the music as the shapes are formed in each group.

ASSESSMENT

- Did your group work well together to create and present your shape sequence?
- Was it difficult to remember your shapes and transition on time?
- What did you learn about the characteristics of geometric shapes?
- Develop a mix-and-match worksheet for geometric shapes where the students will identify each shape.

Assessment Forms

- Participation Assessment form.
- Group Evaluation form.

Extensions

- Add new choices for shapes, such as a star, kite, or free form. Ask students to work independently to create and rehearse a new five-shape sequence. Each group may perform for the class and video camera.
- Instruct students to create a visual art collage (paint, cut paper, markers) of the geometric shapes their group used for the five-shape sequence. They can design the collage using repeating and overlapping shapes of various sizes.

Blast Off!

49

FRACTIONS AND RATIOS OF PARTS TO THE WHOLE.

GRADES: 3 AND UP **LENGTH:** TWO 30-MINUTE SESSIONS

Materials

MOVEnture DVD
- Hand drum
- Gymnastics mat (if desired)

National Standards

Math: 2
Dance: 1, 2, 3

Objectives

The students will be able to do the following:

- Memorize and perform a movement sequence.
- Describe in mathematical terms the concept of *parts to the whole* in fractional representation.
- Describe what is meant by *base of support*.

INTRODUCTION

Explain to students that they will play with the concept of a base of support. *Base of support* is the term used to describe how objects, including the human body, are able to balance in this environment where gravity is so strong. But in this lesson, students will learn about fractions, or how the whole body can use its parts to balance. And because they will use a countdown to do this activity, this lesson is called Blast Off!

Begin by asking the students to look at you while you stand up straight. Ask them how many body parts you have touching the floor. (The answer is two.) Your two feet are touching the floor, so your base of support is two. Bend down and put an elbow or a flat hand on the floor. Ask students how many body parts are touching the floor. (The answer is three, so your base of support is three.) Add another body part and ask students again how many body parts and therefore what kind of base of support you have.

A body part is counted separately when empty space appears underneath the body part. So when you put your whole hand down flat on the floor, that is considered one body part. But if you lift your palm and just have all fingers touching the floor, then the hand alone is considered as having five body parts touching. Remind students that the combination of the body parts we use to hold ourselves up is called *base of support*. Shapes must be able to balance strongly and not fall over. ⚙ **Body Thinking**

THE MOVING ADVENTURE

Session 1

1. Students start in self-space. Ask them to create a base of support of five, so only five body parts can touch the floor. Check each student and give praise for originality.

2. Ask them for a base of support of four body parts. Go around the room and check each one, pointing out the great differences in shapes.

3. Repeat activity with bases of support of three and two, checking their shapes with a quick walk around the room. Finally, ask for the big challenge: the task of one, and only one, body part touching the floor. Of course, most will balance on one foot, but there are some

125

interesting alternative solutions: balancing on one's tailbone, or belly button, or backbone with all other body parts tucked or lifted in some way off the floor. If students try to balance on one hand, remind them that the shape cannot fall over—it must balance on its base of support for a count of three.

Session 2

1. After the experimentation period, tell them they are now ready to begin Blast Off! Students should start standing with feet together, hands overhead in a pointed rocket shape. Request that they each find a balanced shape on a base of support of five body parts, a shape they think is really interesting to look at. Write on the chalkboard, 5 parts = 1 whole body. So 5 represents the denominator, the whole base of support. Each of the body parts touching the floor therefore represents one-fifth of the base of support, so 1 is the numerator. Together, then, all five parts touching the floor would be 5/5, which equals 1. Once they have a balanced shape on a base of support of five, have them memorize their body positions in full detail. After they have held the shape for a few seconds, have them relax and shake out, or "erase." Ask them to repeat the shape exactly. As they reconstruct it, ask if their head is as it should be, if their eyes are looking in the same direction as before, and if every detail is the same. ⚙ **Abstracting**

2. Now reduce the base of support by one, as in a countdown for a rocket launching. So four body parts should now be touching the floor, and the shape should be completely new with a different level and different body parts used to create it. Since four body parts represents the whole, then each body part represents one-fourth. Write it on the board. Students proceed to memorize their shapes for four body parts.

3. Now see if they can remember the five shape. Then ask for the four. Rehearse it by giving a drum roll with quick beats of your hand on the drum and say, "Five!" (They make the five shape.) When all are balancing, give the drum roll again and say, "Four!" (They make the four shape.)

4. Repeat the game all the way down to one body part as a base of support. Keep helping them along the way with reviewing the shapes in order, writing the fractions on the board, and using the drum roll and the excitement of the countdown sequence.

5. When they have completed the countdown, say, "Blast off!" Students should create an

explosion of their bodies into the air, fly through the space, and land on the moon, freezing in a final shape.

6. Break the class into small groups and have them demonstrate their individual dance studies for the rest of the class. Encourage positive feedback directed both at individual students ("I like the way Danny did an upside-down shape for his three shape, or his one-third") and to the group as a whole ("They remembered their countdown really well").

ASSESSMENT

- What did you find challenging in this game?
- What was your favorite part?
- Who can write on the board the correct fraction that represents each body part in the five shape? The three shape?
- Using your own body or a student to demonstrate, create different base-of-support shapes. Instruct students to write what fraction each body part touching the floor represents. (You can introduce numbers higher than five, but be sure the shapes are very clear in terms of the number of body parts touching the floor. The use of separate fingers to increase the number of body parts touching is an advantage here.) Grade the written responses.

Assessment Forms

- Movement Study Assessment form, for student evaluation of the performance.
- Comprehensive Assessment form.
- Self-Assessment form (version appropriate for students' level).

Extensions

- Repeat this entire study in partners. The students now treat their two bodies as the "whole." The only additional element to the activity is that the students must touch each other somehow in each of the shapes. So for the five shape, partnerships must be touching each other and together may only have a total of five body parts touching the floor. As the countdown continues, they will have to solve the problem of having only one body part touch the floor between the two of them! Think it can't be done? The children will surprise you! Many will carry a person piggyback and lift one leg, but others may find creative solutions by lying on their bellies and having their partner sit on their back and then lifting the limbs and head off the floor. Or they might try doing a similar shape while on the back. Another solution is for both partners to clasp onto each other and both stand on one partner's foot. In one instance, a student did a handstand while his partner held his legs up to balance him; then the upside-down boy put his hands on his partner's feet and the partner carefully lifted one foot.
- Blast Off! is a good activity to present at a student–parent event or a demonstration for a PTA meeting. Not only is it visually interesting, but it also can involve the audience. Request the audience to try to figure out what is going on. They may not know it is a fraction study, but they may realize through close observation that the students are reducing the number of body parts touching the floor. Do it once with a few students who are performing solo. Repeat it with the most interesting partnerships from the classroom lesson.

50 Equation Creations

BECOMING NUMERICAL OPERATIONS.

GRADES: 3 TO 5   **LENGTH:** 30 TO 45 MINUTES

Materials

MOVEnture CD track 17
- Audio playback system
- Cardboard symbols: +, –, ×, =
- Number squares of approximately 1 square foot. You need to have a number for each member of the class. (Number squares can be purchased from classroom suppliers or physical education suppliers.)

National Standards

Mathematics: 2, 3

Dance: 1, 4, 7

Objectives

The students will be able to do the following:
- Apply operations efficiently and accurately in solving problems.
- Demonstrate the ability to work cooperatively in a small group.

INTRODUCTION

This lesson has been written for a class of 24 students. It can be easily adjusted to whatever number of students are in your class. You will use the members of the class to develop various types of numerical operations: addition, subtraction, and multiplication. Students will have fun adding movement to their numbers along the way.

THE MOVING ADVENTURE

Descriptive Numbers

1. Using the number squares in a large circle, each student stands on a number from 1 to 24.
2. Go around the circle, each student saying his or her number and adding a movement.
3. Invent a descriptive movement using the same first letter for the words. For example, only one, trembling two, tiptoe three, freaky four, falling five.

Becoming a Number

1. Have students walk around the circle and choose a new number.
2. This time have the students explore their own shape of their chosen numbers through body design. Ask students to use straight and curved lines to make the shape of one of the numbers, such as the number five. They may use a body part or the whole body. They may want to try finding a partner to form the shape together. Then collect the number squares. ⚙ **Empathizing**

Simple Addition Grouping

1. Ask students to tell you the total number of students in the class (24). See how many ways they can be grouped to add up to 24.

2. Divide the class in half (12 students on one side, 12 on the other). Ask students to group themselves to equal 12 (for example, $10 + 2 = 6 + 6$ or $5 + 5 + 2 = 7 + 3 + 2$). On the board, write the equations the students create.

3. Have students move through general space to the music. When the music is paused, gather with students close to you and form a group. For example, groups of $3 + 6 + 6 + 7 + 2$ equal 24. Move again and see what new groups can be created to equal 24.

Equation Creation

1. Create groups for mathematic equations. Have students move through general space to the music. When the music is paused, some of the students form a group and then add another group to their group. For example, a group of $5 +$ a group of 3 equal eight. ⚙ **Body Thinking**

2. Pass out number squares and mathematical signs to small groups.

3. Ask each group to create equations using the number squares and signs; then they dance these equations. The groups may make the body shape of the numbers represented, add a descriptive movement, or form groupings.

4. Share equations created with the class.

ASSESSMENT

- Was it difficult for your group to create equations together?
- Did you enjoy translating your equations into shapes and movements?
- How did teamwork assist you in solving problems?

Assessment Forms

- Participation Assessment form, for teacher use.
- Peer Assessment form.

Extensions

- Ask students to see how many different equations they can create.
- Suggest a simple division equation (such as 24 divided by 4) and demonstrate by placing the class in four groups of six. Invite the students to create another division equation using groupings.

Number Sense

USING BALL-HANDLING SKILLS.

GRADES: 3 TO 5   **LENGTH:** FOUR 20- TO 30-MINUTE SESSIONS

Materials

- Playground balls or basketballs
- Cardboard symbols for addition (+), subtraction (−), and multiplication (×)

National Standards

Physical Education: 2

Math: 2

Dance: 2, 4

Objectives

The students will be able to do the following:

- Work cooperatively and creatively in small groups.
- Demonstrate ascending and descending numbers by manipulating a ball.
- Create and maintain a group ball-handling pattern.

THE MOVING ADVENTURE

Ascending and Descending

1. Begin with ascending number of bounces such as 1 bounce, 2 bounces, 3 bounces, 4 bounces, continuing up to 10. Reverse to descending bounces (10 bounces, 9 bounces, and return to a single bounce). Count the number of bounces aloud for each set.

2. Divide into two groups and ask one group to create the ascending and descending bouncing rhythm while the other group puts the balls away and designs rhythmic movement to accompany the sounds of the bounces.

3. The rhythmic movement can involve body-part isolations or whole-body movements. The groups can switch roles.   ⚙ **Body Thinking**

Patterns

1. Arrange students into groups of three to five.

2. Each group must work together to create a rhythmic pattern using the ball. They can pass, toss, bounce, and roll the ball. They can use a ball for each member of the group or set a few aside.

3. Using any variation that the group agrees on, they set the manipulative ideas into a pattern to be repeated.

4. Have each group perform their pattern and teach it to the other groups.

Equations

1. Set up groups of four in a square formation with one ball per square.

2. One member of the group will place the math sign (addition, subtraction, or multiplication) in the middle of the square.

3. Call out a number (3) for the first student holding the ball. That person will dribble, toss, or do any movement you determine with the ball that number of times and pass the ball to another member of their square.

4. Call out another number (5) for this student, and he or she will manipulate the ball the called number of times. Check the math sign in the middle of the square (×).

5. The student will pass the ball to the next person; this student must manipulate the ball the appropriate number of times for the answer to the equation (15).

6. Every student must have a turn with the ball. ⚙ **Transforming**

Time Measurement

1. Make two circles of 12 students and ask each of them to mark an hour on the clock.

2. Place number squares or tape numbers on the floor.

3. Call out a time of day. The student that marks that hour should perform a movement with the ball representing the time. A student standing on the number 7 would toss the ball in the air seven times.

4. The half hour can have a single movement (like the single chime of the clock) performed by the student on number 6 (6:30). Quarter past and three-quarters past can be signified through a distinctive movement.

5. Try marking the minutes through movement. Invite the students to move around the clock performing dribbles to represent the minutes and toss the ball the appropriate number of times on the hour.

6. The seconds can tick by with a quick, repetitive movement. Follow a second hand on your watch and ask students to pass the ball back and forth between their hands or run in place 60 steps for the duration of a minute.

ASSESSMENT

- Did your group work cooperatively together?
- What was difficult about manipulating the ball to express numbers, patterns, equations, and time?

Assessment Forms

Participation Assessment form. Add these factors to the form: understanding math concepts, ascending and descending, patterns, equations, and time measurement.

Extensions

- Ask students to do a visual representation of numbers, patterns, equations, and time. You may use worksheets to reinforce learned concepts.
- The students manipulate a ball as the prop. Ask students to explore numbers, patterns, equations, and time using another prop (such as a scarf, streamer, or hula hoop).

Pizza Portions

CREATING A PIZZA-PERCENTAGE DANCE.

GRADES: 3 TO 5   LENGTH: 45 MINUTES

Materials

MOVEnture CD track 9
- Audio playback system
- Chalkboard or poster board
- Cardboard wedges of different types of pizza: cheese, anchovies, pepperoni, and vegetable

Objectives

The students will be able to do the following:

- Gather data.
- Construct a chart based on data gathered.
- Write percentages.
- Create a people pizza dance that reflects descriptive words about their favorite pizza.

National Standards

Math: 6

Dance: 7

INTRODUCTION

Review with students the steps in collecting and graphing data. Remind them that data represents specific information about real-world objects or activities. Data comes in many forms and can be collected, organized, and displayed in many ways.

THE MOVING ADVENTURE

1. Ask each student to answer the following question: What is your favorite kind of pizza? Have each student select only one type for their "favorite," despite their possible enthusiasm for all of the possibilities.

2. Divide the class into groups of six or eight.

3. Have one student use the tally method to record the statistics on classmates' favorite types of pizza. Here is an example:
   - Extra cheese...........\\\\
   - Pepperoni..............\\
   - Anchovies.............\
   - Vegetables.............\
   - Total............... 8

4. Have each group construct a bar graph.

132

5. From the statistics, figure out what percentage of the group likes each type of pizza.

6. Transform the bar graph into a pie, or circle, graph.

7. For the People Pizza Dance, have students form groups according to their favorite pizza (all pepperoni together, all cheese together). Each group will explore movement to depict their pizza (for example, hot cheese would be dripping, melting, stretching movements; spicy pepperoni would be sizzling, jumping, hopping movements). ⚙ **Transforming**

8. Each group will choreograph a dance based on their pizza movements. (Use ABA form.)

9. Each group of students will share through performance. Isn't dancing delicious?

ASSESSMENT

- How do you develop a pie chart?
- How do you determine a percentage?
- Describe how the dances represented various types of pizza.

Assessment Forms

Movement Study Assessment form, for teacher to assess each student's performance of the People Pizza Dance.

Extension

Have students collect data, graph the data, determine percentages, and develop a pie chart based on other categories, such as colors or foods.

Adapted, by permission, from Kathleen Isaac, *Math+ Pizza. Movement Me? Why Not!* Workshops of 5 - 9th grade math teachers.

53

Probability Dance

CREATING ONE DANCE OUT OF MANY POSSIBILITIES.

GRADES: 3 TO 5   LENGTH: TWO 30-MINUTE SESSIONS

Materials

MOVEnture CD track 13
- Audio playback system
- Three boxes with the following items in each box:
  - Box 1: Floor plans with stage directions (10)
  - Box 2: Locomotor and nonloco-motor sequences (5)
  - Box 3: Beginning and ending group shapes (8)

National Standards

Math: 7

Dance: 1, 3

Objectives

The students will be able to do the following:
- Apply the concepts of *certain, equally likely,* and *impossible* to occurrences in a dance.
- Determine the likelihood of selecting a specific component of a dance.
- Determine the ratio of selection of a specific component of a dance.
- Create a Probability Dance with randomly selected components.

INTRODUCTION

Introduce the concept of the Probability Dance, which is a dance developed through a chance occurrence. Students will create their probability dance with materials in the boxes. They will try to predict the likelihood of performing a certain floor pattern and a certain locomotor and non-locomotor sequence with a certain beginning and ending shape. Before this lesson, give students information about probability and ratio.

Probability

Equally likely is when each element in a group of outcomes has an equal chance of occurring. For example, a cube with six equal sides is equally likely to land on any side.

Not equally likely is when a group of outcomes do not have an equal chance of occurring. Given a target with a large outer ring and a small inner circle, a thrown dart is more likely to land on the large outer ring than in the smaller inner circle. Therefore, the probability of hitting the inner circle versus the outer circle is not equally likely.

Ratio

Ratio is the number of desired outcomes compared to the number of possible outcomes. For example, you're given five balls (one red, one purple, one green, and two yellow), and your desired outcome is a red ball. A ratio of desired outcomes to total outcomes is as follows:

Desired outcomes	Red balls	1
Total outcomes	Total balls	5

The probability of picking a red ball is 1 out of 5.

THE MOVING ADVENTURE

Create the probability dance. ⚙ **Pattern Forming**

1. Divide students into 10 groups.
2. Distribute the Probability Dance worksheet (pp. 283–285) to each group, and have them complete the three sections.
3. One member from each of the 10 groups will select an item from each box and write the selection on their worksheet, then return the item to the box.
4. Instruct students to cooperate and develop the beginning shape to their Probability Dance.
5. Have students develop a sequence based on the locomotor and nonlocomotor movements they selected. They can increase the numbers of items, but they must maintain the order.
6. Have students design their ending group shape.
7. Perform the dance.
8. One group at a time will perform their probability dance using appropriate stage directions.

ASSESSMENT

- How do you determine a ratio?
- What other ways could you create a Probability Dance?
- Assess answers on the worksheets.

Assessment Forms
- Probability Dance Worksheet.
- Group Evaluation form.

Extension
Groups of students create a new Probability Dance based on other elements, such as qualities, directions, and nonlocomotor movements.

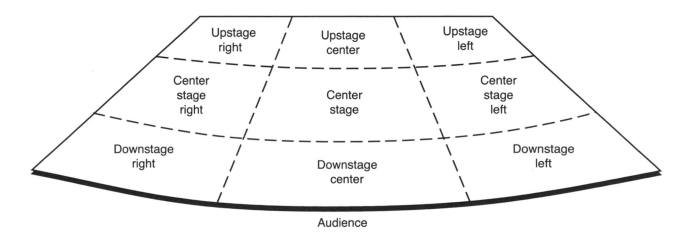

chapter 6

MOVEntures in Social Studies

Dance is first and foremost perceived as motion to express emotion. It transforms everyday body language into a fine art. This language of motion is fundamental to communicating ideas not readily expressed in any other form. Dance bridges the gap between self and others, the individual and the group, and it brings us together as we seek to connect with the world at large. In the process of sharing our similarities and differences, children learn to work in teams, listen to others' ideas, and collaborate to solve problems—all in a dance and movement context. For example, students can explore the concept of oppression firsthand by experiencing a game where the space in which they are moving is systematically reduced to the point that their freedom of movement is significantly compromised.

Today's society is diverse, and it challenges children to increase their ability to handle adversity. Thus, activities that expand their knowledge about history and its heroes; geography; diversity; humanity; and social issues such as poverty, gender, and race are paramount to preparing them for the future.

Universal Circle Dance

54

LEARNING ABOUT THE DANCES OF OTHER CULTURES.

GRADES: K TO 2 **LENGTH:** TWO 20-MINUTE SESSIONS

Materials

MOVEnture DVD

MOVEnture CD track 19

- Audio playback system
- Pictures of different cultures doing circle dances (such as Native American, Greek)

National Standards

Social Studies: 1

Dance: 1, 5

Objectives

The students will be able to do the following:

- Recognize that circle dances are an expression of community life.
- Learn a short dance that is performed with many others in a circle.

INTRODUCTION

As cultures throughout the world have developed, so have their unique dance traditions. One dance form that has evolved universally is a dance performed in a circle. Circle dances celebrate community—community life, unity, and fellowship. By performing the movement in a circle, all members can see each other and feel connected and welcome. In most societies, the circle represents the never-ending cycle, the circularity of life. Share this background and pictures of circle dances with the students.

The following moving adventure is a simple circle dance, which you can use to celebrate *your* classroom community. Though not based on any particular culture or dance tradition, it maintains the spirit and purpose of circle dances while emphasizing rhythm and cooperative skills. ⚙️ **Analogizing**

THE MOVING ADVENTURE

Session 1

1. Form two or three circles with 8 to 10 students in each one. Students hold hands in this formation and stretch the circle open. Arms should be stretched to where the students' clasped hands are at waist level. Once the formation is established, students release hands and place them on their waists. Feet should be close together in parallel position.

2. Start the music. Wait through the 4 beats of introduction. After the introduction, the dance consists of 6 sets of 8 beats. ⚙️ **Body Thinking**

Counts	Suggested Movements
1-8	Clap 8 times on the beat of the music.
1-8	Jump feet apart on count 1, hold count 2, jump feet back together on count 3, hold count 4; repeat for counts 5 to 8.
1-8	All join hands and do 7 slides (sideways gallops) to the right (counter clockwise) for 7 counts, pausing on the right foot on count 8.

Counts	Suggested Movements
1-8	Come into center of circle, swinging hands low and forward and then raising them high together as everyone arrives in a tight group at center on counts 1 to 4. Moving backward, stretch the circle open again to a comfortable distance on counts 5 to 8.
1-8	Repeat the sliding circle to the left.
1-4	Repeat moving into the center of the circle on counts 1 to 4. Students should let go of each other's hands on count 4.
5-8	Students scoot backward out of the circle, no longer holding hands, and sharply make a shape at the edge of the expanded circle on count 7. Hold count 8.

Session 2

Review and practice! Eventually the whole class can do the circle dance together. Initially, it takes some time to get all students to go the same direction at the same moment or to shrink and expand the circle correctly, so it is easier to teach everyone when they are in smaller, more manageable groups. For purposes of performance and assessment, sharing in smaller circles also makes this lesson more manageable and easier to observe.

ASSESSMENT

- What did you like about this circle dance?
- Did you think the members of your circle worked well together?
- Why do you think circle dances were invented by different cultures?

Assessment Forms

- Movement Study Assessment form, for student evaluation of the performance.
- Participation Assessment form. Add these factors to the form: listening, cooperating, clear ending shape.
- Peer Assessment form for oral or written responses.
- Group Evaluation form.

Extensions

- On videotapes, show performances of circle dancing by different cultures.
- Learn an authentic circle dance by inviting a guest from another culture.

Around the World

55

DANCES DONE TO TCHAIKOVSKY'S *Nutcracker*.

GRADES: K TO 2   **LENGTH:** FOUR 20-MINUTE SESSIONS

Materials

- World map
- Tchaikovsky's *Nutcracker* audio recording
- Audio playback system
- *The Nutcracker* story by E.T.A. Hoffman
- Pictures of *Nutcracker* dancers
- Samples of cultural traditions (optional):
    - Chinese gong, chopsticks, fan, silk robe
    - Spanish castanets, red cloak
    - Arabian finger cymbals, recorder
    - Russian Cossack hat

National Standards

Social Studies: 9

Music: 7

Dance: 1, 2, 5

Objectives

The students will be able to do the following:

- Perform dances from various cultures.
- Identify people and customs of other countries.

INTRODUCTION

Introduce your students to the *Nutcracker* by reading the story and listening to Tchaikovsky's score. Focus on "The Land of the Sweets" as a springboard to exploring China, Spain, Arabia, and Russia. Mark the location of each country on the world map and create a bulletin board with pictures from each dance or country.

THE MOVING ADVENTURE

Chinese

1. Ask the students if they have eaten at a Chinese restaurant or used chopsticks. Have they had an egg roll or wonton soup? Greet them with the traditional Chinese bow. Show them a beautiful Chinese silk robe and hand-painted fan. Write a sample of Chinese lettering on the board.

2. Listen to the Chinese segment from the *Nutcracker* audio recording.

3. Begin the dance in a circle formation with the sound of the Chinese gong. Before starting, number the students 1 or 2. ⚙ **Body Thinking**

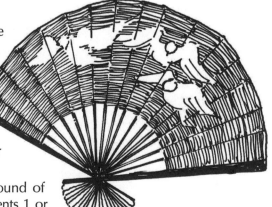

Counts	Suggested Movements
1-8	Students shuffle step with hands pressed together at chest level. Bow toward the audience (outside circle) right with arms folded at chest level.
5-8	Bow left (or toward a neighbor right and left). Repeat shuffle and bow around the circle three times.
1-2	All students face center and jump, bringing feet and arms apart.
3-4	Jump and bring feet and hands together.
5-8	Repeat apart, together.
1-2	All students are facing out; jump and bring feet and arms apart.
3-4	Jump and bring feet and hands together.
5-8	Repeat apart, together. Turn to face center, fanning hands.
1-8	Number 1 students move into the center of the circle and return to their place using the shuffle step. Number 2s circle in self-space while fanning with right hand.
1-8	Number 2 students move into the center and return to their place using the shuffle step. Number 1s circle in self-space while fanning with right hand. Everyone finishes with a bow toward center and then freezes.

Spanish

1. Listen to the Spanish dance on the *Nutcracker* audio recording.

2. Explain to students that Spanish flamenco dance has a flirtatious quality using hand clapping and heel rapping to the rhythm of the Spanish guitar. Castanets, held by the fingers into the palm of each hand, are important to the dance.

3. Galloping is added to the dance to represent the horses present at the bull fight, a famous Spanish tradition. With a kindergarten class, invite all students to gallop in unison around the room clockwise (rather than around a partner) for the full 30 counts. Have them pretend to hold a red cloak, enticing the bull and spin out of the path of the bull at the last moment.

4. In a double-circle formation, face audience (front).

5. Don't be too concerned about placement of the left and right foot for this age group as long as they are changing sides or mirroring the teacher.

Counts	Suggested Movements
1-2	All students step right and then touch together with the left foot. Left arm curves overhead; right arm is in a low undercurve. Fingers click together twice as if playing castanets. Chin is lifted proudly.
3-4	Repeat by stepping left, touching together with the right foot. Right arm curves overhead; left arm is in a low undercurve. Fingers click together twice, and chin is lifted.
5-8	Stamp right foot four times, clap hands over right shoulder 12 times (triple time): "5 and a 6 and a 7 and a 8 and a."

Repeat this phrase three times and pair up students, one from inside circle with one from outside circle.

Counts	Suggested Movements
1-16	Student in outside circle claps hands 16 times over right shoulder, kneeling on one knee. Student in inside circle gallops around partner.
1-14	Partners switch places and repeat.

Repeat beginning phrase.

Counts	Suggested Movements
1-2	All students step right, touch together with left foot. Left arm curves overhead; right arm is in a low undercurve. Fingers click together twice as if playing castanets. Chin is lifted proudly.
3-4	Repeat by stepping left and touching together with the right foot. Right arm curves overhead; left arm is in a low undercurve. Fingers click together twice, and chin is lifted.
5-8	Stamp right foot four times and clap hands over right shoulder 12 times (triple time): "5 and a 6 and a 7 and a 8 and a."
1-2	Finish with step right, and touch together with left foot. Left arm curves overhead; right arm is in a low undercurve. Fingers click together twice as if playing castanets. Chin is lifted proudly.

Arabian

1. Listen to the Arabian dance on the *Nutcracker* audio recording.

2. Disney's movie *Aladdin* helps set the scene for dancing the Arabian dance. Bring in an oriental rug on which the class flies together, or have each student use a carpet square. The can say, "Abracadabra" and pretend to be in Arabia. Show them the costumes of Aladdin and Princess Jasmine. Play the finger cymbals and talk about belly dancing. Use the image of a snake being charmed to exemplify the movement of a belly dancer.

3. Begin seated cross-legged in a circle (on carpet squares).

4. Ask each student to pick up an imaginary snake-charmer flute and pretend to play along with the Arabian music. When the music changes, they put down the flute and become the snake. Using a wiggly torso, arms, legs, head, and neck, they slither through the space at all levels. Have them listen for the flute to play again and be seated with their own flutes. Have them sing the notes of the flute using daah (long)-da (short), daah (long)-da (short), da-daaaah (descending)-da. Repeat the snakelike move-

ment when the music changes. Pretend to play finger cymbals (if possible, borrow finger cymbals from your music teacher).

Russian

1. Listen to the Russian dance on the *Nutcracker* audio recording.

2. Explain that the Russian dance comes from Ukraine, home of the Cossacks. It is exciting and full of competitive spirit, and it requires great endurance. Cossack dancers demonstrate extraordinary leaps and turns and the difficult knee bends, or Prysiadka steps.

3. The students get in scattered formation and perform the dance:

Counts	Suggested Movements
1-2	Jump and reach overhead.
3-4	Hands on waist.
5-6	Jump and reach overhead.
7-8	Hands on waist.
1-8	Spin in self-space with arms extended to the sides.

Repeat four times.

Counts	Suggested Movements
1-2	Cross arms in front of chest, right heel forward, left heel forward.

Continue slow Russian kicks a total of 16 times (32 counts).

Counts	Suggested Movements
1-4	Bend knees and place hands on knees. Do the Russian pose: Extend right heel, extend arms in V shape overhead.
5-8	Do the Russian pose: Extend right heel, extend arms in a V shape overhead.
1-4	Bend knees, hands on knees.
5-8	Russian pose, hands on hips on count 8.
1-2	Jump and reach overhead.
3-4	Hands on waist.
5-6	Jump and reach overhead.
7-8	Hands on waist.
1-8	Spin in self-space with arms extended to sides.
1-28	Fast Russian kicks.
1-2	Bend knees and place hands on knees.
3-4	Russian pose: Extend right heel, extend arms in V shape overhead.

ASSESSMENT

- What can you tell me about the Chinese traditions? What are the customs of Spain, Arabia, and Russia?

- Who can place China, Spain, Saudi Arabia, and Russia on the map?

- Can anyone demonstrate the movement we learned from China? When you hear the music, see if you remember what movements to do to the Chinese music. Try moving to the Spanish, Arabian, and Russian music.

- Match pictures of chopsticks, castanets, snake, and Cossack hat to pictures of dancers in costume.

Assessment Forms

Participation Assessment form.

Extensions

- To explore traditions of China, decorate a fan using watercolors. Discuss and share pictures of the plants and animals in China. Paint something from nature native to China, such as a panda bear, monkey, or flower. Demonstrate the fan-folding technique and fold into fans. Perform the dance with fans.

- Color pictures of dancers in costume from each country.

- Attend a local production of the *Nutcracker* ballet.

- Students in grades 3 to 5 can research the four countries represented and share information about the people and their traditions.

56 The Speaker for the Trees

MAKING GOOD DECISIONS FOR A COMMUNITY.

GRADES: K TO 2   **LENGTH:** TWO 30-MINUTE SESSIONS

Materials

MOVEnture CD track 36
- Audio playback system
- The book *The Lorax* by Dr. Seuss
- Drum
- Rhythm sticks

National Standards

Social Studies: 7

Language Arts: 6

Dance: 1, 2, 3

Objectives

The students will be able to do the following:

- Discuss how people make choices for business purposes.
- Respond to the story *The Lorax* in terms of appropriate and responsible choices.
- Create a story dance depicting a more responsible use of resources.

INTRODUCTION

- Tell or read the story *The Lorax* to the students. It is about decisions made by a business-man—and the consequences of those decisions on a community. Lead a discussion about the action, characters, and story line.

THE MOVING ADVENTURE

Session 1

1. Students will improvise all sections while you act as narrator. Starting position is in scattered formation.
2. Encourage students to use many nonlocomotor and locomotor movements as you read the story. For example, they can mimic trees swaying, bears skipping, and fish jumping and turning.
3. The story ends with all living things eliminated by the poor business decisions of the Once-ler. Students may exit the space or completely collapse to the floor.

Session 2

⚙ **Imaging**

1. Create a new ending. Students are invited to imagine a more responsible way to run business.
2. Post suggestions on overhead projector or chalkboard.
3. Give an example of a possible solution in dance or drama.
   - Students are in scattered formation in rounded body shapes. They are the Truffula Seeds.
   - The seeds grow into beautiful trees. The students rise to middle or high level, swaying in self-space.

- The animals return. Bar-ba-loots skip, slide, and play together.
- The Swomee-Swans circle the room, gliding and flying.
- The Humming Fish jump, turn, fall, and roll.
- All freeze and then become trees.
- As a few trees are cut down, new trees are planted (students collapse, then rise)
- Students form groups representing each animal and the trees.
- The whole community lives in harmony now.

ASSESSMENT

- How should we make decisions about developing new businesses in communities? (Grade 2)
- Did the Once-ler care about the community? Why do you say this? (K to 2)
- How can we be more careful about the people and animals in our communities? (K to 2)

Assessment Forms

- Participation Assessment form.
- Comprehensive Assessment form.

Extensions

- Students draw a picture of the new ending to the story dance.
- People who own businesses can visit the class and describe their business and the impact of that business on the community. Each student can bring one question to ask.

Room to Move

DISCRIMINATION, OPPRESSION, AND THE LOSS OF FREEDOM.

GRADES: 3 AND UP   **LENGTH:** ONE 40-MINUTE SESSION OR TWO 20-MINUTE SESSIONS

Materials

- Drum or musical instrument to provide simple fast and slow accompaniment.
- Easily moveable barriers to expand or diminish the available space, such as orange cones, chairs, and ballet barres.

National Standards

Social Studies: 6, 10

Physical Education: 2

Dance: 1, 4

Objectives

The students will be able to do the following:

- Execute a variety of locomotor movements (walking, running, jumping, hopping, leaping, galloping, sliding, skipping).
- Travel through general space without touching others. (Respect personal space.)
- Define and discuss the issue of discrimination after experiencing a loss of freedom through movement activities.

INTRODUCTION

To introduce the concept of discrimination (unfair treatment of an individual or group based on prejudice), you may want to read one of the books listed in the Extensions section of this lesson. But you can do the activity first, introducing the vocabulary of discrimination and oppression to give a name to what the students will have just experienced.

This activity requires a large space in which students can stand in a scattered formation yet move freely through general space. During the course of the lesson, the amount of space, and consequently the freedom to move easily, will be continually reduced. Establish the size of the initial large space by setting up the moveable barriers at the perimeter. ⚙️ **Analogizing**

Tell the students that this space is their community, which has a fundamental law. The law to be obeyed is *Never touch another person while moving in the space.* Disobeying the law, or touching, has consequences, whether the touching is merely brushing someone on the arm in passing or a larger infringement of personal space.

Consequences can be a variety of punishments:

- Go to jail. The student who touches another student must withdraw for that stage of that activity and watch from the perimeter (that is, be incarcerated). If no obvious fault can be determined, then all persons involved in the touching may have to go to jail.
- Become invisible. The students who touch others must stand frozen like pillars in the space, just as people in society who are not seen or heard have no access to their rights. They now become obstacles within the space, which adds complexity.
- Introduce a consequence not listed here.

THE MOVING ADVENTURE

Session 1

1. Begin by having the students travel through the space using locomotor movements such as walking forward, walking backward and sideways, hopping, skipping, galloping, crawling (introduces a new level), rolling fast and slow, twirling, marching, and finally, running.

2. Beat the drum to help students feel fast or slow speeds, or tickle the drum for twirling. Beat strongly for marching or lightly for galloping. Scratch randomly on the drum skin for crawling, or use no drum beat at all for running.

3. When the space is large, students can accomplish the tasks easily without disobeying the law. Note: Do not stop the activity on each infringement of the law. Wait until the entire series of movements has been explored. After completing the activity, if slight touching occurred, overlook them with a comment that the first time is always a practice run, so you will give no consequences. Repeat the exercise in the large space, making it clear the law will now be applied. Verifying touches and collisions is your responsibility. When finished, apply consequences. If all students were successful, congratulate them for being obedient citizens.

4. Move the barriers to decrease the size of the space by one third. Repeat the exercise in the smaller space, using the same locomotor movements in approximately the same order. Apply the law and seriously implement any consequences.

5. Reduce the space further to only half the original size and repeat the exercise.

Session 2

1. Briefly remind the students of the rules and begin the activity again.

2. Reduce the space three times, making sure the last time that the students are so confined that they feel great difficulty in accomplishing the required task of traveling but not touching others.

3. Bring the dancing to a close and move to discussion.

ASSESSMENT

In the beginning, the students generally have fun with the lesson because they enjoy moving and are excited by the challenge of the rules. But as the space lessens and they become more confined, they feel the loss of freedom, do not want to be embarrassed by going to jail or becoming invisible, and generally become more serious. What at first felt like a game no longer seems so. Encourage them to talk about this. Ask the following questions:

- How did you adjust your movement in order to not touch others, especially when the space was small? (Possible answers are "I moved back and forth rather than around the space," "I noticed we all started moving in the same direction around the room.")

- How did you feel when you were successful? How did you feel when you had to go to jail or become an invisible member of society? ⚙ **Empathizing**

- I was playing the role of the law enforcer, or police. How did you feel about my judgment?

- Did you feel the punishment fit the crime (being sent to jail, whether for an obvious collision or for just barely touching someone)? Elicit discussion of historical racist practices of exclusion or gender, religious, and other discriminatory practices, some of which are at issue in current times. During such discussion, ask the students how they think people feel who are denied the same rights given to other citizens.

- Was this a necessary law for our community (not touching others while traveling)? Would you change the law we had in our classroom community? Would you change how it is enforced?

Assessment Forms

Participation Assessment form. Add these factors to the form: locomotor movements, seriousness of purpose.

Extensions

- The lesson can be repeated either now or later so that the students can be more successful as an entire group. Or repeat the exercise, if appropriate, to let the students try out their own modification of the laws.

- Have the students develop a list of laws they deem appropriate for their school community.

- Have students write an essay or haiku about loss of freedom.

- The following are suggested readings to use as a preface or follow-up for Room to Move:
  - Coleman, E. 1996. *White Socks Only*. Morton Grove, IL: Albert Whitman.
  - Curtis, C.P. 1995. *The Watsons Go to Birmingham—1963*. New York: Delacorte Press.
  - Taylor, M.D. 1976. *Roll of Thunder, Hear My Cry*. New York: Dial Press.

Expedition

58

FOLLOW THE ADVENTURE MAP.

GRADES: 3 TO 5   **LENGTH:** THREE 30-MINUTE SESSIONS

Materials

MOVEnture CD track 10
- Audio playback system
- Torn paper bags
- Watercolor markers
- Locomotor movement cards
- Environmental challenges cards
- Pathway cards (optional)
- Video recorder and equipment

National Standards

Social Studies: 1

Dance: 2

Objectives

The students will be able to do the following:

- Draw sketch maps of the community, region, and nation.
- Accurately demonstrate basic locomotor skills through straight and curved pathways and several directions.
- Identify and clearly demonstrate a range of dynamics and movement qualities.
- Demonstrate the ability to work cooperatively in a small group during the choreographic process.

INTRODUCTION

Scattered throughout general space, dancers walk in a curve, walk in a line, walk in a zigzag, and stop on a dime. Talk about pathways drawn on the floor and the importance of maintaining self-space as they move through the shared space. Review locomotor skills to be included in the adventure, or use lesson 16, Straight, Curved, Zigzag, Dot!, as a warm-up to this Moventure.

Discuss the adventures of Indiana Jones in the movie *Raiders of the Lost Ark* and the environmental conditions that challenge his expedition. These elements of nature demonstrate a variety of dynamics and force. Ask students to demonstrate the vibratory movement of an earthquake, a percussive lightning bolt, and the sustained sinking of quicksand.

THE MOVING ADVENTURE

1. Divide dancers into groups of four to six. Each group should receive a piece of brown paper (torn paper bag), markers, and movement cards including five locomotor movements (walk, skip, leap, crawl, roll) and three environmental challenges (quicksand, tropical storm, lion encounter). Different cards are selected for each group. Ask the groups to sequence their cards into an adventure, design a legend with symbols representing each card (see Legend, p. 150), and create a mapped pathway. Every member of the group must be involved in the design of the map. You can distribute a predetermined pathway card to each group, or the dancers can create their own. ⚙️ **Dimensional Thinking**

Legend

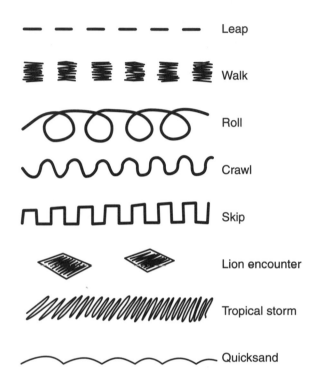

— — — — — — — Leap

▰ ▰ ▰ ▰ ▰ ▰ Walk

◯◯◯◯ Roll

∿∿∿∿∿ Crawl

⊓⊔⊓⊔⊓⊔ Skip

◆ ◆ Lion encounter

⋙⋙⋙⋙ Tropical storm

⌣⌣⌣⌣⌣ Quicksand

2. Introduce music as background for the adventure movement. Ask dancers to determine how they will follow the pathway map as a group. They may want to rotate leaders, move in unison, or break into smaller groups along the way. The group must determine what happens at the end of the adventure. Maybe they will find a hidden treasure or experience an explosion.

3. Give the groups time to rehearse their locomotor movements and the dynamics of the environmental challenges. Sufficient practice is required for learning the map sequence and pathway. When ready for performance, the groups may bring their map but try not to stop the action of their adventures in long pauses by looking at the map. Ask each group to find a starting place on "stage" to represent the spot on their map where the adventure begins. Videotape each group's adventure with music.

ASSESSMENT

- What was the process for creating a map including a pathway and legend?
- Did your group members cooperate on the task?
- Was it difficult to remember the locomotor sequence and pathway of your adventure? How were they performed?
- Were the dynamics demonstrated for environmental challenges clear and appropriate?
- Have classmates try to guess what locomotor movements and environmental elements were included in each group's performance.

Assessment Forms

- Movement Study Assessment form, for teacher use and for student evaluation of the performance.
- Peer Assessment form.

Extensions

- Expedition may represent any geographical area or culture. You may vary the elements of nature and musical accompaniment to fit your region of study.
- You may want to take time to discuss and better understand map design. Give students instruction and experience reading a map.

We the People

59

EXPLORING CIVIC IDEALS THROUGH
THE PREAMBLE TO THE U.S. CONSTITUTION.

GRADES: 3 TO 5   **LENGTH:** TWO 30-MINUTE SESSIONS

Materials

- A U.S. flag on a pole that can be carried
- A copy of the preamble to the U.S. Constitution
- Hand drum

National Standards

Social Studies: 10

Language Arts: 6, 8

Dance: 1, 2

Objectives

The students will be able to do the following:

- Define and perform tableaus using low, medium, and high levels.
- Be able to recognize and recite the preamble in its entirety.
- Work cooperatively in large and small groups.

INTRODUCTION

This lesson supports the study of American government and democratic ideals. Read the preamble to the Constitution to the students as written by the founding fathers. Discuss to clarify or define each phrase. What did the authors of the Constitution mean when they wrote, "form a more perfect Union"? What is "domestic Tranquillity"? What would be included in "general Welfare"? Then explain that the class will create a series of tableaus to interpret the preamble through movement, or a "Preamble Dance." Explain that a tableau is a theatrical tool: All performers on stage freeze in position, as in a snapshot, and then resume the action. ⚙ **Transforming**

THE MOVING ADVENTURE

The following is a simple movement interpretation of the preamble. Feel free to adapt and change any movements to fit your needs.

Session 1

1. Students begin in a single-file line at the side and back of the dance space. The leader of the line holds the flag high and proudly in front. Drum an introduction of 4 strong beats in a marching rhythm on the hand drum. Students march in single file on the 5th beat across the back of the dance space and then curve around to form a large circle. When the leader meets the tail of the line, perform a drum roll. Students stop and face the center of the circle.

2. Students recite, "We the People of the United States . . ." The leader walks into the center of the circle with the flag held high. All freeze for a moment in the tableau.

3. ". . . in Order to form a more perfect Union . . ." As students recite this phrase, they reach straight arms down, then forward, then high, circling them back and down again in one smooth motion. As their arms reach the bottom, they join hands to interconnect the circle as they say the word *union*. Throughout, the leader waves the flag from side to side in the center of the circle and stops on the word *union*. All pause.

4. ". . . establish Justice . . ." As students recite this phrase, all should turn to face the audience and all place the right hand over their heart on the word *justice*. The leader brings down the flag, pounding the pole on the ground three times as if it were a gavel in a courtroom. All pause.

5. ". . . insure domestic Tranquility . . ." One student recites this phrase. Students move out of the circle into smaller groups (four to six students) and show activities that represent happy scenes such as eating together or other ideas that represent community life that they brought up during discussion. Beat the drum three times softly to signal the students to freeze in their activity, forming tableaus.

6. Practice the sequence a couple times to solidify memorization.

Session 2

1. Review the sequence from prior session.

2. Continue with ". . . provide for the common defense . . ." One student can recite. Students stay in their small groups and decide on a level at which to depict soldiers pointing rifles. Each group should point their rifles in the same direction, although that direction may be different from other groups. Decide how to use the flag in one group. Pause.

3. ". . . promote the general Welfare . . ." A single student can recite. Subjects for these tableaus can represent house structures, educational settings, or medical environments, based on ideas from earlier discussion of the meaning of the phrases.

4. ". . . and secure the Blessings of Liberty to ourselves and our Posterity . . ." A single student can recite. The entire class cooperates to build a mountain shape with students at different levels and with one student supported at the highest level (such as by standing on others' backs as a couple students hold his legs to stabilize him). A separate student reaches the flag up toward the student at high level as if trying to hand it off. Pause.

5. ". . . do ordain and establish this Constitution for the United States of America . . ." Give a soft drum roll to signal students to melt out of the mountain shape and form a tight group facing the audience with the flag held by someone at the edge of the group. Have students at the front of the group kneel down on both legs and sit on their heels, students in the middle of the group kneel on one leg, and students at the back of the group stand tall. Break this phrase into two: Have a single student recite, "do ordain and establish," and then all students speak proudly, "this Constitution for the United States of America!"

ASSESSMENT

- Who can tell me what a tableau is? What level did we use in ours?
- Can we all recite the preamble to the Constitution together without movement?
- What did our classroom represent? Whom were we depicting in this dance?

Assessment Forms

- Participation Assessment form.
- Group Evaluation form.

Extensions

- This Moventure, if well practiced, is ideal for sharing with another class or at a PTA, school board, or other school or community event.
- Have students write how they feel about the ideals stated in the preamble. They can include this essay in their portfolios.

Dances of the 1920s

RAGTIME TUMPIE: A STORY OF DANCER JOSEPHINE BAKER.

GRADES: 3 TO 5 **LENGTH:** TWO 30-MINUTE SESSIONS

Materials

MOVEnture CD track 20
- Audio playback system
- The book *Ragtime Tumpie,* a picture book by Alan Schroeder.

National Standards

Social Studies: 1

Language Arts: 6

Dance: 5

Objectives

The students will be able to do the following:

- Discuss the life of Josephine Baker in the context of 1920s America.
- Perform the following dances from the 1920s: two step, Charleston, Suzie Q, and fan steps.

INTRODUCTION

Ask the students if they know of any dances from the 1920s. Explain that they will learn about a dancer, Josephine Baker, through a story titled *Ragtime Tumpie.* They will then learn a few dances from that time period. Read and discuss the book *Ragtime Tumpie.*

Summary of story: Tumpie, a young African American girl who will later become famous as the dancer Josephine Baker, longs to find the opportunity to dance amid the poverty and vivacious street life of St. Louis in the early 1900s.

THE MOVING ADVENTURE

1. Students should have ample space as they all face you.
2. Explain and demonstrate the steps and have students practice without the music. Then have students practice with the music.
3. Face the students while demonstrating by reversing the movements. (For example, if you want the students to use the right hand for a movement, use your left hand as you face them to demonstrate.)
4. You may perform with the students with your back to them.
5. Combine steps to make a 1920s dance.

Dance Steps

Two step: Begin with the right foot. Step right and left, and then repeat. Body sways in the direction of the steps.

Suzie Q: Begin with both feet together, knees slightly bent. Lift up toes of both feet and move right. Lift up heels of both feet and move right. Repeat to the left.

Charleston: Begin with both feet slightly apart. Touch the right toe to the front, then step right foot back in place. Touch the left toe to the back, then step in place. Repeat.

Fan step: Begin facing a partner with legs together and slightly bent, hands on knees. Move knees apart and then back together while hands cross, touching the opposite knee every other time the knees are apart.

ASSESSMENT

- Describe the dances performed by Josephine Baker and others in 1920s America.
- Describe the clothing that people wore in the 1920s.

Assessment Form

- Participation Assessment form.
- Peer Assessment form.

Extension

Have students contact grandparents and great-grandparents and conduct an interview with them regarding the dances performed during their youth. Instruct students to ask the grandparents and great-grandparents to teach them the dances.

A Native American Poem

AN ADDITIONAL ACTIVITY TO A BROADER UNIT ON NATIVE AMERICAN CULTURE.

GRADES: 3 TO 5   **LENGTH:** THREE 20-MINUTE SESSIONS

Materials

MOVEnture CD track 21
- Audio playback system
- "The Planting Song," a Native American poem from the Osage Indian culture
- A variety of simple musical instruments (optional)

National Standards

Social Studies: 1, 2
Language Arts: 6
Dance: 1, 2, 7

Objectives

The students will be able to do the following:
- Interpret a Native American poem through dance and music.
- Describe what a theme is.
- Develop and memorize a movement sequence.
- Work in small groups to create an ending to a dance.

INTRODUCTION

One way to enjoy another culture is by studying its forms of expression. Cultures reflect themselves through their arts and crafts, such as weavings, sculpture, poetry, dance, music, and costumes. In this activity, ask students to listen to a poem by the American Osage Indians; then they will interpret the poem through movement and making shapes. This poem, "The Planting Song," is about something in particular. It has a *theme,* a single idea that was important to the poet. Ask students to think about what the theme is as you read the poem. In other words, what is the poem telling about?

THE MOVING ADVENTURE

1. Session 1: Read "The Planting Song" to the students:

   "The Planting Song"
   I have made a footprint, a sacred one.
   I have made a footprint; through it the blades push upward.
   I have made a footprint; through it the blades radiate.
   I have made a footprint; over it the blades float in the wind.
   I have made a footprint; over it the ears lean toward one another.
   I have made a footprint; over it I pluck the ears.
   I have made a footprint; over it I bend the stalk to pluck the ears.
   I have made a footprint; over it the blossoms lie gray.

"The Planting Song" (continued)

I have made a footprint; smoke arises from my house.

I have made a footprint; there is cheer in my house.

I have made a footprint; I live in the light of day.

Reprinted from *American Indian Love Lyrics and other verse from songs of the North American Indians,* 1925.

2. Promote discussion to determine the theme of respect and reverence for growing corn, a staple food.

3. For the Planting Song Dance, separate students into small groups of five or six. Each group should find their own space in the room and stand next to each other in a cluster. The poem's structure gives the dance a beautiful simplicity and rhythm. Each time the repetitive phrase "I have made a footprint" is spoken, a sound is made just after the word *footprint,* as if the sound represented the semicolon. The rest of the sentence on each line is individually interpreted. The following description is one example of how to interpret the poem through dance, but certainly the students can be allowed to develop their own ideas for solo, partner, or small-group work. Practice each line numerous times and then connect it to the choreography before it.

4. You can extend session 2 into session 3 by learning the poem in smaller increments. For example, learn half the poem, then the other half, then practice for performance. ⚙ **Transforming**

Line	Sound and Movement Description
I have made a footprint;	All children stamp one foot in unison.
(pause)	
a sacred one.	Cross hands over chest, head lowers.
I have made a footprint;	All children stamp one foot in unison.
(pause)	
through it the blades push upward.	Clasp hands together and push them upward slowly until fully extended.
I have made a footprint;	All children stamp one foot in unison.
(pause)	
through it the blades radiate.	Release hands overhead so arms are separate and vertical (many blades).
I have made a footprint;	All children stamp one foot in unison.
(pause)	
over it the blades float in the wind.	Move arms gently overhead.
I have made a footprint;	All children stamp one foot in unison.
(pause)	
over it the ears lean toward one another.	Each group points overhead arms and hands toward another group by bending their bodies.

I have made a footprint; (pause)	All children stamp one foot in unison.
over it I pluck the ears.	Students straighten bodies from leaning and then sharply clench fingers into fists at different times, as if harvesting corn.
I have made a footprint; (pause)	All children stamp one foot in unison.
over it I bend the stalk to pluck the ears.	Bodies bend in any direction and arms pull in sharply toward the body at different times.
I have made a footprint; (pause)	All children stamp one foot in unison.
over it the blossoms lie gray.	All students gently melt to the floor.
I have made a footprint; (pause)	All children stamp one foot in unison.
smoke arises from my house.	Students rise, interpreting qualities of smoke through their bodies.
I have made a footprint; (pause)	All children stamp one foot in unison.
there is cheer in my house.	Students join hands to form circle, facing inward.
I have made a footprint; (pause)	All children stamp one foot in unison.
I live in the light of day.	Each group creates a tableau together, with each member doing a domestic task that would have been part of Native American culture, such as grinding grain, sewing, weaving, forging spearheads. Tableau freezes for ending.

Reprinted from *American Indian Love Lyrics and other verse from songs of the North American Indians,* 1925.

4. Instead of always stamping for the footprint, students can make different sounds. They could slap hands to the thighs, clap the hands, or use a drum. Varying the sound provides aural interest without affecting the rhythm. Besides the sound for the footprint phrase, musical instruments can provide accompaniment for the movement that follows. A wind chime works well for "over it the blades float in the wind" or "smoke arises from my house"; a cowbell ring is nice for "there is cheer in my house." Gather a selection of instruments and let the students help decide which instruments feel right for their movements.

ASSESSMENT

- What is the theme of this poem?
- Do you think the way we danced the poem was how the Osage Indians would have danced it?
- Were you able to remember everything you had to do in the dance?
- How successful was your group in working out a final tableau together?

Assessment Forms

- Movement Study Assessment form, for student evaluation of the performance.
- Participation Assessment form.
- Group Evaluation form.

Extensions

- If the students can handle more complexity, you can introduce other variations. Try changing directions on the mention of *footprint,* changing the speed of the stamp (very fast or in slow motion), or having each group create one line of the poem and then assemble them into the order of the poem.
- Have students write their own simple poem using the "have made a footprint" structure, but they should end each line with their own composition around a single theme.
- Related lesson: Everyday Life in Faraway Times, lesson 96.

The Kaleidoscope of Life 62

CHANT AND DANCE ABOUT ECOSYSTEMS.

GRADES: 3 TO 5   **LENGTH:** TWO 30-MINUTE SESSIONS

Materials

MOVEnture CD track 22
- Audio playback system
- Lyrics to "Kaleidoscope of Life" by Lynnette Overby et al.

National Standards

Social Studies: 2

Music: 1

Dance: 1

Objectives

The students will be able to do the following:

- Create and perform a structured dance.
- Discuss the meaning of the chant and the application of this meaning to their lives.

INTRODUCTION

Ask the students if they know what the word *kaleidoscope* means (constantly changing colors and patterns). Explain that they will perform a chant based on the chant "Kaleidoscope of Life." (Read the lyrics or write each phrase on the board. Lead a discussion about the different aspects of the chant.)

THE MOVING ADVENTURE

1. Students are in scattered formation. Assign them numbers 1, 2, or 3.
2. Start dance. Students clap on upbeat 4 times. 1 (clap 2), 3 (clap 4), 5, (clap 6) 7, (clap 8)

"The Kaleidoscope of Life!"	Suggested Movements
Celebrate! Celebrate! Celebrate!	On the first spoken *Celebrate!* group 1 jumps into a reaching shape, followed by group 2 and then group 3.
Life! Life! Life!	Reverse, changing direction (group 3 moves first).
Celebrate! Celebrate! Celebrate!	On the first spoken *Celebrate!* group 1 jumps into a reaching shape, followed by group 2 and then group 3.
Life! Life! Life!	Reverse, changing direction (group 3 moves first).
The kaleidoscope of life comes in many shapes and sizes.	Form two circles: one outside and one inside circle. The circles slide in opposite directions, depicting a kaleidoscope.
Microbes! Seeds! And sharks!	Change shapes on each of these words.
In a world of great surprises . . .	Circle arms while moving to a scattered formation.

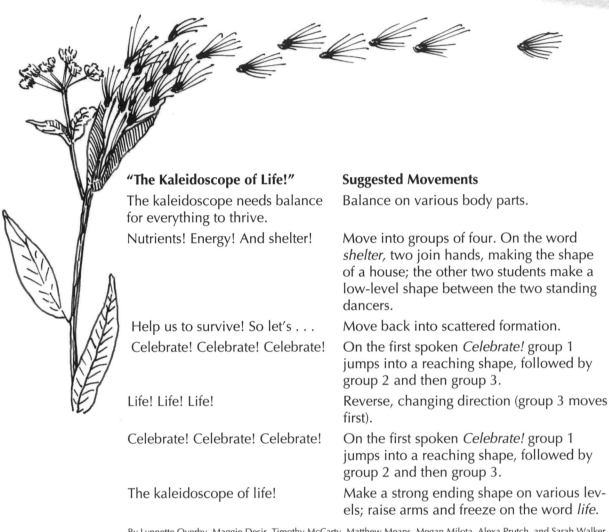

"The Kaleidoscope of Life!"	Suggested Movements
The kaleidoscope needs balance for everything to thrive.	Balance on various body parts.
Nutrients! Energy! And shelter!	Move into groups of four. On the word *shelter,* two join hands, making the shape of a house; the other two students make a low-level shape between the two standing dancers.
Help us to survive! So let's . . .	Move back into scattered formation.
Celebrate! Celebrate! Celebrate!	On the first spoken *Celebrate!* group 1 jumps into a reaching shape, followed by group 2 and then group 3.
Life! Life! Life!	Reverse, changing direction (group 3 moves first).
Celebrate! Celebrate! Celebrate!	On the first spoken *Celebrate!* group 1 jumps into a reaching shape, followed by group 2 and then group 3.
The kaleidoscope of life!	Make a strong ending shape on various levels; raise arms and freeze on the word *life.*

By Lynnette Overby, Maggie Desir, Timothy McCarty, Matthew Means, Megan Milota, Alexa Prutch, and Sarah Walker

ASSESSMENT

- What did the chant mean to you?
- What did the chant and dance say about life?
- In what ways did you and the other students need to cooperate to perform the dance?

Assessment Forms

Movement Study Assessment form for teacher use. Videotape the assessment.

Extension

Students can focus on the natural resources in their state. Have them develop a portfolio of pictures and news articles about the status of their state's natural resources. With this information, they can complete the portfolio with an essay titled "What I Can Do to Preserve Natural Resources in the State of _____."

63

It's The Law

INTERPRETING LAWS THROUGH MOVEMENT.

GRADES: 3 TO 5   **LENGTH:** 30 TO 45 MINUTES

Materials
- Traffic signals
- Whistle

National Standards
Social Studies: 6

Dance: 3, 7

Objectives
The students will be able to do the following:
- Explain how laws and rules helps people maintain order and manage conflict.
- Describe fair ways for groups to work together and make decisions.
- Demonstrate kinesthetic awareness and concentration in performing movement.

INTRODUCTION

Ask students what purpose laws serve within our society. (Laws allow us to live together peacefully.) How do the rules in our student handbook affect the school community? (They help us work together as kind, safe, respectful citizens within our community.) Laws and rules are designed to help us maintain order and protect people, property, and tradition.

THE MOVING ADVENTURE

You can and should adapt these ideas to your class situation. Pick one or two ideas from the following possibilities.

Possibility 1
1. Traffic laws can be easily interpreted through movement. Ask everyone to find a partner.
2. One student represents the driver, putting hands on the shoulders of the partner (the car).
3. Students begin driving on imaginary roads throughout the general space.
4. Hold up or call out signals: ⚙️ **Modeling, Body Thinking**
   - Go, yield, and stop (move, slow down, and freeze).
   - Speed limit: 10 miles per hour (same speed).
   - Low bridge (move at a low level).
   - Slow curve (in slow motion).
   - Yield to pedestrians (pathways).

- No trespassing (limit general space).
- Merging traffic (group cars together).
- Buckle seat belts (wrap arms around partner's waist).
- No parking zone (no stopping).
- One-way traffic (same direction).

5. Create a simple sequence of signals and test the students' responses. Use a whistle (be the traffic officer) to signal a violation and issue an imaginary ticket. Discuss what happens if the laws are broken.

Possibility 2

1. Separate students into groups of four to six. Ask them to consider three laws for their community to present through movement.
2. They may use actual laws (rules):
   - Lifejackets are required (one student wraps arms around another's back).
   - Drivers must come to a complete stop at a stop sign (one student holds up a stop hand gesture; all remaining students stop).
   - No running in the hallways (all students walk in a line).
3. They may also create movement laws:
   - All citizens must move forward through general space.
   - All citizens are required to move quietly (they must jump up and down as a punishment for breaking the law if they talk).
   - Citizens must not touch anyone (they must make an upside-down shape if they touch anyone else).
4. Have each community present their three movement laws to the class. Ask the class to guess the wording of the laws.

Possibility 3

Invite one student from each community (group) to break a law. Each community repeats the demonstration of their three laws with a violation. Ask the class to discuss how the community is affected by the violation.

Possibility 4

Working with the same groups, develop three laws that are unfair or discriminatory. For example, all citizens that are wearing red must remain in their self-space while others are free to travel through general space, or only girls are allowed to drive above the speed limit.

ASSESSMENT

- What did you learn about the importance of traffic laws?
- How did your community government work to create their laws?
- What are the consequences when laws are broken? How did it feel when laws were unfair?

Assessment Forms

- Group Evaluation form.
- Movement Study Assessment form, for student evaluation of the performance.
- Peer Assessment form.

Extensions

- This is the perfect opportunity to review classroom rules and discuss their importance. Ask students to consider three laws for the classroom to present through movement.
- Revisit the classroom rules throughout the year and reinforce them by re-creating the "laws" movement phrase.

64

Time Scrolls

A GOOD BEGINNING-OF-THE-YEAR ACTIVITY.

GRADES: 3 TO 5   **LENGTH:** FOUR 30–MINUTE SESSIONS

Materials

MOVEnture CD track 23
- Audio playback system
- A room large enough for all students to lay out their materials and work on their individual figure drawing on the floor at the same time
- For each student, a length of three-feet-wide paper, cut two feet longer than the height of that student
- Felt-tip markers
- Magazines of interest to the age of students; their own pictures, photos, postcards, and easily glued decorative items from home that reflect their interests and their world (sequins, beads, bits of cloth, small jewelry, a piece of doll clothing, charms, string, leather, parts of favorite but broken toys, comics, baseball cards, gum wrappers, favorite CD covers, computer game boxes, television guides, cereal boxes)
- Lots of bottles of glue or glue sticks
- Scissors, enough pairs for all students
- Double-sided cellophane tape

National Standards

Social Studies: 2
Dance: 1, 2

Objectives

The students will be able to do the following:
- Describe the contents of a time capsule and its historical and cultural purpose and usefulness.
- Describe elements of their culture through verbalization and visual arts media.
- Perform and identify a variety of locomotor movements.
- Develop a dance sequence with a beginning, middle, and end.

INTRODUCTION

Ask students if they know what a time capsule is. What types of things are contained in it? Why do we make time capsules? Explain that they will send messages to the future about their lives today—how they live them and what their home, state, country, or world is like. So they will include commonplace items as well as newsworthy ones.

Tell the students that their messages are not capsules (containers with things inside). Their messages will be called Time Scrolls.

THE MOVING ADVENTURE

Session 1

Students should work in partners to each draw their silhouettes on their three-feet-wide pieces of paper. Roll out the paper and weight the corners with books. The student lies down on the paper with body in an open yet interesting shape. A student can lie on the back with arms by sides, but it is more interesting to have one arm bent overhead. Or they can lie on one side in the shape of running, or on the belly with arms and legs in different directions, as long as the entire body fits within a six-inch border from the perimeter of the paper. The partner, using a wide-tip marker, draws around the edge of the student's body, picking up details such as spaces between fingers, lines around the cuffs of pants, or a ponytail streaming onto the paper.

Sessions 2 and 3

1. Conduct sessions 2 and 3 in a large space, and instruct students to roll out their papers and secure the edges by either weighting them down or taping with tape that will not ruin the edge of the paper when pulled up from the floor. Now for the fun part: Students use the magazines and personal paraphernalia from their lives to fill in the silhouette using collage techniques—cutting out select pictures and graphics and then gluing; overlapping; and decorating with markers, crayons, string, and sequins. Remind the students that the silhouettes are symbolic, representing who they are and what their life is like at this moment in time. Archeologists who discover these time scrolls 100 years from now should understand what life was like, what children were interested in, what things might have cost, and what was going on in the world—the purpose of a time capsule. ⚙ **Modeling**

2. To preserve the clean lines of the silhouettes and provide continuity when the scrolls are hung, students should leave the negative space outside the silhouette free of decoration. How to hang the scrolls is your choice. You can tape them up using teachers' sticky tack, or each scroll can be wrapped around a dowel at each end and stapled firmly, and then wire strung at the top to hang it like a picture. The bottom dowel gives weight to the scroll and prevents rolling. You may have other options for hanging artwork that already exist in your school.

Session 4

1. *Let's dance!* After the scrolls are hung on the walls, instruct students to start by finding self-space and lying on the ground in the shape of the figure on their scrolls. Start background music. In slow motion, each student should find a way to rise from the floor and make the

same shape as the one on their scroll. When all students are frozen in their scroll shapes, each student chooses a locomotor movement to use to travel through general space, stopping to make a shape that reflects something from the scroll (an activity depicted on it like reading, a sporting activity, or reacting to a favorite movie). ⚙ **Transforming**

2. Students repeat this task two more times, changing the locomotor movement each time as well as the shape depicting an activity.

3. After the students have performed their phrases, instruct them to turn and face their scroll. On a signal (drum roll, tambourine, gong), students run to their individual scrolls and stop suddenly in front of them as if smashing into an invisible wall. Then they melt to the ground and finally regrow to finish in the shape of the figure on their scroll. Fade the music as they finish.

4. Split the class in half and have each group perform for the other half.

ASSESSMENT

- Do you think an archeologist 100 years from now would get a good idea of what your life was like at this time in history from the personal perspective of your time scroll?
- What locomotor movements did you see used or did you use yourself during this dance?
- What did you learn about yourself from this activity?
- Time Scrolls artwork and Time Scrolls dance can be evaluated separately.
- Photograph each scroll for student portfolios.

Assessment Forms

- Movement Study Assessment form, for teacher use and for student evaluation of the performance. Add these factors to the form: locomotor movements, clear shapes, following directions, confidence in execution.
- Self-Assessment form (version appropriate for students' level). Include comments on their Time Scrolls artwork.

Extensions

- These scrolls can be hung in a variety of places: in the school's halls; around the gym for a special event; or at a local business such as a bank, restaurant, hospital, wherever they can be appreciated. They look best hung closely side by side, like a frieze on the side of a temple.
- The scrolls offer a nice backdrop to a performance for parents or other classes.
- Have students write about what was going on 100 years ago in their community.

20th-Century Celebration

DECADES IN HISTORY.

GRADES: 3 TO 5   **LENGTH:** TEN 30-MINUTE SESSIONS
(MAY BE TIME VARIATIONS WITH EACH DECADE
LESSON)

Materials

MOVEnture DVD

MOVEnture CD tracks 24-34 or music from the decades of the 20th century

- Audio playback system
- Celebration of the 20th-Century Time Line of Events
- Celebration of the 20th-Century People in Dance
- Pictures from decades of the 20th century

National Standards

Social Studies: 2

Dance: 1, 5

Objectives

The students will be able to do the following:

- Understand highlights in 20th-century history.
- Perform dances representative of each decade.
- Answer questions about dance and dancers of the 20th century.

INTRODUCTION

Tell students that they will be looking back at the 20th century, the 1900s through 1990s, and reflect on highlights in U.S. history. As they follow the time line of the decades, they will discover the world of dance and be introduced to just a few of the dancers who influenced the dance of today.

THE MOVING ADVENTURE

Pass out the Celebration of the 20th-Century Time Line of Events and the Celebration of the 20th-Century People in Dance to your students and briefly discuss the history of events. Celebration of the 20th-Century Time Line of Events and the Celebration of the 20th-Century People in Dance present highlights from the century in concert and popular dance. The scope of the time line and the chart of influential people allows for only a few representative historical people and events to be discussed. Feel free to research any of the influential personalities not included in this selection and add them to the appropriate decade in the 20th-century history.

The following selection of dance styles are aligned with a decade or an important dance personality. Ask your students to find self-space, and lead them through the basic steps. Practice with the suggested musical accompaniment and have each half of the class take turns performing for the other half.   ✿ **Body Thinking, Recognizing Patterns**

Celebration of the 20th-Century Time Line of Events

Events in dance	Decade	Events in history
• 1904: Isadora Duncan opens school • 1905: Pavlova and Fokine's *The Swan* • 1906: Ruth St. Denis performs *Radha* • 1909: Diaghilev's *Ballets Russes* • Ragtime music	**1900**	• 1903: Wright Brothers' first flight, first base-ball World Series • 1908: Henry Ford's Model T • Immigration
• Jazz music emerges • 1912: Nijinsky in *Afternoon of a Fawn*	**1910**	• Halley's comet • Decline of rural life • 1914: World War I, Panama Canal opens • 1919: Treaty of Versailles ends war
• Tap dancer Bill "Bojangles" Robinson • 1926: Martha Graham's first recital • Charlie Chaplin, silent-movie star • The Charleston, "flappers" • 1929: First Academy Awards • Henry Ford helps bring square dancing back into popularity.	**1920**	• Golden age of radio • Prohibition (illegal alcohol) • Women's right to vote • 1929 stock market crash, Great Depression
• Fred Astaire and Ginger Rogers • 1934: George Balanchine and Lincoln Kirstein open School of American Ballet	**1930**	• By 1933, 25% unemployment • Dust bowl, farmers lose land • National idols: boxer Joe Lewis, track star Jesse Owens
• Big-band music, swing dance • Jukeboxes, bobby socks, saddle shoes • 1949: José Limón's *The Moor's Pavanne*	**1940**	• 1941 Japanese attack Pearl Harbor • U.S. enters World War II • Women in the workforce
• Rock 'n' roll takes over popular music • Elvis Presley • 1958: Premiere of Martha Graham's *Clytemnestra*	**1950**	• Postwar baby boom • Television becomes popular
• 1960: Alvin Ailey creates *Revelations* • Jerome Robbins' *West Side Story* • Chubby Checker does the twist • 1961: Rudolf Nureyev defects to the U.S. • The Beatles	**1960**	• 1963: President John F. Kennedy assassinated • Civil rights movement • 1969: Neil Armstrong first to walk on the moon
• 1973: Twyla Tharp stages *Deuce Coupe* • Paul Taylor • Disco dance craze (the bump, hustle)	**1970**	• 1973: Agreement to end Vietnam War, renewed fighting in Middle East • 1974: Watergate scandal • Platform shoes, bell bottoms
• Mikhail Baryshnikov • Andrew Lloyd Webber's *Cats* • Michael Jackson on MTV • Break dancing	**1980**	• Presidents Ronald Reagan and George Bush • Berlin Wall brought down
• 1996: Savion Glover wins Tony award • Hip-hop dancing, rap music • Mark Morris	**1990**	• End of the Cold War • L.A. riots • Operation Desert Storm • Technology: computers, cell phone • President Bill Clinton

From *Interdisciplinary Learning Through Dance: 101 MOVEntures*, by Lynnette Young Overby, Beth C. Post, and Diane Newman. 2005. Champaign, IL: Human Kinetics.

Celebration of the 20th-Century People in Dance

Years	Person in dance	Dance contributions
1872-1929	Serge Diaghilev	Director of Ballets Russes; dominated European dance. Remarkable manager and organizer. Contributed to the international art movement. Collaborated with a long list of composers and painters including Stravinsky and Picasso.
1877-1968	Ruth St. Denis	Modern dance innovator. Devoted half a century to promoting new dance forms. Codirected the Denishawn Company with Ted Shawn, which was a proving ground for the next generation of dancers
1878-1927	Isadora Duncan	Pioneering talent in modern dance. She broke from the traditions of ballet by freely using her whole body and dancing barefoot in a flowing Grecian tunic to the music of the great masters.
1878-1949	Bill Robinson	Internationally renowned rhythm tapper. Danced in vaudeville, Harlem clubs, Broadway shows, and Hollywood movie musicals.
1880-1942	Michel Fokine	Dancer and choreographer of standard masterpieces such as *Les Sylphides* and *Petrouchka.* Reformed the stereotypical methods for creating ballet; marked the beginning of the modern movement.
1881-1931	Anna Pavlova	A great ballerina known for her dramatic passion. Her solo in *The Dying Swan,* choreographed for her by Fokine, is her most famous role.
1889-1977	Charlie Chaplin	Silent-movie actor. Won international fame for his pantomime. In 1914, he created the role of a tramp named Charlie. Among Chaplin's most famous movies were *The Kid, The Gold Rush,* and *City Lights.*
1890-1950	Vaslav Nijinsky	Legendary dancer known for his technical accomplishments, particularly his elevation and powers as an actor. Career lasted less than 10 years.
1894-1991	Martha Graham	Major influence in modern dance technique, choreography, and performance. Her technique incorporates the breathing cycle and principle of contraction and release.
1899-1987	Fred Astaire	Masterful tap and ballroom dancer. Considered one of world's greatest dancers. With dance partner, Ginger Rogers, perfectly expressed the romance of ballroom dancing. Became an international star.
1904-1983	George Balanchine	One of America's finest ballet choreographers for more than 50 years. Worked extensively with abstract ballets, created works of profound significance, and influenced generations of dancers. Director of New York City Ballet.
1908-1972	José Limón	Dynamic Mexican-born dancer. Danced with Doris Humphrey (created fall-recovery technique) and Charles Weidman company. Formed his own company in 1946; worked to strengthen the image of the male dancer.
1919-1991	Margot Fonteyn	Ballerina with a career that spanned more than four decades. Danced for Frederick Ashton's Royal Ballet. Known for her quiet radiance and partnership with Rudolf Nureyev.
1930-	Paul Taylor	Known for a choreographic style that uniquely uses wit, satire, repetition, and logical placement of movements.

(continued)

From *Interdisciplinary Learning Through Dance: 101 MOVEntures*, by Lynnette Overby, Beth Post, and Diane Newman. 2005. Champaign, IL: Human Kinetics.

(continued)

Years	Person in dance	Dance contributions
1931-1989	Alvin Ailey	African American dancer, teacher, choreographer. Best-known works *Revelations, Lark Ascending,* and *Cry* present the human spirit and black themes. Director of the popular company that still bears his name.
1938-1993	Rudolf Nureyev	Magnetic stage presence. Came to U.S. from the Kirov Ballet in 1961. Legendary partnership with Margot Fonteyn; guest performer with many of the world's major companies
1942-	Twyla Tharp	Reputation for complex abstract choreography. Her *Deuce Coupe,* first created for the Joffrey Ballet, was danced to music by the Beach Boys against a subway-car graffiti backdrop.
1948-	Mikhail Baryshnikov	Born in Latvia. Came to U.S. in 1974 from Kirov Ballet. Unparalleled technique; performed ballet and modern works with all major companies. Artistic director of American Ballet Theatre for almost 10 years.
1956-	Mark Morris	Choreographer, dancer, director. Acclaimed for his use of music, using dancers of all shapes and sizes often in nontraditional ways.
1973-	Savion Glover	Has redefined tap dance with his speed, clarity, and inventive quality. Won the Tony award for his performance and choreography in *Bring in 'da Noise, Bring in 'da Funk.*

From *Interdisciplinary Learning Through Dance: 101 MOVEntures,* by Lynnette Overby, Beth Post, and Diane Newman. 2005. Champaign, IL: Human Kinetics.

1900s: Ballet

This dance consists of three 20-minute sessions. Refer to MOVEnture CD track 24 for music to accompany this lesson.

Session 1: Introduction

During the early 1900s to 1920, the art of ballet became increasingly popular both in Europe and in the United States. Ask students if they know what ballet is, and ask them if they have ever seen a live performance by a ballet company.

If they have never been to see ballet, how would they recognize it as different from other dance forms, like tap dancing, jazz dancing, or folk dancing? Specific characteristics of ballet help us recognize it. Look at pictures of ballet dancers and costumes and sets and identify some of those characteristics.

1. Turned-out legs. In everyday life when we walk or run, our feet and knees point straight forward. But ballet dancers turn out their legs so that their knees and feet point more to the side. Why? Because that gives them a wider and more stable base of support to dance on. So we see that ballet dancing shows legs that are turned out.

2. Pointed feet. To extend the shape of the leg and make it look longer and sleeker, ballet dancers point their feet whenever they lift their feet off the floor. (In sports like gymnastics and diving, athletes also point the feet to create a beautiful line.)

3. Erect spine. Ballet was born in the courts of France during the 1600s, which is why the names of all the ballet steps are in French. Royal people at the courts participated in the ballets at that time, and it was considered proper to move in a very tall and regal way, so they kept their spines very erect. Today's ballet dancers keep the spine erect also, because it helps them to find the balance necessary to spin and jump well.

4. Pointe shoes. As ballet developed, the dancers and choreographers wanted to make the dancing look as light and weightless as possible. Pointe shoes were invented to help the female ballet dancers rise even higher than tiptoe. Eventually the men lifted the women off the floor to create even more of a sense of dancing in the air instead of on the ground.

Tell the students that they will learn some of these ballet characteristics for themselves so that they can better appreciate this beautiful art form.

1. Begin in a large circle, sitting on the floor. Students should draw their legs together in front of them. Keeping their knees straight, they should try to point their ankles and feet to look like the dancers in the ballet pictures. Have them practice lifting a leg into the air with the foot pointed and the knee straight.

2. Now have the students stand up and move into a scattered formation facing the front of the room. Show them the five turned-out positions of the legs pictured here; have students try to do these positions. It helps to tighten the buttocks (gluteal muscles) to rotate the inner thighs to the front. Introduce students to the language of ballet and show them the movements.

   • Plié (plee-AY). Students start in first position. Plié means "to bend." As the students bend their knees, the knees should go sideways over the toes. Heels stay on the floor. The empty space between their legs should look like a diamond shape. Students then straighten the knees. Practice plié with the following rhythm: plié on count 1, straighten on count 2. Do this four times in a slow 8-beat phrase to the music.

   • Elevé (el-a-VAY). Rise, lifting heels and balancing on the balls of the feet, keeping the knees very straight. Lower down to first position again, heels touching as they reach the floor. Elevé requires balance, so try to keep the spine straight too! Have the students practice one slow elevé to the music: Rise on counts 1 to 2, balance counts 3 to 6, lower on counts 7 to 8.

   • Tendu (ton-DOO). Stretch a straight leg to the side with the foot pointed and heel underneath.

   • Grand battement (grahn bott-MA). Try lifting the leg in the tendu shape without bending the standing leg. Repeat with leg lifting to the front and to the back.

   • Grand jeté (grahn zha-TAY). Run and then leap from one leg to the other with straight knees and pointed toes while airborne.

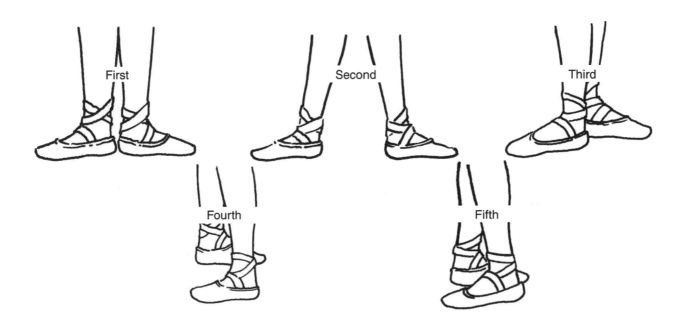

First   Second   Third

Fourth   Fifth

Session 2: Ballet Poem (First and Second Verse), by Diane Newman

Refer to the MOVEnture DVD for a demonstration.

Students recite while performing, starting in first position with hands on hips.

Ballet Poem, first verse	Suggested Movements
Plié is to bend.	Bend knees on the word *bend.*
Elevé is to rise.	Straighten knees and elevé on the word *rise.*
Tendu is to stretch, or stretch, or stretch.	Lower elevé with heels together and tendu to right side, then left, then right.

Ballet Poem, second verse	Suggested Movements
First position.	Close tendu to first position.
Second position.	Set right foot to side into second position and open arms wide to the sides at the same time.
Fifth en bas (on bah)	Lower arms to a circular shape while standing straight. (En bas means "low" in French.)
Losing my balloon.	Lift circle to high overhead.
(Gasp)	Pop hands open as if balloon were suddenly let go, looking up sharply.
Is port de bras (por duh brah)	Lower arms wide to the sides and down to bottom circle again (en bas)

Session 3: Ballet Poem (Third and Fourth Verse)

Ballet Poem, third verse	Suggested Movements
Sauté (so-TAY) is to jump.	Jump by bringing feet to first position and arms wide. (Body looks like the letter T.)
Grand battement to kick.	Kick right leg forward, knee straight, toes pointed.
I like when we do retiré (reh-teer-AY).	
Very quick!	On the word *very* lift right knee, pointing right foot and touching it to the left knee (legs look like the number 4); return to first position quickly on *quick.*

Ballet Poem, fourth verse	Suggested Movements
All in all . . .	Step right foot to right side.
I like to dance.	Boys place left foot next to the right one and bow with one arm in front of waist and one in back. Girls point left foot forward in tendu and delicately bend body forward to curtsy, arms out to side to balance.
It's fun even when it's tough!	Feet together, thrust the right hand, fisted, across body on the word *tough.*
So I listen well	Step right leg to side into a lunge with right hand to ear for *listen* gesture.
And I practice hard	Students do a single spin of their own in self-space, ending in a squat with hands on floor and knees between elbows.
And I never get enough!	All jump up to the letter X shape.

1920s: The Virginia Reel

Square dancing first came to America with the colonists and then spread with the settlers across the continent. These lively dances became so popular and varied that the participants required a caller who would announce the steps as they changed. Eventually, however, the popularity waned. It was Henry Ford who renewed the interest in the dances during the 1920s, bringing the public back to square dancing in a fad-like frenzy. Refer to MOVEnture CD track 25 for music to accompany this lesson.

Formation: Six couples in two lines facing each other. Partners on one end of the set are designated the head couple.

Counts	Measures	Action
1-16	1-4	Take three steps forward; curtsy or bow. Take three steps back and close.
1-16	5-8	Move forward to partner, turn once in place using a right forearm grasp, and return to position.
1-16	9-12	Repeat measures 5 to 8 with a left forearm grasp.
1-16	13-16	Partners join both hands, turn once in a clockwise direction, and move backward to place.
1-16	17-20	Partners pass each other right shoulder to right shoulder and then back to back and move backward to their place.
1-16	21-24	Repeat the action of measures 1 to 4.
1-32	25-32	The head couple, with hands joined, take eight slides down to the foot of the set and eight slides back to their place.
1-128	33-64	The elbow reel: The head couple begins the reel with linked right elbows and turns one and a half times to face the next couple in line. Each member in the head couple then links left elbows with the person facing and turns once in place. The head couple meets again in the center and turns once with a right elbow swing. The next dancers down the line are turned with a left elbow swing, and then the head couple returns to the center for another right elbow turn. The head couple thus progresses down the line, turning each dancer in order. After the head couple has turned the last dancers, they meet with a right elbow swing, turn halfway around, and sashay (slide) back to the head of the set.
1-128	65-96	March: All couples face toward the head of the set with the head couple in front. The person on the right turns to the right while the person on the left turns to the left and goes behind the line followed by the other dancers. When the head couple reaches the foot of the set, they join hands and make an arch, under which all other couples pass. The head couple is now at the foot of the set and the dance is repeated with a new head couple.

1920s: Tap Dance

Tap dance began on the streets of the city by African American youth. The young people put bottle caps on the soles of their shoes, and tap dancing as a form of expression began. Here are a few basic tap steps. Refer to MOVEnture CD track 26 for music to accompany this lesson.

- Front and back brush. Begin with weight on left foot. Bend right knee by bringing right foot off the floor. (The right toe should be at the left ankle.) Sweep the right foot on the floor toward front, making one sound. Reverse for the back brush.

- Flap front and back. Begin with weight on the left foot. Brush right foot forward, and then step on right foot as you transfer weight to right foot, making two sounds. Reverse for the back flap.
- Step. Begin with weight on left foot. Raise right foot off floor and then transfer weight to ball of right foot.
- Dig. Begin with the weight on the left foot. Tap the floor with the ball of the right foot (the right knee is bent in order to do this) without transferring weight.
- Shuffle. Brush right foot to front, then brush right foot to back. This is faster than front and back brush, with a quicker action of the ankle. The shuffle has two sounds.
- Ball change. Step on the ball of right foot, and then transfer weight quickly as you step on ball of the left foot slightly in front of right, making two sounds.
- Heel drop. With feet together, raise the right heel in air with the ball of foot on floor. Drop right heel on floor and bend both knees.
- Shuffle dig. Weight on left front foot with right knee bent, right foot off floor, right toe at the left ankle. Brush right foot to front; then brush right foot to back; then step on ball of right foot without transferring weight to add a dig after the shuffle. Be sure to keep the feet close together.

1930s: Ballroom

Ballroom dance began with the court dances during the Renaissance period. With changing trends in music, social dances disappeared and reappeared in a variety of styles and variations throughout history, especially with the help of Hollywood star Fred Astaire.

Waltz

The waltz was made popular in Germany and Austria with the music of Johann Strauss. The waltz is a smooth, gliding dance that weaves an even pattern in triple time. The accented first beat of the music has a corresponding accented movement with a reaching step forward, backward, sideward, or a turn. The American-style waltz is danced in a box, or square, pattern. Refer to MOVEnture CD track 27 for music to accompany this lesson.

Counts	Movements
1, 2, 3 (even beats)	Step forward left, step side right, close left to right.
1, 2, 3	Step backward right, step side left, close right to left.

Square pattern cue: forward side close, backward side close.

Foxtrot

The foxtrot is the only truly American form of ballroom dance. The basic foxtrot steps can be used with variations in position, direction, and tempo.

Counts	Movements
1 quick	Step forward on left.
2 quick	Close right to left.
3, 4 (slow)	Take the weight on right, step left.

Repeat on right.

1940s: Swing (Jitterbug)

Jitterbug, also known as swing, originated in old ragtime, a music popular in the early 1900s. The syncopated quality of swing (that is, the accent on upbeat instead of the downbeat) varies with the style. The single lindy set the *slow, slow, quick–quick* rhythm as basic for all other styles. Swing steps do not carry the dancers around the dance floor but swirl and roll, covering a circular space in one area. Refer to MOVEnture CD track 28 for music to accompany this lesson.

Single Lindy

Counts	Movements
1, 2 slow	Step left sideward.
3, 4 slow	Step right sideward.

Rock Step

Counts	Movements
1 quick	Step left backward, a little behind right heel.
2 quick	Step right in place.

Step Cue

Side, side, rock step

1940s: The Polka

A folk dance originally from Bohemia, polka traveled to France, then England, and then to America. European immigrants that came to America after World War II brought a renewed interest in the Polka with them. Refer to MOVEnture CD track 29 for music to accompany this lesson.

Children's Polka (Kinderpolka)

Formation: Single circle with partners facing, both arms extended sideward, and hands joined.

Counts	Measures	Action
1-6	1-2	Take two slides toward the center and step lightly three times.
1-6	3-4	Take two slides away from center; step lightly three times.
1-9	5-8	Repeat actions of measures 1 to 4
1-6	9-10	Slap own knees once, clap own hands once, and slap partner's palms three times.
1-6	11-12	Repeat actions of measures 9 and 10.
1-3	13	Jump, placing right heel forward; place right elbow in left hand, and shake right index finger three times.
1-3	14	Repeat actions of measure 13 with left foot.
1-6	15-16	Turn in place with four running steps, and step lightly three times.

1950s and Early 1960s: Twist, Jerk, and Mashed Potato

All dances may be performed alone or with a partner. Refer to MOVEnture CD track 30 for music to accompany the Twist and the Mashed Potato. Refer to MOVEnture CD track 31 for music to accompany the Jerk.

Twist

1. The starting position is knees bent, arms flexed at waist.
2. Shift pelvis to right. Move left arm forward. Shift pelvis to the left as left arm moves back and right arm moves forward. Repeat several times.
3. Rhythm is even.

Counts	Movements
1	Shift right.
2	Shift left.
3	Shift right.
4	Shift left.

Variation: Begin on balls of feet. With knees bent, move heels, legs, and pelvis right, then left.

Jerk

1. The starting position is knees bent, arms in by sides.
2. Use syncopated rhythm.

Counts	Movements
1	Arch back; eyes look up; bring right hand by face.
2	Snap fingers on right hand jerking back and forward as hand and arm travel down, eyes looking forward.
3	Arch back; eyes look up; bring left hand to face.
4	Snap fingers on left hand jerking back and forward as hand and arm travel down.

Mashed Potato

1. The starting position is knees bent, weight on balls of feet.
2. Twisting action continues throughout step.
3. Twisting action involves toes on both feet turning in, then toes on both feet turning out.

Counts	Movements
&	Shift weight to left foot as right foot releases from the floor.
1	Brush right foot in.
&	Brush right foot out.
2	Brush right foot and shift weight to right foot.
&	Brush left foot out.
3	Brush left foot in.
&	Brush left foot out.

1960s: Modern Dance

Modern dance is a vital American art form. Modern dance began as a revolt against ballet. Instead of the ballet slipper, the modern dancer performed barefoot. Instead of performing in a turned-out position with specific body movements, modern dancers used alternative movements like contraction and release (associated with Martha Graham's choreography) and fall and recovery (associated with Doris Humphrey's choreography). Today there is much crossover between modern dance and ballet, as many ballet companies have included choreography by modern dance choreographers in their repertoire, and many modern dancers study the techniques of ballet.

The focus of this lesson is on evaluating and critiquing a professional modern dance performance. The following questions provide guidelines for the critique.

The Dance As a Whole

- Was there a unifying theme that you could identify?
- What is your idea of what the dance is about? Did the title adequately reflect the idea of the work?
- Did the spatial elements (levels, directions, floor patterns, shapes) promote a clear understanding of the theme?
- Was there a clear beginning, middle, and end?
- Were the individual movements and movement patterns original and visually interesting?

Technical Considerations

- Did the music or sound enhance the performance?
- Was the lighting design suitable for the work?

- Did the costumes contribute to or detract from the piece?
- Were the props an integral part of the work?
- Were the makeup and hair design appropriate for the dance?

Performance Considerations

- Were the dancers well trained for what they were asked to perform?
- Did the dancers work well together during the performance?
- Did the dancers seem to be well rehearsed?
- Did the dancers seem secure and at ease with the movement and the piece?

1970: Disco

The Hustle

Refer to MOVEnture CD track 32 for music to accompany this lesson.

Counts	Movements
1-3	Walk forward three steps right, left, right.
4	Touch left.
5-7	Walk backward three steps left, right, left.
8	Touch right.
1-4	Grapevine right.
5-8	Grapevine left.
1-2	Point right toe forward, tap two times.
3-4	Point right toe backward, tap two times.
5	Right toe forward.
6	Right toe backward.
7	Right toe side.
8	Raise right knee high and make a quarter turn.

The Bump

Counts	Movements
1	Gently bump a body part together with your partner on the beat.
2	Step back, prepare, and bump with your partner again.
3	Change levels or directions and continue to bump together on the beat.

Be spontaneous about what body part bumps. Enjoy the interaction with your partner and the beat of the music.

1980: Moonwalk

A popular form of traveling is moonwalking, made famous by singer Michael Jackson. Refer to MOVEnture CD track 33 for music to accompany this lesson.

1. Stand with back to the direction of travel.
2. Pop the right heel up, keeping the right toes on the floor.
3. Drag the right toes backward along the floor and back a step.
4. Lower right heel to the floor, simultaneously popping the left heel up, keeping left toes on the floor.
5. Drag the left toes backward along the floor and back a step.

6. Lower left heel to the floor, simultaneously popping the right heel up, keeping the right toes on the floor.

7. Repeat, creating a fluid motion, as if gliding backward across a slippery floor.

1990s: Jazz and Hip-Hop

Contemporary Jazz and Hip-Hop dance

Start with feet together, arms at side. Refer to MOVEnture CD track 34 for music to accompany this lesson.

Counts	Movements
1	Slide sideways to wide knee bend, hands on knees; body dips to center.
2	Feet together, arms at side.
3-4	Repeat side slide, together.
5	Parallel arms straight overhead.
6	Drop right arm to side, look over right shoulder.
7	Open to wide stance, feet hip-width apart; extend left arm at shoulder height; look over left shoulder.
8	Drop body over, left arm behind back.
1	Reach right arm front; extend right foot side; bend left knee.
2	Pull right arm to chest; lift right knee front and then step down.
3	Reach left arm front; extend left foot side; bend right knee.
4	Pull left arm to chest; lift left knee front and then step out left.
5-6-7	Three-step turn left.
8	Freeze in a pose (with attitude!).

ASSESSMENT

- What can you tell me about the early 1900s (1900 to 1920)? 1930s? 1940s? Other eras?
- Can you match the dance style with the decade it represents?
- Can you name a dancer who was influential in the 20th century?

Assessment Forms

- Movement Study Assessment form, for teacher use. Add these factors to the form: a review of historical events, important dancers, and dances of each decade.
- Self-Assessment form (version appropriate for students' level).

Extensions

- The historical events detailed in the time line offer many social studies connections in learning about the highlights of the 20th century. Select an event on the time line (Great Depression, World War II, civil rights movement). Discuss, research, and develop an understanding of the time period with your students.
- Reinforce the students' learning by exploring literature, video, and visual aids (such as artifacts like props, photographs, and costumes) representative of the time period.

chapter 7

MOVEntures in Science

Science and dance may seem to be disciplines at opposite ends of a spectrum—one based on logical, concrete outcomes and mathematical determinants, the other aesthetic and creative, with the human body as the expressive tool. However, scientists and dancers use the same toolbox of skills, skills that illuminate similarities and break down the usual boundaries that too often promote separation rather than integration of the disciplines. The skills of observing, imaging, abstracting, empathizing, modeling, and transforming are as prevalent in scientific investigation as in the creation and performance of a new dance work.

The integration of science and dance is supported by research on active learning strategies. Active processing results in a consolidation and internalization of information that becomes both personally meaningful and conceptually coherent to each student. For example, the lesson about the water cycle can enhance understanding of the process of evaporation, condensation, and precipitation by having the students create dance movements for each of those processes. Furthermore, when dance is integrated with such scientific concepts, a transformation occurs as the dance and the scientific concept are merged into one learning experience.

179

66 Dynamics of Sound

PLAYING WITH SOUND WAVE QUALITIES.

GRADES: K TO 2   **LENGTH:** 20 TO 30 MINUTES

Materials

- Musical instruments including a drum, triangle, xylophone, maracas, or tambourine
- Picture of sound waves
- List of movement dynamics: percussive, sustained, vibratory

National Standards

Science: 9

Music: 6

Dance: 1

Objectives

The students will be able to do the following:

- Describe sounds in terms of their properties: pitch and quality.
- Understand qualities of movement dynamics.

INTRODUCTION

Have the students listen to the soft sound of a triangle or xylophone. They move their heads in a slow, smooth movement (sustained) for as long as they can hear the sound. Sustained movement is slow, smooth, and continuous. The sound waves are stronger for those who are close to the triangle, where the sound was produced. The sound waves are absorbed by things like carpeting and people. They bounce off things that are hard, like the walls or cabinets.

THE MOVING ADVENTURE

1. Repeat the sustained movement of the sound of the triangle; this time students move their shoulders. Then they move arms, a leg (while balancing on the other), or the torso while maintaining continuous movement as long as they hear the sound. ⚙ **Analogizing**

2. The pitch of the triangle is high. The pitch of the xylophone ranges from the longest bar as low, the shortest bar as high. Explore pitch by adding levels in movement. When the long bar or low pitch is played, your students should move with a sustained quality at a low level. You can select a body part that they should move or allow the dancers to choose one. Explain that as you move up the xylophone, the pitch becomes higher and their level should become higher. They should remember to always move with a sustained quality.

3. Next, play the strong, sharp sound of the hand drum. Students respond to the beat by moving the head in a sharp, strong movement. Sharp, strong movement is percussive movement. The drum is a percussion instrument.

4. Explore shoulder movement and then movement of the arms, legs, and torso. Change movements on the percussive sound of the drum. Ask students what the drum does when it makes sound. We hear sound when a moving object makes the air vibrate. The strike of the drum causes vibrations. These vibrations travel through the air in the form of waves. The shape of the sound wave determines the pitch. What is the pitch of the drum? (Low.) Does it create a loud or soft sound? (Loud.)

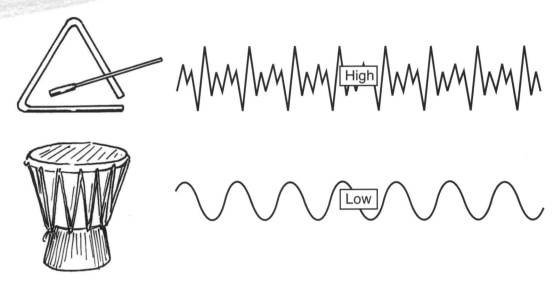

5. The maraca or tambourine produces a shaking sound. Shaking movement is called vibratory movement. Ask students to try moving their heads with a vibratory quality to the sound of the maraca. Continue by moving shoulders, hands, a foot, hips, or torso to the sound of the maraca.

6. Review the dynamics of sound by playing the instruments in an order of your choice while the students perform the appropriate accompanying movement. They can use the body part of their choice. Remind them that listening skills are essential. The sound of the instrument is their musical cue.

ASSESSMENT

- Which movement dynamic did you enjoy performing the most: percussive, sustained, or vibratory?
- How did your movement change with the change in the pitch of the xylophone?
- What are the properties of sound waves?
- Create a form with different sound waves pictured. Students circle the correct sound wave picture in response to the sound played.

Assessment Forms

Movement Study Assessment form, for teacher use. Add this factor to the form: movement dynamics aligned with sound quality.

Extensions

- Describe sounds using visual art design. Students interpret a percussive sound with a strong brushstroke design or sharp-edge design. Play the triangle and then have students paint the sustained sound. Play the drumbeat; students paint percussive designs. Play the maraca; students paint vibratory designs. Sound waves can be added to the designs.

- Create a pattern using a repetition of dynamics in a movement sequence (such as sustained, percussive, percussive, vibratory, sustained). Perform with instrumental accompaniment.

- Related lesson: Fractions Sounding Off, lesson 46.

67

Traveling in Many Directions

MOVING FORWARD, BACKWARD, UP, DOWN, RIGHT, AND LEFT.

GRADES: K TO 2   **LENGTH:** 30 MINUTES

Materials

MOVEnture CD track 8
- Audio playback system
- Chart with direction words listed
- One four-feet-long piece of string for each student
- Drum

National Standards

Science: 10

Dance: 1

Objective

The students will be able to identify and move in the six directions (forward, backward, up, down, right, left).

INTRODUCTION

Ask the students how many directions they can move. Explain that they will explore moving forward, backward, up, down, right, and left.

THE MOVING ADVENTURE

Painting

1. Students put imaginary paint on their hands in a color that feels good. In their self-space, they paint in front of them, behind them, up high, down low, right side, left side.

2. Instruct students to put paint on their noses. They draw straight lines in different directions with their noses.

3. Ask them if they can draw with their elbows quickly and slowly. Try other body parts (knees, shoulders, head, legs, arms, wrist, toes, torso, feet).

4. Students put paint on the whole body. They travel through general space using different locomotor movements as they move in all six directions.

5. They decide which body part will move them forward, backward, up high, down low, to the right, and to the left.

6. Dancers can change the paint as they move in the different directions, or the class can choose a color. ⚙ **Imaging**

Painter and Paint

1. Dancers find a partner. One partner is the painter; the other is the paint. The painter uses his or her arm as a huge brush. The painter paints directions in space.
2. As the painter is painting in the various directions, the partner who is the paint will follow the directions using his or her whole body to create the directions.
3. After each design has been painted, the dancers change roles. ⚙ Imaging

String

1. Each dancer receives a piece of string four feet long.
2. Dancers hold the string in front of them, behind them, up high, down low, to the right, and to the left.
3. Dancers make a straight line on the floor with the string.
4. Give them challenges: Can you jump in a straight line along the string? Can you move backward slowly and then quickly? Can you perform low movements along the string? Can you perform high movements along the string? Can you jump from the right side to the left side?

Creating

Using a streamer, dancers dance freely to music, moving in all directions. They move until the music ends, then freeze into a strong shape.

ASSESSMENT

- What are six directions we worked on today?
- Which body parts were leading as you moved in the different directions?
- The students perform a "good-bye dance" across the floor in groups of two. Call out different directions for the students to perform.
- Create an assessment form to indicate each student's ability or inability to perform the concept.

Assessment Forms

Participation Assessment form.

Extension

- Create a dance to a poem about directions using haiku (see lesson 34), cinquain, or diamante form.
- Related lesson: Rope Dances, lesson 40.

Cinquain

Cinquain poems have five lines and the following pattern. You can use syllables or words to create this type of poem.

Line 1—Title	2 syllables	1 word
Line 2—Description of the title	4 syllables	2 words
Line 3—Action about the title	6 syllables	3 words
Line 4—Feeling about the title	8 syllables	4 words
Line 5—Synonym for the title	2 syllables	1 word

Diamante

Diamante poems are diamond-shaped, and have seven lines. This type of poem combines two opposing or different themes. The following pattern can be used to create a diamante poem.

Line 1   one noun (theme A)

Line 2   two adjectives (theme A)

Line 3   three verbs (theme A)

Line 4   four nouns (two from theme A and two from theme B)

Line 5   three verbs (theme B)

Line 6   two adjectives (theme B)

Line 7   one noun (theme B)

For example:

Dance

fast, slow

leaping, jumping, sliding

ballet, jazz, haiku, diamante

imaging, creating, writing

sensitive, simple

Poetry

by Lynnette Overby

The Snowflake Dance

68

A LESSON ON SNOWFLAKES AND THE WINTER SEASON.

GRADES: K TO 2   **LENGTH:** TWO 20-MINUTE SESSIONS

Materials

MOVEnture CD track 4
- Audio playback system
- Six-sided paper snowflakes of various sizes (diameters of 2 inches, 4 inches, or 6 inches), cut with decorative and interesting designs
- Various musical instruments: drums, wind chimes, maracas, finger cymbals

National Standards

Science: 1

Visual Arts: 1

Language Arts: 6

Dance: 1, 2, 3

Objectives

The students will be able to do the following:
- Describe the scientific process by which snowflakes, a form of precipitation, are created.
- Create a story dance about snow that has a beginning, middle, and end.

INTRODUCTION

Ask students if they know how a snowflake is made. It starts with a particle of dust suspended in the atmosphere, around which tiny ice crystals begin to stick. As the crystals grow, they form symmetrical and interesting patterns, and they are always six-sided, a hexagon. Have them look at paper samples you have cut and notice how each one is different. So are snowflakes. How the crystals freeze into patterns is unique to each snowflake. Just like humans, no two are exactly alike. Study the paper snowflakes with the students, observing closely, like a scientist, to notice the characteristics of pointed designs, symmetry, and beauty. ⚙ **Observing**

THE MOVING ADVENTURE

Session 1

1. Students start in self-space. Standing on a chair, hold a paper snowflake up high and release it. Instruct the students only to watch it fall. Ask them to describe its motion with action words, such as it rocks back and forth, loop-de-loops, twirls, dives, it is graceful.

2. Ask the students to put one hand up high. Tell them to watch the paper snowflake fall all the way to the ground. When it finally lands and stops, instruct them to imitate

the motions of the paper snowflake as it fell using only their hands. Repeat with the different sizes of snowflakes because each will behave very differently when it falls.

3. Ask the students to repeat the exercise just completed using the whole body. You can further ask what the snowflake looks like when it has landed. Did part of it melt when it touched the ground? How could you dance that? Repeat with each differently sized snowflake. ⚙ **Empathizing**

Session 2

1. Perform the Snowflake Dance. This activity is easily structured into a dance form by adding music and a beginning-middle-end sequence. The snow can begin by falling gently, becoming a blizzard, and blowing into beautiful group shapes of snowdrifts. It could further melt into the ice of a skating pond (the students roll away to the edges of the dance space after melting), and then they can skate, play hockey, and play on it.

2. The Snowflake Dance can be accompanied by your live musical instrumentation or by a recording of your choice, classical or new age music, or a recording of the classical piece "Les Patineurs (The Skaters)" by Giacomo Meyerbeer for the skating-pond scene. The recorded music can fade up (beginning) or down (ending) to match the students' performance.

3. Divide the class in half (or in smaller groups) and have each group perform the snowflake studies for the other groups (share through performance). Teach appropriate audience skills of sitting straight and attending, applauding at the end. Encourage them to comment positively about what they saw and liked.

ASSESSMENT

- How is a snowflake created in nature?
- Did our dance tell a story?
- Did it have a beginning, middle, and end? (Have them identify each section.)
- What part of the story did you enjoy dancing the most: the soft falling, the blizzard, the snowdrift, or the skating pond? Why?
- Distribute a paper with drawings of snowflakes, some of which display an incorrect number of points. Have the students indicate which snowflakes are incorrect.

Assessment Forms

- Movement Study Assessment form, for teacher use and for student evaluation of the performance. Add these factors to the form: memory skills, clear shapes, confidence in movement, use of energy (for different qualities such as gentle falling, blizzard, hockey).
- Participation Assessment form.
- Self-Assessment form (version appropriate for students' level).

Extensions

- Have students play the musical instruments to accompany the dance. Using their voices to make the sound of the wind can be very magical for the blizzard.
- This lesson can be used as a springboard for visual arts activities as well. The students can cut their own snowflakes from paper (six-sided, please!), spatter paint the shapes onto a larger group work, or draw the winter scene. You could introduce the students to Currier and Ives paintings of winter scenes.
- This lesson also may lead to further questions such as "What is a crystal?" That may lead to a discussion of frost on a windowpane or other examples of crystalline form.

In the Cloud Crowd

69

FILL IN THE SPACE.

GRADES: K TO 2   **LENGTH:** TWO 25- TO 30-MINUTE SESSIONS

Materials
- Triangle or finger cymbals for signal
- Pictures of cloud formations
- *Sometimes It Looked Like Spilt Milk* by Charles G. Shaw

National Standards
Science: 1
Language Arts: 6
Dance: 1, 7

Objectives
The students will be able to do the following:
- Use improvisation to discover, invent, and solve movement problems.
- Describe the cloud formations and weather conditions.
- Collaborate as a small group to create cloud shapes.
- Demonstrate kinesthetic memory in performing group compositions.

INTRODUCTION

Introduce the concept of positive and negative space by playing a game called Fill in the Space. Ask one student to come into the middle of the space ("on stage") and make a shape. Ask the other students to look for the space that surrounds this student's shape, not just around the outside of the shape but between body parts. This space that is not being used is called the negative space. The space that is filled by the student's shape is the positive space. Have another student come "on stage" and make a shape that somehow fills in some of the negative space. That student might place an arm under the first student's arm or next to the first student's head. Continue to build the group shape with four or five more students. Remind them to explore different levels as they fill in the space.   ⚙ **Dimensional Thinking**

THE MOVING ADVENTURE

1. Share pictures of cloud formations with the class and discuss the shape variations.
2. Start with cumulus (fair-weather clouds). They form in warm air on sunny days and are thick and puffy in shape. Invite the students to work in groups of three to five. Begin by forming a positive/negative shape that represents the cumulus cloud. Sometimes cumulus clouds pile up to form shapes like a cauliflower which are cumulonimbus clouds (thunderheads). See if the students in one group can overlap or "pile up" with other cumulus groups to form cumulonimbus clouds. Remind them to move like a cloud and maintain positive and negative space (don't touch!).
3. They finish by lifting into high wispy shapes, thinning out, and spreading away from the other students. Allow much more negative space between shapes. This is a cirrus cloud and looks like horse tails blowing in the wind. They're also known as mare's tails.
4. Read Charles G. Shaw's book *Sometimes It Looked Like Spilt Milk*.

187

5. Talk to the students about shapes they might see in the clouds. Select four or five shapes to create in cooperative groups. They can be from the book or a suggestion from some of the students. The members of each group must work together to form the shapes and remember what part they play in the composition. Start with "sometimes it looked like spilt milk." Create, with the students, a group shape and a collapsed movement that can be repeated for "spilt milk." Continue through a performance of the selected four or five shapes. 🜚 **Recognizing Patterns**

6. Talk to the students about moving from one shape to the next with smooth transitions. Allow students enough practice to accommodate forming the group shapes without dialogue. Finish with the "spilt milk" shape and movement, then slowly explore improvised cloud shapes that continually change positive and negative space.

ASSESSMENT

- Did your group members cooperate and work together?
- Was it difficult to remember the shapes?
- What other cloud shapes could have been created?
- Students will label pictures of cloud formations or circle the correct picture as the name is read aloud.

Assessment Forms

- Movement Study Assessment form, for teacher use and for student evaluation of the performance.
- Group Evaluation form.

Extensions

- As students watch the groups perform, ask them to use their imaginations and look for new images in the cloud shapes. Their perspective may be very different from the intended image of the group.
- Kindergartners may be more successful at creating cloud shapes individually rather than in cooperative groups.

Shadows

70

CREATING A SHADOW DANCE.

GRADES: K TO 2   **LENGTH:** 45 MINUTES

Materials

MOVEnture CD track 3
• Audio playback system

National Standards

Science: 9

Language Arts: 6

Dance: 1, 2, 3

Objectives

The students will be able to do the following:

• Describe how shadows are made.

• Create a dance about shadows.

INTRODUCTION

Before this lesson, the students should spend time outside exploring shadows. Explain that they will explore shadows through movement. Ask students what a shadow is and how it's formed.

• Show the effect of a flashlight on the wall.

• Students are prompted to provide many examples of shadows.

THE MOVING ADVENTURE

1. Shadow Dance. Partners become a person and shadow. The shadow is on the floor with feet touching the standing partner. The standing partner moves arms and torso slowly, and the shadow copies the nonlocomotor movements.
   ⚙ **Dimensional Thinking**

2. Trio Shadow Activity. Students are divided into groups of three. Each student takes on a role—the person, the sun, or the shadow. The sun slowly changes position, and the shadow changes position in correspondence with the blockage by the person.

3. Shadowing (moving through space in partners). The leader dances through general space slowly at a high and middle level. The follower moves on a low level on the floor, as a real shadow does, trying to copy the leader's movements. The leader needs to move slowly.

4. Poem: "My Shadow" by R. Stevenson. Partners work together to express words to a poem:

Student A	Student B
I have a little shadow	that goes in and out with me.
And what can be the use of him	is more than I can see
He is very, very like me	from my heels up to the head.
And I see him jump before me	as I jump into my bed.

Reprinted from R.L. Stevenson, 1885. My Shadow, *A Child's Garden of Verses.*

On the last line, student B (the shadow) might take the jumping movement first, with student A following on the second half of the line.

5. Choreography for Shadow Dance. The students work with a small group and create a dance based on shadows. The students use material from previous explorations regarding shadows to create a dance with a beginning, middle, and end. (Distribute the Movement Study Assessment form, and encourage students to use the list as they create and assess their dances.)

ASSESSMENT

- What is a shadow?
- How are shadows formed?
- Have students describe (in their journals) how shadows are made.

Assessment Form

Movement Study Assessment form, to assess students on their choreography.

Extensions

- Students draw a picture depicting the relationship between the person, the sun, and the shadow.
- Students present their shadow dance to another class.

The Fall Season

71

A LESSON ON LEAVES.

GRADES: K TO 2   **LENGTH:** 30 MINUTES

Materials

MOVEnture CD track 35

- Audio playback system
- Freshly fallen leaves of different tree families; include a couple that have become dried
- Scarves in many different colors, enough for at least one per student
- Drum

National Standards

Science: 1, 7

Dance: 1, 2, 3

Objectives

The students will be able to do the following:

- Recognize the leaves of common tree families.
- Describe the scientific process by which leaves change color and fall in autumn.
- Create a story dance about leaves that has a beginning, middle, and end.

INTRODUCTION

Study the leaf shapes with the students, identifying the tree species of oak (round-lobed or pointed), maple, ash, or sassafras. Ask them to practice observation as a scientist would, helping them to notice the special features of veins, edges, shape, and other characteristics of classification. Explain to them the scientific reasons that the leaves of deciduous trees change color and fall during the autumn season (shorter day length, reduction of chlorophyll production). ⚙ **Observing**

Beyond scientific aspects, appreciate with them the aesthetic component of autumn—the beauty of the colors and shapes, the sounds of leaves when they rustle, the curliness of dried leaves, or the interesting shape of the broken leaf. Hold each leaf up high and watch it fall: the motion, the softness with which it lands.

THE MOVING ADVENTURE

1. Tell the students to pretend to be a maple leaf, still hanging on the tree. How might it fall? When it lands, does it still have its pointed tips? Have the children imitate the falling motion of the leaf and then create its shape with their bodies, as if they had fallen from the tree to the ground. Ask them what the leaf looks like when it has dried. (It becomes curly, more three-dimensional.) What if it was broken on the way down? How could you dance that? (Repeat the exercise with each type of leaf.) ⚙ **Empathizing**

2. Leaf Dance. Structure this activity into a dance form by adding music and a beginning-middle-end sequence. You may use music you select or the one recommended to accompany this lesson. Pass out the scarves, one or two per student. Students should start in self-space.

3. This music is in three parts. Song 1: As the first song begins, the students imagine themselves as rooted trees whose leaves (scarves) blow in the wind. As the first song ends, there is a falling sound in the music and the students fall softly to the ground, creating a leaf shape at the end.

4. Song 2: Students pick up scarves and travel through space as if the wind is tossing them about, and then they descend to the ground again with the falling sound in the music.

5. Song 3: With the sharp music, students jump, throwing leaves (scarves) into the air as if the wind is gusty. On the falling sound, students fall and then roll into a pile of leaves. You might pretend you are raking them together, and then get down in the pile with them for an ending.

6. Divide the class in half (or in smaller groups) and have each group perform the dance for the others (share through performance). Teach appropriate audience skills of sitting straight, paying attention, and applauding at the end. Encourage the children to comment positively on what they saw.

ASSESSMENT

- Why do the leaves of many trees change colors and fall during the autumn season?
- When you were observing the leaves like a scientist, what did you notice that made them different from each other?
- Did our leaf dance tell a story?
- Did it have a beginning, middle, and end? (Have them identify each section.)

Assessment Forms

- Movement Study Assessment form, for student evaluation of the performance.
- Participation Assessment form.

Extensions

- Use this lesson as a springboard for visual arts activities. Spatter-paint the shapes of the leaves, brush paint onto the leaves directly, and stamp them onto paper or fabric surfaces.
- Gather leaves on the way to school and classify them according to the appropriate tree family. Investigate unfamiliar ones by using a tree-identification book or field guide.
- Distribute a sheet with drawings of various common leaves and have students identify the correct tree family for each.

Seed to Flower

72

THE GLORIOUS GARDEN.

GRADES: K TO 2   **LENGTH:** 30 MINUTES

Materials

MOVEnture CD track 3
- Audio playback system
- Poem "The Glorious Garden," by Lynnette Overby

National Standards

Science: 5

Dance: 1, 3

Objectives

The students will be able to do the following:

- Describe the elements that seeds and flowers need for healthy growth and development.
- Create a dance to a poem about seed growth.

INTRODUCTION

Explain to students that they will explore the elements that a seed needs in order to grow. Then they will look at pictures of the many varieties of flowers. Finally, they will dance to a poem about the development of a seed into a flower.

THE MOVING ADVENTURE

1. Imaginary Journey. Students are in scattered formation, lying down on the floor. Tell the students that they will take an imaginary journey as a seed. Give them the following cues: Relax your feet, ankles, calves, knees, and thigh muscles. Everything from the waist down should be totally relaxed. Now relax your abdomen, chest, arms, neck, and face. Now we will begin our imaginary journey. You are a tiny seed ready to be planted. The little boy who is going to plant you carefully picks you up and turns you around to make sure you are very healthy. (Students get up and turn around.) Then the little boy takes you to rich soil and digs a hole for you. Then he carefully plants you. (Students make a low-level round shape.) He waters you every day, and soon you begin to grow. (Students slowly move from low to high level.) You have become a beautiful flower. (Students make beautiful flower shape). ⚙ **Imaging**

2. Students gather in close to you. Have a copy of the poem "The Glorious Garden" written on a chalkboard or chart paper (large enough for the students to see). They dance to the poem as you read it.

3. Discuss with students the elements that a flower needs in order to grow.

4. Show pictures of many types of flowers.

5. Invite the students to suggest movements that will interpret the words of the poem.

6. Read the poem and write appropriate suggestions from the students on the board, opposite the line of poetry.

7. Have students find self-space in preparation for the dance.

"The Glorious Garden"

Lines of poem	Suggested Movements
Shapely solid	Various shapes on middle level and low levels.
Deep in soil	
Warm moist weather	
Helps our toil	Slowly turning shapes.
Sunshine streams	Begin unfolding.
Through cloudless skies	
Finding green	
a-peeking by	Roll on low level.
Slowly reaching	
Toward the rays	Stretching.
The whistling winds	
Cause gently sway	Swaying.
Scampering squirrels	
Amongst the leaves	Sudden bending.
We shake and bend	
As we achieve	Shake, twist, bend, and turn.
Reaching, stretching	
Toward the rays	Reaching and stretching, middle to high level.
Unfurling glory	
Salutes the day!	Form a flower shape in groups of five. All parts of the flower should be apparent: stem, leaves, blossom.

By Lynnette Overby

8. Share through performance by having the students perform with music and poetry. Have half of the students perform while the other half observe and then comment on the performance.

ASSESSMENT

- What does a seed need in order to grow?
- Describe how the movements fit the words to the poem.

Assessment Forms

- Seed to Flower Assessment form.
- Participation Assessment form.

Extensions

- Children plant a seed in a paper cup and observe the growth of the seed over the next three days. They should water the plants.
- Read and explore movement to Eric Carle's "A Tiny Seed."
- Related lesson: Flower Dance, lesson 8.

Wacky Weather Forecast

73

DEMONSTRATING CHANGING WEATHER CONDITIONS.

GRADES: K TO 2 **LENGTH:** TWO 25- TO 30-MINUTE SESSIONS

Materials

- Map of the United States
- Chart of dynamics
- Weather pictures (such as lightning, blizzard, tornado, and hurricane)
- Weather symbols
- An assortment of percussion instruments

National Standards

Science: 1

Music: 2

Dance: 1, 2, 7

Objectives

The students will be able to do the following:

- Use improvisation to discover, invent, and solve movement problems.
- Demonstrate an understanding of weather conditions and climates through movement qualities.
- Use percussion instruments to provide sound texture.

INTRODUCTION

Ask the students to describe the weather conditions that happen in their home state throughout the year. Make a list of weather changes in line with seasons. Take a look at the map, locate your home state, and mark it on the map. Review the country by regions and list weather conditions that occur in the northeastern states, southeastern states, midwestern states, northwestern states, and southwestern states. Don't forget the Hawaiian islands and Alaska!

Design a weather symbol for each of the conditions listed. You can use official symbols used by meteorologists or create your own. The children can be involved in designing the symbols to be used.

Snow
(Green)

Snow shower
(Green)

Lightning
(Red)

Thunderstorm
(Red)

Tropical storm
(Red)

Hurricane
(Red)

Review the chart of dynamics and movement qualities:

Percussive: strong, sharp	Swinging: suspended and released
Sustained: smooth, continuous	Frozen: no motion, still
Vibratory: shaking, vibrate	Collapsed: drop energy, release

Have the students spread out, find their self-space, and explore the movement quality of a lightning bolt (percussive), a gentle snowfall (sustained), the strong wind of a hurricane (percussive, swinging, vibratory), or a tropical storm (swinging, collapsed). ☼ **Body Thinking**

THE MOVING ADVENTURE

1. Put together a weather map using different weather conditions for each region and meteorology symbols. Determine how you will present the sequence of weather conditions, and review the order with the students. The students will then need to improvise a movement interpretation for each weather condition in the forecast.

2. Begin by introducing yourself, "Hi, I'm Sally Sunshine with today's Wacky Weather Forecast." Read through the forecast slowly, stopping to comment on the students' movement interpretation. Remind them to use the appropriate dynamic energy and coordinate their movement with their classmates as they move through the general space. "The citizens of Boston, Massachusetts, are experiencing a delay in school and business this morning caused by thick fog rolling in." (Dancers move sustained, low to the ground, reaching and stretching through the space.) "Lansing, Michigan, has developed a storm front overnight with crashing thunder and lightning." (Dancers use vibratory for the rumble of thunder, and percussive jumps and slashing arms for lightning.) "Look out, Dorothy. Kansas has reported three tornado touchdowns in the past hour." (Spin, changing level from high to low; houses and trees collapse.) "Seattle, Washington, has a light drizzle with heavy cloud cover." (Dancers create the pitter-patter of raindrops by tapping hands on different areas of the body: knees, shoulders, and head. They finish by coming together in a cloud formation.)

3. Ask your music teacher if she might share some percussion instruments or look into purchasing a small selection from a music education supplier. Divide the class in half and distribute musical instruments to one half. For example, triangles could accompany fog, drums and cymbals could accompany thunder and lightning, a tambourine could accompany the tornado with added drumming as it touches down, a xylophone could accompany the raindrops, and a gong could accompany a forming cloud.

ASSESSMENT

- Were the weather conditions accurately demonstrated through the movement qualities used by the students?
- Did the musical instruments provide a sound texture suitable to the weather conditions?
- Did the dancers stay in character (no voices) and seem to complement the musicians?
- Perform the Wacky Weather Forecast with musical accompaniment twice so that each dancer has an opportunity to enjoy watching and adding musical dynamics.

Assessment Forms

- Movement Study Assessment form, for teacher use and for student evaluation of the performance.
- Self-Assessment (version appropriate for students' level).

Extensions

- You may want to revisit Wacky Weather Forecast each season to explore the changes in weather from season to season.
- Invite students to create a scene representing a weather condition using painting or torn-paper composition. What does a thunderstorm, a blizzard, or fog look like?

74 The Water Cycle

DANCING A WATER CYCLE STORY.

GRADES: 3 TO 5   **LENGTH:** TWO 30-MINUTE SESSIONS

Materials

MOVEnture DVD

MOVEnture CD track 36

- Audio playback system
- Scarves for each student

National Standards
Science: 1

Dance: 1, 2, 3

Objectives
The students will be able to do the following:
- Discuss the water cycle (list it on board).
- Identify movement elements of the water cycle.
- Explore the element of flow.
- Perform a story dance of the water cycle.

INTRODUCTION

Explain to students that they will learn about the water cycle through dance. Ask the students if they can describe the water cycle. The parts of the water cycle are precipitation, evaporation, and condensation. Ask them why it is called a cycle. (The sequence of events repeats.)

Before moving, students complete the chart by connecting the dance vocabulary to the movement concepts (see the Connecting Water Cycle Science With Movement chart).

Connecting Water Cycle Science With Movement

Movement concepts	Stream	Evaporation	Condensation	Precipitation
Space: place, levels, directions, pathways	General space, middle and low level	General space and self-space; low level to high level	Self-space; high level	General space; high to low level
Time: slow, medium, fast	Slow	Fast	Slow	Medium to fast
Force: energy, weight, flow	Smooth, light, free	Smooth, light, free	Smooth	Sharp
Body movement: locomotor, nonlocomotor, shapes	Stretching, bending, gliding	Floating, rising	Shapes	Bending, jumping to low level, pounding the floor

THE MOVING ADVENTURE

Move and Balance

Give the students the following movement cues:

1. Swing and stop, and then glide and stop.
2. Move freely through space. When you hear the signal, stop and balance in a shape. Can you hold the shape? Are you on balance? It's hard to stop a free-flowing movement. What can you do to help? (Bend knees, contract abdominal muscles, pull body parts in.) Now move through space with bound flow. When you hear the signal, stop and balance. Is it easier to balance after moving with bound flow? (Alternate free-flowing movement and and balancing.)

Chance Dance

1. Give each part of the water cycle a number. 1 = precipitation, 2 = evaporation, and 3 = condensation.
2. Randomly assign students to various combinations of the numbers 1, 2, and 3. Possible combinations include: 1-2-3, 1-3-2, 2-1-3, 2-3-1, 3-2-1, or 3-1-2.
3. Students should come up with movements that represent the three parts of the water cycle.
4. Five to seven dancers should simultaneously perform their interpretation of each stage of the cycle, in the order you told them.

Story Dance: The Water Cycle

Lines	Suggested Movements
The water in the stream moves gently as it flows down the river.	Use free-flowing, slow locomotor movements.
Molecules of water become hot and move into the air, then spread out moving faster.	Use fast movement, light movement, high-level movement.
As the water vapor rises higher, it reaches cooler air. The cool air makes the water vapor slow down and move closer together. A cloud is formed.	Group makes shapes with scarves.
Soon the water drops become too heavy to remain in the air as clouds, and gravity brings them down to earth as rain.	Students perform movements to suggest that their clouds are slowly becoming heavier.
Raindrops strike the ground like tiny bombs, flinging up the earth.	High- to low-level movement hitting the ground.

Some raindrops seep slowly into the
ground while others form tiny streams,
and others cling to plant leaves.

By Lynnette Overby

Take on shape of a plant.
⚙️ **Modeling**

ASSESSMENT

- Describe the components of the water cycle
- Relate the dance vocabulary to the water cycle.

Assessment Forms

Participation Assessment form.

Extension

Students imagine that they are a drop of water. They draw a picture about their trip through the
water cycle.

Molecules in Motion

75

THE STATES OF MATTER.

GRADES: 3 TO 5   **LENGTH:** 30 TO 45 MINUTES

Materials

- Hand drum, xylophone, tambourine
- Create a States of Matter chart using the template on p. 277

National Standards

Science: 8

Dance: 1, 2, 7

Objectives

The students will be able to do the following:

- Describe common physical changes in matter: solid, liquid, and gas.
- Explain how visible changes in matter are related to atoms and molecules.
- Improvise, create, and perform dances based on concepts from other sources.
- Apply the elements of space, time, and relationships in movement to changes in matter.

INTRODUCTION

Introduce the molecular structure of states of matter. Discuss molecules in motion and how the speed of the molecules determines the form that matter will take. Gas particles are far apart and move fast and freely. Liquid particles are loosely clustered and move at a medium speed and more freely than solid matter. Solid particles move in a pattern in a restricted space. Heat changes the speed of the movement of molecules. The most common heat source in nature is the sun.

THE MOVING ADVENTURE

1. Explain that students will build a group shape representing a glacier or frozen water. Remind them that solid particles are within a restricted space and move slowly in a pattern. Establish the boundaries of the restricted space as a quarter of the classroom. Students make a shape in self-space within the restricted area and move in a pattern. Remind them that solid particles move very slowly. Tell them to listen to the drum for the signal of the movement of solid molecules.

2. Gradually the sun melts the glacier. As the particles warm, students demonstrate the movement of liquid molecules. They move at a medium speed, cover half of the class-room space, and gently bump into each other. The outside molecules will feel the heat first and melt away before the core. The xylophone will cue the movement of liquid molecules.

3. Continued exposure to the heat source causes the liquid to evaporate. Dancers move as gas molecules by speeding up and traveling throughout the entire space. Explore moving at different levels and in different directions. Play the tambourine for the movement of gas molecules.

ASSESSMENT

- How did the limited space change the way you moved?
- What happened to your relationship with other students as the speed of your movement changed?
- Was it difficult to move as the states of matter? If so, why?
- Students draw and describe the molecular structure of solid, liquid, and gas as states of matter.

Assessment Forms

Participation Assessment form.

Extensions

- Express other properties of matter through movement. Start with atoms that combine to form molecules. Have the students spread out, find self-space, and represent atoms. Upon your signal, they should form groups that represent molecules. Within their groups, ask them to design a way to hold on to each other as molecular bonds. The strength of the bonds determines the states of matter.
- Demonstrate how the process of cooling changes the state of matter.

Weather Vanes

76

USING WIND DIRECTION TO EXPLORE CONCEPTS OF NORTH, SOUTH, EAST, AND WEST.

GRADES: 3 TO 5   LENGTH: 20 TO 30 MINUTES

Materials

- Wind chimes
- Pictures or examples of different weather vanes
- Signs with the letters N, E, S, and W on them, posted in geographically correct positions in the room

National Standards

Science: 1

Dance: 1, 2, 3

Objectives

The students will be able to do the following:

- Demonstrate knowledge of directions north, east, south, and west.
- Describe the function of a weather vane.
- Create shapes that point using levels and directions of the body.

INTRODUCTION

In your own words, give the following background on geographical directions. It's important to know geographical directions. If you get lost, you may find that knowing which way is north, east, south, or west may help you find your way. It's also helpful if you want to read a map. In weather forecasting, or meteorology, the direction of the wind determines where the weather will travel next. Ask students if they know what a weather vane is. Does the weather vane point toward where the wind is coming from or where it is going?

Continue discussion to get to a point of general understanding. You may want to connect the discussion historically to agriculture and why farmers used weather vanes. Many of the shapes of weather vanes have livestock as the subject. Students will make their own special weather vanes using their bodies to create pointed shapes.

THE MOVING ADVENTURE

1. Have students find self-space. Request that they find the signs with N, S, E, and W posted in the room. Play a game that requires them to use different body parts to point to a geographical direction. (For example, use an elbow to point north, then a finger to point east, a hip to point south, a tongue to point west.) The students will have lots of suggestions for other body parts.

2. Instruct the students to make up a shape with the whole body that points toward north. As they create, remind them to play with the level and direction of their bodies. (For example, use a backward or sideways shape to make the point.) Ask them to make the shape very strong so that it could stand gusty winds. When all students have successfully created their shapes pointing north, have them hold very still and memorize it with all its details.
   ⚙ **Playing, Imaging**

3. Repeat the exercise creating a shape to point south, asking the students to make a change of level.

4. Repeat the exercise for east. But instead of the expected final shape pointing west, ask the students to point northwest. The students should now have four shapes they have memorized in the specific order of N, S, E, and NW.

5. Instruct the students to start the sequence, holding each shape until they hear the sound of the wind chimes. North shape . . . wind chimes . . . south shape . . . wind chimes . . . east shape . . . wind chimes . . . northwest shape.

6. Have the students watch others' creations in groups of four to six. Encourage the watchers to comment positively about what they observed.

ASSESSMENT

- What are the four basic geographical directions?
- Can you identify directions that are even more specific (WSW, NNE)?
- What does a weather vane indicate?
- Besides pointing with different body parts to make your weather vane shape, what else did you use to make the shape interesting?

Assessment Forms

- Movement Study Assessment form, for teacher use and for student evaluation of the performance. Add these factors to the form: clear shapes, listening, sequence memorization.
- Peer Assessment form (use oral or written responses).

Extensions

- You can spend a whole unit on studying geographical directions because the concept is integral to so many other areas of learning, including meteorology, latitude and longitude, agriculture, and mapping skills. Students could draw weather vanes they would like to see. They especially enjoy creating ones of animals such as dinosaurs, dragonflies, snakes, and other unconventional livestock.
- Though this Moventure is only a fundamental introduction to wind, you could further develop this topic by focusing on how winds are created, or types of winds, such as breezes, gusts, gales, and tornadoes.

77

Magnetic Force

BODY PARTS ATTRACT.

GRADES: 3 TO 5   **LENGTH:** 15 TO 20 MINUTES

Materials

- Hand drum
- Create a Magnetic Forces worksheet using the template on p. 277.

National Standards

Science: 10

Dance: 1, 2, 7

Objectives

The students will be able to do the following:

- Demonstrate magnetism through movement.
- Use focus and body-part isolation to present magnetic force.

INTRODUCTION

Bring in examples of magnets, including a bar magnet, horseshoe magnet, and a compass. Demonstrate magnetic force with objects that are attracted to a magnet (such as nails, paper clips, a key, or a spoon) as well as those objects that are not attracted to a magnet (such as paper, erasers, and fabric).

THE MOVING ADVENTURE

1. Students begin by finding self-space on the floor and lying on their backs.
2. Tell the students to imagine that the ceiling in the room is a giant magnet and their elbows are made of metal. As you play the drum, the students start being pulled toward the ceiling by an elbow. Remind them that the magnetism becomes stronger the closer the elbow gets to the ceiling (the magnet). They must focus the magnetic force on the elbow and hang from the elbow. When the drum stops beating, the magnetic force releases and they must carefully collapse to the floor.
3. Talk about possible choices for falling and collapsing safely. They need to catch themselves by bending a leg and collapsing on the bent leg, placing a forearm on the floor, rolling down to their side. Continue to play with magnetic force using a new body part. Ask students to suggest body parts to be attracted to the magnet (such as a hand, foot, belly, back, shoulder, or knee). ⚙ **Empathizing, Body Thinking**

ASSESSMENT

- What did it feel like to be the magnet or an object being drawn to the magnet?
- Was it difficult to isolate one body part in an attraction to the magnet?
- Students identify objects attracted to magnetic force: Primary grades color magnetic objects, and intermediate grades identify a temporary magnet and poles that attract and repel.

Assessment Forms

- Movement Study Assessment form, for student evaluation of the performance.
- Participation Assessment form.

Extensions

- Change the location of the magnet to a wall or an object in the room.

- Change body parts within one pull. Start with a nose being attracted to the magnetic force, then change to a knee, then to fingers. Notice the focus change on the body part being pulled as a new body part is called.

- Explain that a temporary magnet is an object that is attracted by a magnet and then becomes a magnet itself. Try having one dancer represent the temporary magnet and have others add on, like a chain of paper clips. The magnet will pick them all up as long as the first object remains in contact with the magnet.

- Demonstrate how like poles repel each other and unlike poles attract each other. Explore how like poles repel by having all students represent north poles and travel throughout the classroom repelling each other as they move. Have them move as unlike poles, half north and half south. Watch the magnetic force draw dancers together as they move. Give them a signal to release the force, move, and draw together again. Think of unique ways to connect.

Zap, the Electric Current

78

ELECTRONS ALIVE.

GRADES: 3 TO 5   **LENGTH:** 20 TO 30 MINUTES

Materials

None.

National Standards

Science: 9

Dance: 1, 7

Objectives

The students will be able to do the following:

- Use improvisation to discover, invent, and solve movement problems.
- Demonstrate an understanding of electrical currents and circuits through movement.

INTRODUCTION

Explain electricity beginning with the structure of the atom. A nucleus is composed of protons and neutrons with tiny electrons orbiting around it. Protons represent the positive charge (+), and each electron represents a negative charge (–). Neutrons are neutral with no charge. The electrons jump from atom to atom, flowing with the current in search of something positive. Negatively charged atoms have more electrons than protons. When these extra negative electrons pass through a conductor and flow to atoms that have a positive charge, there is an electric current.

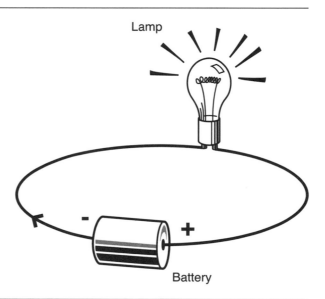

Lamp

Battery

THE MOVING ADVENTURE

1. Ask the students to tell you what types of material are good conductors. Electrons pass through copper and silver easily. When a copper wire carries electricity, the electrons charge in the same direction traveling through the wire. The wire must be insulated with rubber or plastic so that we don't get a shock. Have them try moving like an electric current.

2. The class forms a circuit by connecting in a circle to represent a wire (conductor). Explore different ways of connecting. ⚙️ **Modeling, Empathizing**

3. Select students to travel along the wire as electrons. Each electron follows the circuit path performing a locomotor pattern (such as hop, jump, hop) and briefly connects with each member of the "wire" (perhaps with a hand slap) as they form the current. If the pattern is broken, the flow of electricity stops and the circuit is broken.

ASSESSMENT

- Was the electric current clearly demonstrated through the movement ideas used by the dancers?
- What other properties of electricity could be explored through movement, and how?
- Have students draw an electric current.

Assessment Forms

- Participation Assessment form. Add this factor to the form: movement demonstration of an electrical circuit.
- Self-Assessment form (version appropriate for students' level).

Extensions

- Pathway: Add resistors to the circuit by limiting the pathway and catching the electrons as they travel. Resistors form a bridge. Electrons must crawl under resistors as they travel through the circuit. Demonstrate the energy (heat) buildup as atoms doing vibratory movement.
- Force: An ampere represents the strength of the electric current. Change the force of the locomotor pattern depending on the amp strength selected.
- Time: Vary the timing of the electrons by moving in slow motion when representing a poor conductor like tin.
- Ask students to move as superconductors. Superconductors charge with no resistance; powerful magnets cause the flow. These electrons move very fast.

79

Dinosaurs

DANCING THE RISE AND FALL OF THE DINOSAURS.

GRADES: 3 TO 5   **LENGTH:** 40 MINUTES

Materials

MOVEnture CD track 37
• Audio playback system

National Standards

Science: 7

Dance: 1, 2, 3

Objectives

The students will be able to do the following:

• Describe the evolution of dinosaurs.
• Name and describe various dinosaurs.
• Explore movement associated with specific dinosaurs.
• Perform a dance depicting the life and extinction of dinosaurs.

INTRODUCTION

Tell students that they will apply their knowledge of dinosaurs to a movement experience. Review the history of the dinosaurs.

Rise and Fall of the Dinosaurs

The Paleozoic era (550 to 248 million years ago) was the first era in which plant and animal life flourished. During the Mesozoic era, Triassic period (248 to 208 million years ago), a number of pioneering reptile groups evolved and became extinct. Longer-lasting groups such as turtles, crocodilians, pterosaurs, ichthyosaurs, and dinosaurs appeared in the late Triassic period. Flowering plants became widespread during the Cretaceous period (144 to 65 million years ago). The end of this era was marked by the mass extinction of dinosaurs, pterosaurs, large sea reptiles, and other animals. The immense crater from an asteroid that fell in Mexico 65 million years ago is a possible explanation for the mass extinction of animals. Dust from the explosion may have caused a worldwide winter, unsurvivable for almost all large animals.

Review the various types of dinosaurs. Ask the students if they can name and describe the various dinosaurs (see the Connecting Dinosaurs and Other Reptiles With Movement chart).

Connecting Dinosaurs and Other Reptiles With Movement

Types of dinosaurs and other reptiles	Movement concepts
Birds (flying reptiles): archaeopteryx and pterosaurs	Smooth, gliding, flying; body shapes; self-space and general space
Plant eaters: barosaurs	Large shape; reaching high level; slow movement
Sea dwellers: ichthyosaurs and plesiosaurs	Low-level; directions; smooth and sharp force
Meat eaters: tyrannosaurs	Fast moving; zigzag pathway; runs and leaps

THE MOVING ADVENTURE

Students are in scattered formation.

Imaginative Journey

Students are dinosaurs living in a warm environment. It is morning, and the sky is a brilliant blue with clouds. The air is warm with the slightest breeze. (Movement begins.) The plant eaters move slowly through the forests, gathering food from high branches (pause). Next the meat eaters move quickly in a zigzag pathway through the forests (pause). The flying reptiles take to the air and soar through the forest (pause). Finally, the sea-dwelling reptiles move smoothly through the water. ⚙ **Empathizing**

Dinosaur Dance

Place students into four groups. The first group is the plant eaters, the second group is the meat eaters, the third group is the flying reptiles, and the fourth group is the sea-dwelling reptiles.

Part 1

- In self-space, dancers make shapes with their bodies as the various dinosaurs and reptiles.
- Moving in general space, plant eaters move slowly, in a large shape, gathering food from high branches.
- In a zigzag pathway, meat eaters move quickly, run and leap, run and leap.
- Flying dinosaurs and sea-dwelling reptiles move through general space. (Dancers change levels and directions, using smooth and sharp force.)

Part 2

- An explosion occurs. (Use a loud drumbeat as dancers leap into the air.)
- The dinosaurs move in slow motion from a high level to a low level. This depicts the extinction of the dinosaurs.

ASSESSMENT

- Describe the various types of dinosaurs and reptiles.
- Describe a theory of the extinction of the dinosaurs.

Assessment Forms

- Comprehensive Assessment.
- Participation Assessment form.

Extensions

- The students create a portfolio of pictures of dinosaurs, with descriptions of habitats.
- The students develop a time line that visually displays the rise and fall of the dinosaurs.

Save the Rain Forest

80

A STORY DANCE.

GRADES: 3 TO 5   **LENGTH:** 30 MINUTES

Materials

MOVEnture CD track 38
- Audio playback system
- Props (several artificial plants to be held by "trees")
- Background information about the rain forest

National Standards

Science: 2

Dance: 1, 2, 3

Objectives

The students will be able to do the following:
- Connect scientific concepts with movement and dance concepts.
- Describe various components of the rain forest.
- Describe humans' negative effects on the environment.
- Perform a story dance about the rain forest with appropriate use of space, time, force, and body movement.

INTRODUCTION

Invite students to look at a globe with you. Point out the locations of several rain forests. Review the Connecting Rain Forest Science With Movement chart.

Connecting Rain Forest Science With Movement

Movement concepts	Trees	Gorilla babies	Tropical birds	Tree kangaroos	Snakes
Space: place, levels, directions, pathways	Self-space; high level	General space and self-space; low level	General space; low, middle, and high levels	General space	General space
Time: slow, medium, and fast	Slow, medium, and fast	Slow and medium	Medium	Medium	Slow to medium
Force/dynamics: energy, weight, flow, qualities	Smooth, light, and bound	Smooth and sharp	Smooth, light, free	Sharp, light, free	Smooth
Body movement: locomotor, nonlocomotor, shapes	Swaying, shaking, bending, stretching	Walking, running, stretching, sleeping positions	Running and leaping, flying, soaring, shaped with outspread wings	Jumps, body shape	Curving arms and torso

Describe the various parts of the rain forest where the trees grow to be over 200 feet tall:

- The forest floor: insects and large mammals
- Understory: anteaters, lemurs, and tree kangaroos
- Canopy: tropical birds, monkeys, and snakes
- Emergent layer: eagles, butterflies, monkeys, and snakes

THE MOVING ADVENTURE

In this story, students dance various parts of the rain forest. Starting in a scattered formation, they move to all of the different sections, and then they divide into groups for the final performance.

Save the Rain Forest, by Lynnette Overby

✿ Empathizing

Narrate the story, or assign a narrator to read, as all the students perform all sections.

Lines	Suggested Movements
It is beautiful in the rain forest, a wild garden zoo filled with exotic plants and animals. It's a place in perfect harmony with nature.	Sway in the breeze like the trees.
On the forest floor, the gorilla babies stretch, yawn, and sleep in various positions.	Stretch and make three different sleep positions.
The tree kangaroos play together in the understory.	Jump and move in general space with a partner.
In the canopy, exotic tropical birds fly from tree to tree looking for food.	Fly in general space, land, then take off again.
In the emergent layer, snakes move slowly around the tree limbs.	Students make curving designs with arms and torso.
	Students freeze on signal.
One day, loggers arrive in the rain forest with big chainsaws. They cut down every tree.	Students become trees in the forest; you (the teacher) become the logger. Children slowly fall to the floor when logger pantomimes cutting down trees.
The animals look around and find no shelter because there are no trees. The animals cannot live without trees, so one by one they die.	Students remain still.
After many years, new trees are planted. The trees grow and the animals and plants return one by one.	Students slowly rise to become trees again.
Once again, the gorilla babies stretch, yawn, and sleep in various positions.	Repeat all sections.

The tree kangaroos play together in the understory, the beautiful tropical birds fly from tree to tree looking for food, and the snakes curl around the tall tree limbs.

We must preserve our beautiful rain forests by caring for the environment. Each of us can make the world a better place for you, for me, and for everyone on Earth.

Repeat all sections.

Students freeze in their shapes for the end of the dance.

Performance

1. Students are divided into the following groups: Trees, gorilla babies, tree kangaroos, tropical birds, and snakes.

2. Narrator repeats story.

3. The trees are scattered in general space, swaying and moving to a slight breeze. The other creatures wait on the sides until they are cued to enter the space, one group at a time.

ASSESSMENT

• Describe the various components of the rain forest.

• Describe the negative effects humans have had on the rain forest.

• Students discuss the movements they selected to perform in the rain forest dance.

Assessment Forms

Comprehensive Assessment.

Extensions

• Students construct a diorama (or miniature model) of a rain forest.

• Older students will enjoy a more open approach to the rain forest. Have students create a movement story with students acting out the parts of the plants and animals in the rainforest.

• Read and explore movement to Lynne Cherry's "The Great Kapok Tree."

81

Ecosystem Explorers

DESERT USA.

GRADES: 3 TO 5   **LENGTH:** 30 TO 45 MINUTES

Materials
- Hand drum or triangle to signal
- Desert cards

National Standards
Science: 6
Dance: 1, 2, 7

Objectives

The students will be able to do the following:

- Demonstrate the ability to work cooperatively in a small group during the choreographic process.
- Create a sequence with a beginning, middle, and end both with and without rhythmic accompaniment. Identify each of these parts of the sequence.
- Create a sequence that reflects an understanding of an animal from the desert biome (an ecological community).

INTRODUCTION

The desert biome has plant and animal communities that exist in a dry, barren region. These plants and animals interact with one another through food chains and webs. As the class becomes familiar with the characteristics of the plants and animals that form the desert communities, begin to make desert cards for each one. You may want to create the desert cards for the students in advance as a resource or give them a homework assignment to research one desert plant or animal. Sort the desert communities into animal eaters, plant eaters, and plants.

Refer to the elements of dance and apply them as you describe the desert plants and animals. For example, what is the shape of Gila monster and how does it move? Where does it travel and at what speed? You can determine how simple or complex to be with your description.

THE MOVING ADVENTURE

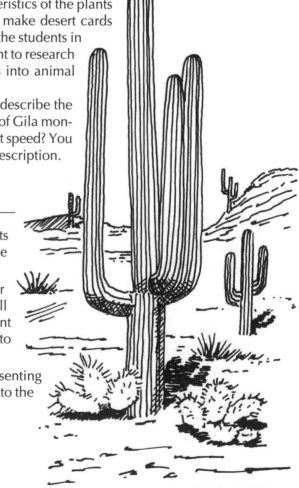

1. Describe the desert habitat. Visualize how the plants and animals fit into the environment and adapt to the climate.

2. Place the students in small groups throughout your room. Give each group a desert card, making sure all three categories are represented—animal eaters, plant eaters, and plants. (See sidebar for a list you can use to create these cards.)

3. Ask each group to create a movement phrase representing their desert plant or animal and prepare to present it to the class. ⚙ **Empathizing, Forming Patterns**

The following are examples:

- The king snake (animal eater) hisses, strikes, and vibrates its tail when threatened. When attacked, it rolls into a ball with its head in the center. It is found near clumps of vegetation and under rocks or logs. Dancers begin in a snake shape under a "rock," move with a hiss, vibrate tail, and roll into a ball.

- The bighorn sheep (plant eater) is known for its head-to-head combat. It is primarily a grazer, using its hooves and horns to remove spines from cacti. The bighorn sheep is commonly found in herds of 8 to 10. Dancers in a group of 8 begin grazing, use their "hooves and horns" to remove spines, and pretend to engage in head-to-head combat. (Use the "close but not touching" rule.)

- The saguaro cactus (plant) begins its life in the shelter of a "nurse" tree or shrub and grows very slowly to a great height of 15 to 50 feet. It has a surprisingly shallow root system and its smaller roots wrap around rocks. The night-blooming flowers attract birds, bats, and insects. Each dancer germinates in the shade of another dancer and slowly grows very tall (dancer on piggyback or held between two dancers). Other group members become the shallow roots, and finally one dancer represents the flower on the stem tip.

Desert Cards

Animal Eaters

King snake	Collared lizard	Elf owl
Armadillo	Hummingbird	Scorpion
Termites	Cougar	Honey ants
Turkey vulture	Spade foot toad	Roadrunner
Long-nosed bat	Golden eagle	Gila monster

Plant Eaters

Bighorn sheep	Prairie dog	Jackrabbit
Desert tortoise	Kangaroo rat	Sphinx moth
Ringtail	Antelope squirrel	Desert iguana
Peccary	Cactus wren	

Plants

Mesquite	Creosote bush	Prickly pear cactus
Fan palm	Mariposa lily	Saguaro cactus
Lupine sage	Desert marigold	Evening primrose
Joshua tree	Indian rice grass	

ASSESSMENT

- How did the dance elements apply to your desert card movement phrase?
- What did you like about the movement phrases you observed?
- Did your group members work together?
- Students perform the desert biome movement phrase.

Assessment Forms

- Movement Study Assessment form, for teacher use and for student evaluation of the performance.
- Self-Assessment form (version appropriate for students' level).
- Group Evaluation form.

Extensions

- Describe the tundra habitat. Visualize how the plants and animals fit into the environment and adapt to the climate. Place the students in small groups throughout the room and give each group a tundra card. Pass out a few cards from each category: animal eaters, plant eaters, and plants. Create a movement phrase representing the tundra plants or animals; prepare to present it to the class.
- Describe, visualize, and create a movement phrase representing the ocean plants or animals; prepare to present it to the class.
- Describe, visualize, and create a movement phrase representing the forest plants or animals; prepare to present it to the class.
- Create an ecosystem mural representing the animal eaters, plant eaters, and plants of the desert biome.

82

The Kelp Community

ECOSYSTEM INTERDEPENDENCE.

GRADE: 3 TO 5   **LENGTH:** TWO 30-MINUTE SESSIONS

Materials

- Musical instruments for various parts of the Kelp Community (drum for the shark, chimes for the kelp, kazoo for the sea otter, shaker for the sea urchin)
- Lightweight material or streamers for kelp
- Background information about the kelp community

National Standards

Science: 6

Dance: 1, 2, 3

Objectives

The students will be able to do the following:

- Connect scientific concepts with dance concepts.
- Describe various components of the Kelp Community.
- Perform the Kelp Community story dance with appropriate use of space, time, force, and body movement.

INTRODUCTION

Tall brown algae called kelp grows in such thick stands that they form underwater forests in cold coastal waters. Kelp provides living spaces for hundreds of different types of creatures (see the Connecting Kelp Science With Movement chart).

Parts of the Kelp

- The blade contains the leaves.
- The stipe is the stem.
- The float is the air-filled bladder at the base of each blade that buoys the plant up toward the surface.
- The holdfast is a rootlike structure that sticks to rocks and other hard surfaces on the ocean floor.

Kelp Forest Layers

- At the bottom layer of the kelp forest live the brittle stars and sea urchins.
- In the middle of the forest live snails and many kinds of fish.
- The top layer, or canopy, houses marine mammals, young fish, and seabirds.

Locations of Kelp Forests

- Northwestern North America
- Japan
- South America
- Great Britain
- New Zealand

Connecting Kelp Science With Movement

Movement concepts	Kelp	Sea urchin	Sea otter	Shark
Space: place, levels, directions, pathways	Self-space; high level	General space and self-space; low level	General space; low, middle, and high levels; moving backward	General space
Time: slow, medium, fast	Slow, medium, and fast	Slow and medium	Medium	Fast
Force/dynamics: energy, weight, flow, qualities	Smooth, light, and bound	Sharp (like the prickly spines)	Smooth and sharp, light, free	Sharp, strong, free
Body movement: locomotor, nonlocomotor, shapes	Swaying, shaking, bending, stretching	Kick, slash	Waving arms, walking	Running, jumping

Kelp Forest Creatures

- The sea urchin is a prickly invertebrate with red or purple spines. The sea otter eats the sea urchin.
- The sea otter is a mammal with thick brown fur and webbed hind feet.
- The white shark is a large gray or brown fish with a white belly. It feeds mainly on fish and marine animals.
- The giant kelpfish is a long slender fish that eats small fish, shellfish, crabs, and shrimp.
- The brittle star is a yellow, brown, or green relative of the sea star and sea urchin. It has long, spiny arms and lives in the holdfast region of the kelp.

THE MOVING ADVENTURE

1. All students dance all parts of the story and then divide into groups.
2. Students start in scattered formation in self-space. They move like the kelp: smooth, light, and bound.
3. Narrate the story, or appoint a narrator to read "The Kelp Community" while the students perform the movements.
4. Once performed a first time, repeat dance with students divided into the various parts. Begin with the kelp in a line at center stage. The sea urchins are at stage right, the sea otters are at stage left, and the white shark is upstage.
5. The sea urchins move stage left, then end at a low level near one of the students who is kelp. The sea otters move toward stage right, face front for shellfish cracking, and then end scattered among the kelp.

6. The shark moves downstage and jumps, facing the other creatures.

7. All students end by forming a circle and bowing.

The Kelp Community by Lynnette Overby

⚙️ Empathizing

Lines	Suggested Movements
Kelp grows in such thick stands that a forest is created under the sea. The kelp provides nourishment and shelter for many types of creatures.	Sway as if a rope of kelp underwater.
	Students freeze on signal.
Here come the sea urchins. They are prickly invertebrates with red or purple spines.	Students move with sharp arm and leg movements through general space.
They live at the base of the kelp and feed on all parts of the plants.	On a low level, students make a shape with their spines.
Now here come the sea otters. They swim on their backs and have thick brown fur and webbed hind feet.	Students smoothly swim, moving backward in a circular pattern in general space.
When they are hungry, they break open a shellfish on a rock.	Students pantomime cracking the shellfish on a rock.

Lines	Suggested Movements
And when they are sleepy, they wrap themselves in the kelp to stay put in the waves.	Students perform a wrapping motion in self-space and then pantomime falling asleep.
The king of the kelp community is the white shark. The white shark feeds mainly on fish and marine animals. It moves very fast.	Students run in a zigzag pattern in general space; then on a signal they jump in the air and land in a strong medium-level shape.
The kelp, sea urchin, sea otter, and shark all make up the kelp community. They depend on one another for food and shelter.	Students form a circle holding hands.
Together they make a circle of life under the sea.	Students walk two steps into the center of the circle and then two steps out; they repeat and then open the circle to one line and bow.

ASSESSMENT

Describe the creatures in the Kelp Community.

Assessment Forms

- Comprehensive Assessment form.
- Movement Concept Chart. Connect science concepts to movement by completing a blank movement chart.

Extension

For this activity you need pictures of the animals and plants in the kelp community; writing paper; drawing paper; pencils, markers, or crayons; and examples of sea myths. Reference books should also be available. In groups of four, students create and write a myth about a sea animal. Each member of the group can add on to the myth until the story is complete. They dance the sea myth while one member reads the narration. The students then write a final draft of their sea myth.

Microscopic World

83

DANCING THE AMOEBA, THE PARAMECIUM, AND THE HYDRA.

GRADE: 3 TO 5 **LENGTH:** TWO 30-MINUTE SESSIONS

Materials

MOVEnture CD track 39
- Audio playback system
- Water sounds
- Background information about microbes

National Standards

Science: 5

Dance: 1, 2, 3

Objectives

The students will be able to do the following:

- Connect scientific concepts with movement and dance concepts.
- Describe various microorganisms: the amoeba, the paramecium, and the hydra.
- Create a movement sequence with appropriate use of space, time, force, and body movement.

INTRODUCTION

1. Background information: Show pictures and discuss the Connecting Microscopic Science With Movement chart.

2. What is a microbe? *Micro* means small; *bio* means life. Microbe is simply small life.

3. Where can you find microbes? Microbes can be found everywhere: in the soil, air, rivers, and oceans. They are so small that they can only be seen under the microscope. There are more microbes than any other living thing in the world.

   - An amoeba is a living organism made up of a single cell. The amoeba looks like a shapeless blob of jelly. An amoeba creeps along slowly. It lives for only a day or two and survives by splitting into two smaller amoebas.

   - A paramecium is a microscopic organism that looks like a miniature slipper. The body is covered with short, hairlike structures called cilia. The cilia move back and forth and allow the paramecium to glide smoothly through the water.

   - The hydra looks like a monster with many heads. It has a long, thin body and many tentacles that extend near the hydra's mouth. The hydra usually moves slowly, but it can move quickly by turning somersaults in the water.

Connecting Microscopic Science With Movement

Movement concepts	Amoeba	Paramecium	Hydra
Space: place, levels, directions, pathways	General space; high, middle, and low levels	General space and self-space; low level	General space; low, middle, and high levels
Time: slow, medium, fast	Slow	Slow and medium	Medium to fast
Force/dynamics: energy, weight, flow, qualities	Smooth, light, free	Smooth, light, free	Smooth and sharp; free
Body movement: locomotor, nonlocomotor, shapes	Stretching, bending, gliding	Floating, gliding	Gliding; somersaults to move faster

THE MOVING ADVENTURE

Students are in scattered formation in self-space.

Warm-Up Exercises

Include stretches in self-space and various locomotor movements in general space.

Relaxation Exercise

Dancers lie on the floor on their backs with their arms at their sides, legs uncrossed, and eyes closed. They tighten and relax each body part, beginning with the feet. Use the following cues to guide their relaxation: Tighten your feet and legs; now release. Continue to your belly, chest, arms and hands, face, and finally your entire body. Take a deep cleansing breath. Rise, open eyes, and prepare for the imaginative journey.

Imaginative Journey

⚙ Empathizing

1. Explain to students that they will move like the amoeba, paramecium, and hydra—microscopic organisms that live in a pond.
2. Students first move like the amoeba: They make a wide shape with the body and then move slowly through the general space. (Freeze.) Instruct them to look at the person next to them; that is their partner. Each student makes a large amoeba shape with their partner; they move together through space. On the signal, they divide into two. (Use a drumbeat as the signal.)

3. They move like a paramecium, swimming and gliding and turning slowly like a top. Tell them to imagine they see a rock. They run into the rock, back up, turn slightly, and try again. Their arms are the cilia, swaying back and forth in rhythm to create movement.

4. Finally, students move like a hydra. They lift their arms over their heads to form the shape of the hydra with tentacles, and they glide smoothly through the water. To move faster, they cartwheel in general space and then glide smoothly again. (Instruct students to watch out for their neighbors.)

Creating

Individually, students design a short dance about one of the microbes.

1. They form a beginning shape.
2. They dance using various levels, directions, pathways, and dynamics.
3. They form an ending shape.

ASSESSMENT

- What is a microbe?
- Describe an amoeba, a paramecium, and a hydra.
- Observe and label microorganisms. For this activity you'll need microscopes and slides of various microbes. You should also have reference books available.

Assessment Forms

- Movement Study Assessment form, for teacher use.
- Movement Concept Chart. Connect science concepts to movement by completing a blank movement chart.

Extensions

- Create a microbe puppet and write dialogue for the microbe puppet.
- Visit a pond, collect the water, prepare slides, and use microscopes to identify microorganisms.

84

Roller Coaster

PHYSICAL SCIENCE ACTIVITY.

GRADE: 3 TO 5   **LENGTH:** 10 MINUTES

Materials
Roller coaster script.

National Standards
Science: 10
Dance: 7

INTRODUCTION

1. This activity can be used as a supplement to an in-class physical science lesson.
2. Students stand next to their desks and create movements that match the words.
3. Read through the script twice. During the first read-through, have the students imagine the types of movement they will perform during the second read-through.
4. Post movement suggestions on the board. Encourage them to focus on space, time, dynamics, and locomotor and nonlocomotor movements and body shapes.

MOVING ADVENTURE

Ask the students if they've ever ridden a roller coaster. As students stand next to their desks, use the following cues to guide them on their imaginary roller-coaster ride.

Roller Coaster Script

Imagine that you're waiting in line for an hour and a half for a terrific roller-coaster ride. As you nervously stand there clenching your ticket and hearing the terrifying screams coming from the cars that hold the other passengers in the roller coaster, you wait for your turn. "All aboard!" Your turn! You get comfortable in your seat, and suddenly the car takes a great lurch forward. Clink, clink, clink, clink! A chain slowly pulls your shaky car to the top of the first steep hill of the ride, clinking the whole way. You're getting so high that you can see the tops of all of the houses, trees, schools, and buildings. Maybe you aren't thinking about physics right now. You're probably thinking, *Get me out of here!*

But it's too late! And you're about to experience many examples of physics on this wild and crazy ride. The moving chain that pulls the car runs on electricity. As the chain pulls you to the top of the steep hill, the chain changes electrical energy to potential energy. That is the stored energy you have when you're in position to fall. Suddenly gravity steps in, and bam! It tugs you, pulling you swiftly. See it! Feel it! Use your imagination! You are zooming down the steep hill, changing your potential energy to kinetic energy! That's the energy you have when you are working.

When you were at the top of the incline you felt completely weightless. That was because the inertia kept you going in the direction you were headed—up! But only for a minute. Another force interrupts the process; it's the car going down, and it pulls you in that same direction.

Now the force is centripetal, which means directed or moving to the center of an object. Inertia will be disturbed and changed. When your car suddenly enters a steeply banked turn, you actually feel like you might tip right out of your seat! Actually, the tilted track forces the car to turn and pushes against the car with centripetal force. Thank goodness for that because if the inertia hadn't stopped, your car would have gone straight and jumped right off the track.

Now the car swiftly enters a loop, and you are upside down! You have to be traveling at a very fast speed for this to work. Do you know why you don't fall out? Inertia and centripetal force are busy at work once again! Inertia tries to keep your car moving outward and in a straight line. The track acts against inertia and centripetal force pushes the car around the track in a circle. Finally the hills start to get smaller and smaller and the roller coaster slows your car to a stop. (Students take their seats.)

ASSESSMENT

- Ask students to write down everything they experienced during that imaginary ride.
- Students define the following words: kinetic energy, potential energy, inertia, friction, and centripetal force.

Assessment Forms

None.

Extensions

- Create a story dance about the movement of simple machines.
- Visit an amusement park and write about the applications to physical science.

85

Rocks Rule!

THE PROCESSES OF IGNEOUS, SEDIMENTARY, AND METAMORPHIC ROCK.

GRADES: 3 TO 5   **LENGTH:** 30 MINUTES

Materials

- Musical instruments: drum, rain stick, wind chimes
- Examples of all three types of rocks, either real or pictured, for students to examine

National Standards

Science: 2

Dance: 1, 2, 3

Objectives

The students will be able to do the following:

- Perform shapes that reflect the dominant characteristics of the three forms of rock.
- Sequence shapes they have created into a movement study with a beginning, middle, and end.

INTRODUCTION

As we study the earth's rocks, we become interested in how they were formed. There are three types of rock, and they are named after the processes by which the earth created them:

- Igneous rock is formed by the heat of volcanic activity; it is hardened lava and magma. (Show examples of igneous rocks and invite students to describe the characteristics they observe. Connect their observations to how these rocks were formed.)
- Sedimentary rock is formed from bits and pieces of other rocks, often appearing layered as sediments of organic and inorganic matter are pressed together and then cemented with minerals from water. (Observe and describe examples of sedimentary rocks.)

- Metamorphic rock means changed rock. Almost all metamorphic rocks are formed from igneous and sedimentary rocks as they are broken down by the agents of weathering, such as wind, water, heat, chemical erosion, and pressure. (Observe and describe.)

Exploring rocks with the body is fun. Have students create a study about rocks and their formation.

THE MOVING ADVENTURE

1. Have the students start in a scattered formation. Instruct them to interpret the igneous rocks they examined by making very strong, hard shapes with their bodies, requiring their muscles to be very tense (bound energy). These are igneous rocks. After they have experimented with three or four shapes (encourage them to use low, medium, and high levels), they should each choose one shape and, while holding it very still, memorize it in detail. ⚙ **Body Thinking**

2. Move on to interpreting the sedimentary rocks, emphasizing the characteristic horizontal layering of many sediments lying on top of one another and pressing into linear designs. After experimenting with many ideas and change of level, again have them select just one shape and memorize it.

3. Finally, repeat the shape-making process with metamorphic rock. Students can create shapes that reflect processes of erosion such as hollows, holes, scrapes, and broken-off edges.

4. Students create a sequence, a complete phrase, from what has been memorized. As individual words are connected to make a sentence, so are shapes and movement. Assemble the memorized rock shapes into this sequence: igneous shape, sedimentary shape, and metamorphic shape. Students should be able to move from one shape to the next cleanly, including all the details of each shape.

5. After they have succeeded in memorizing the sequence of their shapes, ask them to make the movement changes between the shapes (transitions) as interesting as the shapes themselves. Suggest using the idea of the natural forces at work as inspiration for how the igneous or sedimentary rocks may have eroded through glacial scraping or wind, or how heat may have melted them into a metamorphic rock. Suggest that one transition could include a series of sharp movements while a different transition moves smoothly.

ASSESSMENT

- What are the three forms of rock?
- What are the characteristics of each form?
- What processes cause each rock to form?
- Which rock shape did you prefer? Why? (Possible answers are "It felt good" or "I liked how my muscles felt in that shape.")

Assessment Forms

- Movement Study Assessment form, for teacher use and for student evaluation of the performance. Add these factors to the form: originality of rock formations, clear shapes, transitions.
- Self-Assessment form (version appropriate for students' level).
- Peer Assessment form.

Extensions

- Take the students on a field trip to a museum with geological exhibits of rocks, minerals, gems, and fossils.

- Show a video on volcanoes.

- The movement study can be expanded to form the students' memorized shapes into a dance with a beginning, middle, and end as follows:

  - Students work together to make the shape of a volcano, which erupts with explosive movements (use a drum roll followed by powerful drum strikes, or have the students use their voices by starting low and rumbling and then increasing in pitch until they explode (boom!).

  - The students become liquid lava, which slithers and cools (sound of rain imitated by rain stick), hardening into various igneous rocks (their memorized shapes) about the general space.

  - Through pressure and the crushing of rock into smaller bits (tambourine or maraca), sedimentary rocks are formed as they are stretched, flattened, and layered.

  - Finally, through the actions of natural forces such as wind (wind chimes), the rock erodes into a metamorphic form.

- Students can develop an ending beyond the metamorphic shape that gives a sense of completion, perhaps by adding one more transition to a powerful shape and then, as a strong chorus, saying the words *Rocks Rule!* Ask the students for their ideas about what would be a good ending for this rock study. They'll have plenty of ideas!

86

Spaceship Ahoy!

EXPLORATION OF PLANETS IN THE SOLAR SYSTEM.

GRADES: 3 TO 5   **LENGTH:** 45 MINUTES, OR TWO 20-MINUTE SESSIONS

Materials

- Background music and audio playback system
- The book *Dogs in Space,* by Nancy Coffelt
- Poster-sized list of planet descriptions to post on the wall, or smaller version of list for handout

National Standards

Science: 3

Dance: 1, 2, 3, 7

Objectives

The students will be able to do the following:

- Become familiar with the planets in the solar system.
- Demonstrate the ability to work cooperatively in a small group during the choreographic process.
- Demonstrate partner skills by taking and supporting weight.
- Create and perform a dance based on a scientific concept.

INTRODUCTION

Ask the students if they've ever wished they could be an astronaut and fly on a spaceship to visit other planets. Explain that they will use their bodies, their imagination, and a little help from friends to do just that. First they must decide on a planet in our solar system that they would like to visit. Then they must build spaceships so that they can go there. They will study a little bit about the planets and what makes each one unique.

Read the story *Dogs in Space* to the students. At the back of the book, all the planets are briefly described in terms of temperature, size, distance from the sun, and unique characteristics. You may have other resources to help you develop their understanding.

For this Moventure, students will (1) build spaceships in small groups, (2) visit a planet either by landing on it or exploring it from orbit, and (3) decide on an ending to their journey. As an example, students could pretend they will visit Saturn. After they build their spaceship and travel there, it might be fun to ice skate on its rings, which are made up of a lot of dust and ice particles. For an ending, they might decide to return to Earth, or they might continue to other planets. But maybe they get so cold from ice-skating that they have to build a fire and warm themselves up while roasting marshmallows. (Post the most interesting characteristics of each planet on the wall for students' reference or distribute as a handout. For example, Mars is very hot, Uranus spins on its side, and Neptune has the fastest winds in the solar system.)

THE MOVING ADVENTURE

Session 1

1. Group the students into threes or fours. Have them find their own space in the room in which to work.

2. Build the spaceship. The task at hand requires trust. If your students have an extensive background in dance, each group can develop a structure with their bodies in which one member is lifted completely off the floor. The structure must be able to travel through the room. All must be involved in the formation of the ship, whether as a structural element (holding someone else's weight), as a design element (such as wings or tail), or as a passenger. Tell students that the objective is to work cooperatively in small groups to solve problems. If your students are newcomers to dance, they can create a connected shape that moves together across space. ⚙ **Body Thinking**

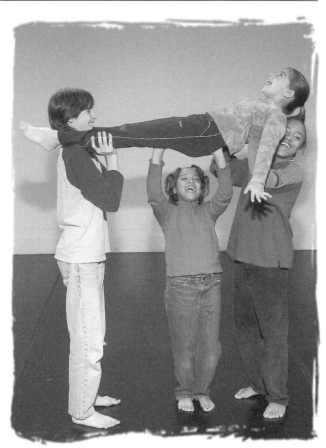

Session 2

1. Journey. Review the spaceship shapes from session 1. Then instruct the students to take off, fly through space, and arrive at a planet of their choosing. Referring to the list of planet characteristics, students decide on movements that they think will reflect the environment they encounter.

2. Journey's end. Students should develop an ending to the journey. As you move among the groups to support their learning, you may want to prod their thinking beyond the simplest solution.

3. Put on background music as students rehearse for sharing through performance.

ASSESSMENT

- Without looking at the list on the wall, see if students can name the planets in the solar system.
- Did your group work well together? Did you like the spaceship journey you agreed on?
- Did your dance have a beginning, middle, and end?
- Did you ever think that a person could create a dance about the solar system?
- As students observe each group's performance and the way the group moves, have them guess which planet the group is visiting.

Assessment Forms

- Movement Study Assessment form (evaluate as a group). Include these factors: cooperation, originality, spaceship shape, clear ending.
- Group Evaluation form.

Extensions

- Students can repeat this activity to explore other bodies in the galaxy, including constellations (what if the constellations came to life, like the Big Bear, or Orion, or the signs of the zodiac?)
- You can structure the activity for performance for parents by having each group perform their dance in succession, without stopping the background music.
- For an even more creative experience, have the groups imagine a planet that has unusual characteristics and travel there to explore it. The imaginary planet may have a surface of quicksand, banana peels, glue, or aliens. After creating their dance with beginning, middle, and end, they should give their planet a name. Have each student write the story of the journey from his or her own perspective.

87 Levers and Games

EXPLORING THIRD-CLASS LEVERS.

GRADES: 3 TO 5   LENGTH: 45 MINUTES

Materials

MOVEnture CD track 8
- Audio playback system
- Can opener
- Nutcracker
- Pictures of a child performing throwing, kicking, and striking movements

National Standards

Science: 10

Dance: 1, 2, 3

Objectives

The students will be able to do the following:
- Discuss simple machines.
- Explore third-class levers in the human body.
- Create a dance about levers in the human body.

INTRODUCTION

A machine is a device that does work. It doesn't have to have a motor to work. A machine produces a force and controls the direction and speed of the force. The lever is the most efficient machine. There are three different types of levers:

- First-class lever. (Show a can opener.) A can opener is a first-class lever with a resistance arm, a force arm, and a fulcrum. The resistance is the top of the can. The fulcrum is the edge of the can where the opener hooks around the edge. The force comes from our hand at the end of the opener. First class equals resistance, fulcrum, and force.

- Second-class lever. (Show a nutcracker.) A nutcracker is a second-class lever. The fulcrum is the closed end. The nut (resistance) is in the middle. The hand (force) is at the end of the handle. Second class equals fulcrum, resistance, and force.

- Third-class lever. (Show pictures of a child throwing, kicking, and striking a ball.) Arms and legs are third-class levers. The fulcrum is the body joint, the force is the muscles, and the resistance is the ball at the end. Third class equals fulcrum, force, and resistance.

THE MOVING ADVENTURE

Students are in scattered formation.

Creating a Space Ball

1. Students work individually to focus on the space substance (the air) between the palms. They sculpt the substance into a ball (pantomime).

2. Students throw and catch the space ball to themselves (higher, faster, slower). Instruct students to throw the ball against the wall and catch it. (They catch it in slow motion; they let the ball become very light and very heavy.)

3. Direct students to form partners and throw and catch to their partners. (They throw and catch in slow motion, let the ball become very light, and very heavy, keep their eyes on the ball, use their whole body to throw and catch.) ⚙ Imaging

Creating a Dance

1. Direct students to create a beginning shape (8 counts).

2. The game begins with throws and catches with a partner (32 counts).

3. They vary movements: slow, fast, heavy (change to strong), light.

4. Have students run and freeze in reaching and catching shapes—four different shapes, 4 counts each.

5. Students run in a curved pathway for 8 counts, then form a group of six members.

   • Group 1 is made up of a catcher, batter, and pitcher and first-, second- and third-base players. (Develop a 32-count game.)

   • Group 2 is tennis players. (Three pairs play a game of tennis for 32 counts.)

   • Group 3 is soccer players: two players on offense, two players on defense, and two goalies. (Develop a 32-count game.)

6. Students run to self-space and freeze in a shape (8 counts). ⚙ Modeling

ASSESSMENT

   • Describe a third-class lever.
   • Describe the third-class levers that were used in the dance.
   • You can give students pictures of various types of levers to label appropriately.
   • Students may collect pictures of various simple machines and place them in a portfolio.

Assessment Forms

Movement Study Assessment form may be used by teachers to assess choreography.

Extension

Have students explore first-class and second-class levers by creating a dance.

chapter 8

MOVEntures in Music, Theater, and Visual Arts

A relationship with the arts gives us a unique perspective with which to interpret the world. The arts (visual, creative writing, and performing) combine sensory and intuitive perceptions to encourage students to scale the logical and leap to the aesthetic, that plane where unconventional answers may lie. The interrelated arts curriculum follows a theme-based approach to learning, incorporating self-expression across the arts disciplines. For example, students can explore the concept of pattern in visual art design, in a dance sequence, and in a phrase of music. The curriculum accommodates diverse learning styles through visual, musical, and kinesthetic modes, the benefit of which is potential success for every student.

Living the arts is a way of being, a way of seeing. It allows children to trust their creative impulse and apply it to the everyday life of family, work, spirit, and play. As they see the value of their own special ideas and feelings, they are more able to respect the ideas and feelings of others. An interrelated arts curriculum prepares our students not only to move into the future but also to grasp it confidently.

Creating Across the Arts

88

A MULTIAGE, MULTIARTS LESSON.

GRADES: K TO 2, 3 TO 5   **LENGTH:** THREE 30- TO 45-MINUTE SESSIONS

Materials

- Visual arts media: paper, crayons, paint, markers, pastels
- Audio playback system and music (an American theme is recommended, such as Sousa's *Washington Post,* Copland's *Rodeo,* or Grofe's *Grand Canyon Suite)*

National Standards

Music: 7

Visual Arts: 3

Theater: 1, 5

Dance: 2, 3, 4, 7

Objectives

The students will be able to do the following:

- Create a dance sequence with a beginning, middle, and end.
- Improvise, create, and perform a dance based on ideas and concepts from other sources.
- Make connections among the arts.
- Listen to, analyze, and describe music.
- Select and use subject matter and ideas to communicate meaning.
- Explore writing a script.

INTRODUCTION

Have students listen to a piece of music you brought. (If it is a very long selection, just give the students' the flavor by listening to an excerpt.) Ask them what they heard, and have them list the instruments in the selection. Have them consider the loudness and softness, musical phrasing, and mood of the selected music. Did they picture anything specific as they listened? How did it make them feel?   ⚙ Imaging

THE MOVING ADVENTURE

⚙ Transforming

Session 1

Interpret through visual arts. Play the music again. Have students make a list of at least four ideas or images inspired by the music. Have the students illustrate the images. Distribute materials for an exploration of visual arts using the medium of your choice, such as pastels, crayons, paint, and markers. This could be a literal interpretation (in which students actually draw objects and images) or an expressionistic interpretation (in which students use splashes of color or create designs with lines).

Session 2

1. Interpret through dance. Play the music as the students observe their drawings or paintings. Have them visualize movement and still shapes inspired by the music and the subject of their piece of visual art. Instruct them to explore their movement ideas with the music both in self-space and general space. Caution them to respect each other's space while moving.

2. Once they have explored movement possibilities, students should create a phrase composed of both motion and frozen shapes that they can remember. Have them develop a composition that includes a beginning and an end. (Note for upper-elementary students: If their artwork is abstract in nature and they seem unsure about how to interpret it, suggest dancing the lines, curves, designs, or overall ideas and emotions within the painting through shapes and movement.) The beginning or end can be a shape or an entrance or exit. The composition or movement study is as follows: beginning, memorized movement phrase, end. Students rehearse with the music in the background to prepare for sharing.

Session 3

1. Interpret through drama. Returning to the original list of words or pictures in session 1, students should develop a story either individually, in small groups, or as an entire class. Upper-elementary students could write a script, defining characters and a plot.

2. Depending on your goals for this lesson, the students can perform the dance compositions they have developed, or act out the script they have written, or just appreciate the process of creating across the arts. They can perform individually or in small groups.

ASSESSMENT

- Did your dance have a clear beginning, middle, and end?
- How did we get to the point of writing a script? What started this whole process?
- How did your ideas differ from other students' interpretation of the music?

Assessment Forms

- Participation Assessment form.
- Self-Assessment form or Peer Assessment form.

Extensions

- Repeat the interrelated arts activity with a different genre of music.
- Repeat the process, starting from an image of visual art (Picasso). Use musical instruments to interpret the piece of art, then dance as a reflection of the music and piece of visual art. Repeat with a very different type of artist (such as Rembrandt or Warhol).
- Try another variation beginning with a dramatic scene. Create a visual arts representation of the scene. Explore the essence of the scene through abstract movement, and add musical accompaniment.

89

Color Me

A RAINBOW OF EXPRESSIONS.

GRADES: K TO 2   **LENGTH:** TWO 30-MINUTE SESSIONS

Materials

- Crepe-paper streamers or scarves
- Tempura or watercolor paint, paintbrushes, water, white paper

National Standards

Art: 1, 2

Dance: 1, 2, 3

Objectives

The students will be able to do the following:

- Describe how different colors have expressive features.
- Understand the importance of color in the world around us.
- Use self-expression in movement and visual art.

INTRODUCTION

Artists use color in many different ways to express their ideas. The colors around us affect the way we perceive our world and the way we feel. What color choices do we make during the day? The color of a book cover in the library might catch your eye. Maybe the color of a piece of pizza looks inviting for lunch. Color contributes to our personal choices all the time.

THE MOVING ADVENTURE

1. In scattered spacing, students explore ways that color makes them want to move. Give each student a colored streamer or scarf. The students with red streamers or scarves stand up and show everyone how red makes them want to move. Maybe red makes them think of a mad movement or something loving, like a valentine heart. The students with blue streamers or scarves stand up and move to represent their color. Ask the students for movement ideas to share how each color makes them feel. ⚙ **Body Thinking**

2. Students perform their color dance. When you call out a color, students with that color dance the way the color makes them feel and say, "Color me _____." They freeze in an ending shape using their streamer or scarf as a part of the shape. Call out each color individually for their color dances. Finish with everyone repeating their movement at the same time throughout the general space and saying, "Color me beautiful!"

3. Students share a chosen mood by painting their feelings. Using tempura or watercolor paints, they can use images from their movement exploration or create the painting first and then dance it. Encourage them to experiment with painting techniques and colors. ⚙ **Transforming**

ASSESSMENT

- What feelings were you dancing to interpret your color?
- What do you think of in the world around you that reflects your color?
- How did your painting reflect your color dance and the feelings you were expressing?
- Create a gallery showcase of mood paintings.

Assessment Forms

- Participation Assessment form.
- Self-Assessment form (version appropriate for students' level).

Extensions

- Create a "rainbow" movement sequence by determining one movement for each color and dancing from one color to the next. You can sing, "Violet (quiet shape), indigo (ocean waves), blue (reach to the sky), and green (blades of grass or a tree), yellow (bumble bee), orange (flickering flames), and red (heart shape)." The dancers can have streamers of all the colors together to manipulate as they move, designing the space with beautiful rainbow colors.
- Read *Hailstones and Halibut Bones: Adventures in Color,* by Mary O'Neill and John Wallner or *My Many Colored Days,* by Dr. Seuss, Steve Johnson, and Lou Fancher. Explore new interpretations of colors and how they make us feel.

Rain Dance

90

RHYTHM PLAY.

GRADES: K TO 2   **LENGTH:** 30 MINUTES

Materials

Rhythm (lummi) sticks

National Standards

Music: 2

Social Studies 1

Dance: 1, 5

Objectives

The students will be able to do the following:

- Demonstrate moving to a musical beat.
- Play a rhythm independently.
- Describe Native American music and dance.

INTRODUCTION

Discuss the role of dance and music in the Native American culture. Most tribes observe ceremonies that are connected with the changing seasons, planting crops, and animals they hunted. They dance in celebration of important events in daily life. Native American Indians use many kinds of drums made of natural materials such as animal skins, wood, or clay. The rhythm of the drum provides the pulse for the dancers' feet. Gourd rattles, bells, and bones might be added for rhythmic sounds. Ceremonial dances are often long. Dancers use small steps, close to the ground, to conserve energy. The headdress, costumes, and masks symbolize the traditions of the tribe.

THE MOVING ADVENTURE

1. Sit in a circle, which represents a powerful connection to life to the Native Americans. Dances are often performed in circular patterns. The rain dance was performed in the growing season as a way of asking for rain and giving thanks at harvest time.

2. The rhythms complement the syllables of each phrase. Try clapping the rhythm first, then introduce the rhythm sticks. If drums are available, half the students can modify the rhythm for drums while the other half dances. Think about adding accents to the drum rhythm. ⚙ **Recognizing Patterns, Body Thinking**

Rain Dance	Rhythm Stick Patter	Foot Pattern
On the Mountain	1-2 tap sticks on floor twice; 3-4 tap sticks together.	Stomp-stomp right; stomp-stomp left.
On the Plain	1-2 tap sticks on floor twice; 3 tap sticks together; hold count 4	Stomp-stomp right; stomp together.
Hear the Thunder	1 tap on floor with right stick only; 2 tap left, 3 tap right, 4 tap left.	Stomp left, hop left; stomp-stomp right.
Bring the Rain	1-2-3 tap sticks together; hold count 4.	Clap hands; reach and look up.

Rain Dance	Rhythm Stick Patter	Foot Pattern
For the Harvest	1-2 tap sticks on floor twice; 3-4 tap sticks together.	Walk 3-step circle (right, left, right, touch left).
For the Grain	1-2 tap sticks on floor twice; 3 tap sticks together; hold count 4.	Walk 3-step circle (left, right, left; touch right).
From the Clouds High	1 tap floor right only; 2 tap left; 3 tap right; 4 tap left.	Circle arms high.
Bring the Rain	1-2-3 tap sticks together; hold count 4.	Clap hands; reach and look up.

By Beth C. Post

3. Repeat the dance sequence with rhythm sticks only (no lyrics).

ASSESSMENT

- Could you play the rhythm of the chant with your lummi sticks?
- Were you successful at demonstrating the steps of the rain dance?
- What did you learn about the importance of dance to the Native American culture?

Assessment Forms

- Movement Study Assessment form, for teacher use.
- Self-Assessment form (version appropriate for students' level).

Extensions

- Write lyrics to celebrate an important event in life, an animal, or a season.
- Compose a rhythmic accompaniment for sticks or drums.
- Choreograph simple steps to dance with the rhythm composition.
- Related lessons: Universal Circle Dance, lesson 54, and A Native American Poem, lesson 61.

91

A Spider's Life

LEARNING TO BLOCK A DANCE ABOUT SPIDERS.

GRADES: K TO 2   **LENGTH:** TWO 30-MINUTE SESSIONS

Materials

MOVEnture CD track 14
- Audio playback system
- Chalkboard or poster with stage directions
- Streamers

National Standards

Theater: 4
Science: 6
Dance: 7

Objectives

The students will be able to do the following:
- Perform a story dance about the life cycle of a spider.
- Describe symbols used for blocking.

INTRODUCTION

Begin class with students seated in front of a chalkboard or poster with stage directions and symbols. Explain that directors bring a play to life by blocking the action of the performers. Blocking is a technique used to move the performers from one location to another and to make certain the stage picture is interesting. (See figure of stage setup in Probability Dance, lesson 53 in chapter 5, page 135.)

Each movement is designated by a number at the appropriate place in the script and is detailed on the facing page in an entry carrying the corresponding number. Each script page is numbered separately.

THE MOVING ADVENTURE

Session 1: Practice Moving to Various Parts of the Stage

Students start at center stage. Ask them to move on a low level to downstage right. Move on a high level to upstage left. Move smoothly back to center stage. Now move quickly to downstage right. Move sharply to upstage right. Move slowly back to center stage. Move freely to downstage center. Move in a bound way to upstage center. Move while twisting and shaking back to center stage. Form a circle and sit down. (Continue to have students practice moving to various parts of the stage individually, in small groups, and as a whole class.)

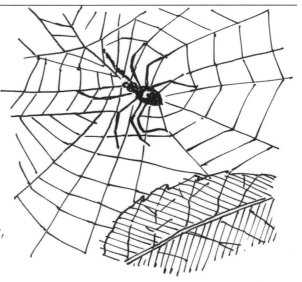

Session 2: Blocking A Spider's Life

⚙ **Body Thinking**

Block the action to "A Spider's Life." Divide students into partnerships for later in the dance.

Narration	Suggested Movements
(No line.)	Half of the dancers enter stage right and the other half enter stage left and cross to center stage.
In the bushes silken balls burst open.	All dancers are seated in a circle at center stage—round shape. On cue of "burst open," the dancers sharply raise both arms.
They stretch one leg at a time.	All dancers turn to face out of the circle, stretching one leg at a time.
Dance along the branches.	Dancers gallop facing out of circle.
On silken streamers tiny spiders . . .	Using streamers, dancers float in general space
. . . fly, they float above the homes of other spiders reeling in their lines. The spiders twirl, floating down to places of their own.	Dancers float in general space, then float down in a scattered formation, facing down stage.
They explore their field.	Dancers make a shape that focuses up.
Their place.	Dancers make a shape that focuses out.
Their home.	Dancers make a shape that focuses down.
They eat and become larger.	Dancers stretch and rise to a wide shape.
Twitching, twisting, twirling the swollen spiders kick and kick their way out of their skin.	Dancers twist, twirl, shake, and jump.
Two spiders dance their own . . .	Dancers take partners in scattered formation.
. . . dance inside the web.	Dancers perform mirroring movement.

Finally, the spiders lay a hundred eggs inside a yellow fluffy ball and hide them from the wind and the rain.	Partner 1 shapes partner 2 into a ball.
So very tired, they bow and leave the eggs behind.	Partner 1 moves slowly downstage and then performs a suspended and collapsed movement. (All dancers freeze.)
In the wintertime the cold bare bush . . .	All dancers move back into center stage.
. . . displays the spider's gift,	Dancers use circular formation and round shapes.
. . . a yellow ornament full of life, waiting for spring when tiny spiderlings will creep and fly and dance. The end.	

From J. Ryder and R.J. Blake, 1981, *The spider dance.* By permission of J. Ryder.

ASSESSMENT

- Why is blocking important?
- How did the blocking help to tell the story?
- Students label the parts of the stage.

Assessment Form

Participation Assessment form.

Extensions

- Students create stage directions for a previously learned dance.
- Students develop a dance with stage directions about another living thing.
- Related lessons: African Folktale, lesson 29, and Probability Dance, lesson 53.

The Animal Tale

CREATING A STORY DANCE ABOUT ANIMALS.

GRADES: K TO 2   **LENGTH:** TWO 30-MINUTE SESSIONS

Materials

 MOVEnture CD track 23 or another environmental music selection (forests, oceans, wind)

- Audio playback system
- Cards with quality and time words (one for each student)
  - Quality: sudden, sustained, strong, light, bound, free, percussive, sustained, vibratory, swinging, suspended, collapsed, heavy, powerful, jerky, shaking, gentle, explosive, soft
  - Time: fast, medium, slow, gradually slowing down, gradually getting faster, in slow motion, even, uneven

National Standards

Theater: 2

Science: 6

Dance: 3

Objective

The students will be able to create a story dance about animals.

INTRODUCTION

Ask students who their favorite actors are and why. Actors must make the audience believe that an imaginary place, time, and person really exist. They accomplish this by learning as much as possible about the characters they portray before they begin to act. Explain that students will use movement to help them become good actors as they create an animal story.

THE MOVING ADVENTURE

Session 1

Exploring Quality and Time Words

1. Students are in scattered formation. Distribute the quality and time cards to each student.

2. Instruct students to move in self-space like the quality or time word on their cards. (Signal to start and stop.) ⚙ **Body Thinking**

Animal Exploration

1. Students are seated in scattered formation.

2. Have students think about an animal that moves like the element on their cards.

3. Give students examples, such as "Slow and strong are words that describe an elephant."

Moving in General Space

Have students move in general space like the animals that they chose. (How would the animal move if it were happy? How would it move when searching for food? When tired? When agitated?)
⚙ **Empathizing**

Session 2

Designing the Animal Tale

1. The students form groups of four and improvise and create an animal tale. (Make sure they have a beginning, middle, and end.)

2. Have each group form a beginning shape, and on signal the students tell their tale through movement (and through the use of animal sounds if appropriate).

3. When each group finishes their tale, they hold an ending shape until all groups are finished. ⚙ **Pattern Forming**

Sharing the Story

Each group shares their tale while the other students become audience members.

Discussion

After each group performs, the students describe what they saw happening in the animal tale.

ASSESSMENT

- How did the quality or time cards help you create a believable animal character?
- How did your group develop your story?
- Did the use of the quality and time cards promote a movement-inspired interpretation of the animals?

Assessment Forms

Movement Study Assessment form, for teacher use.

Extensions

- The students write their animal tale as a group writing project.
- The students connect with science by creating an animal tale based on animals studied in science class.
- Related lesson: Express Yourself!, lesson 17.

93 Bodies in Motion

A SPORTS DANCE.

GRADES: 3 TO 5   **LENGTH:** THREE 30- TO 45-MINUTE SESSIONS

Materials

- Pictures or videotape of athletes in action
- Tagboard (light-weight poster board), drawing paper, and pencils or thin markers

National Standards

Art: 1

Dance: 3

Objectives

The students will be able to do the following:

- Relate dance to other forms of human movement (such as sports and common gestures).
- Use different media and techniques to communicate ideas.
- Understand and demonstrate gesture drawing, contour outline, and use of repetition.

INTRODUCTION

Talk about a particular sport and determine the movements that happen in the sport. For example, in a football game, the action might include kicking, passing, tackling, and running.

THE MOVING ADVENTURE

1. Invite the students to perform a few of these movements in their self-space. The students can create a sequence of movements from the chosen sport and vary it by performing at a different level, in slow motion, in a new direction, or in a different pathway.

2. Select a sport movement such as a football pass. Ask a student to perform the action; say, "Freeze" during the execution of the pass. Demonstrate a gesture drawing of the position in which the student is frozen. Remember that a gesture drawing uses just a few lines to show a figure in motion. Assign partners and have students practice different sport movements. They take turns being the models.

3. Draw the contour outline of the body shape from the chosen sport on tagboard and cut it out. Trace the outline in repetition at least three times, following the action through space as in freeze-frame photography. Add details to the figure, and design the environment where the sport is performed. ⚙ **Abstracting**

ASSESSMENT

- What dance elements did you apply to vary your sport movement?
- Can you see the sport movement represented in your gesture drawing?
- What was difficult about drawing the contour outline of your athlete in action?
- Did you complete the gesture drawing successfully?
- Did you complete the contour outline repetition drawing successfully?

Assessment Forms

Movement Study Assessment form, for teacher use.

Extensions

- In an Olympic year, share pictures depicting Olympic sports. Students can interpret movements from sports such as speedskating, downhill skiing, or synchronized swimming. Take time to learn about the history and traditions of the Olympic Games.
- Watch sport segments on video to analyze the action. Check the local video store for examples of athletes in action.

94

Dance TV

INTERPRETING MUSIC AND DANCE STYLES.

GRADES: 3 TO 5   **LENGTH:** 30 TO 60 MINUTES

Materials

MOVEnture CD track 40 or another collection of various music genres such as country, jazz, classical, popular, cartoons, favorite sitcom themes

- Audio playback system

National Standards

Music: 7

Dance: 1, 5

Objectives

The students will be able to do the following:

- Improvise, create, and perform dances based on their own ideas and concepts from other sources.
- Demonstrate perceptual skills by moving to music of various styles.

INTRODUCTION

The music collage should reflect a variety of music styles to give the students a broad perspective for music appreciation. Play selections of country, classical, and popular music, and ask the students to identify the music genres. Invite them to explore moving in ways that they think best reflect the selections of music.

THE MOVING ADVENTURE

1. Ask students to imagine they are tuning in to different television channels. As they listen to the music from each channel, they should think about how they would interpret the style of music through movement.

2. Work together to share ideas and choreograph a movement phrase for each style in the music collage. For example, they can square dance or line dance to the country music channel. They can create a ballet movement phrase for the classical music channel. They can dramatize exploration in outer space or freeze in a tableau respresenting the sci–fi channel.They can perform a superhero dance to the cartoon channel.

3. Play the entire collage once and ask students to improvise movement. ⚙ **Playing**

4. Watch their ideas to see what movement vocabulary they have for each genre. You may want to experience the music variations through improvisation only. Compliment the students on their inventiveness and sensitivity to the music styles. Or you may want them to develop their ideas into a set movement phrase by using their ideas in a choreographed sequence.

5. Depending on your students' ages and their ability to generate movement ideas, have suggested movements prepared to assist them in the choreographic process. Refer to the 20th-Century Celebration, lesson 65 in chapter 6, for dance styles.

ASSESSMENT

- Who has a movement phrase they would like to share for a music channel in our collage?
- With each change of music style, could you think of ways to move to reflect the style?
- Have the students write a journal reflection on a music and dance genre.

Assessment Forms

- Movement Study Assessment form, for teacher use.
- Self-Assessment form (version appropriate for students' level).

Extensions

- Divide the students into groups of three to five. Ask each group to coordinate their own movement interpretation to the music collage. Remind them to work cooperatively and strive to include everyone's ideas. Each group will perform their Dance TV choreography for the class.
- Ask students to share other styles of music they could include on new Dance TV channels. They can work within their small groups to create their own Dance TV collage. Select three or four different pieces of music (students can bring music from home to share). Students create short movement phrases to interpret the music. Finally, they transition from one movement phrase to the next with the change of the Dance TV channel.

95

Masquerade

MASKS, CHARACTERS, AND TRANSFORMATION.

GRADES: 3 TO 5 **LENGTH:** THREE 30-MINUTE SESSIONS

Materials

MOVEnture CD track 23 or other percussion music
- Audio playback system
- Pictures of masks from a variety of cultures (Japanese, African, Aboriginal, Native American)
- Premade theatrical eye masks in a variety of colors (available in assorted packs at a dime store)
- Glue, scissors, and tape
- Lightweight decorative items such as beads, feathers, strips of colored paper, yarn, cotton balls, sequins, and leather strips

National Standards

Visual Arts: 3
Theater: 2
Language Arts: 6
Dance: 1, 2, 3, 4, 7

Objectives

The students will be able to do the following:
- Create a mask.
- Develop a unique theatrical character through dance.
- Define the concept of transformation.
- Perform a dance with a beginning, middle, and end.

INTRODUCTION

This can be an exciting lesson to develop with help from the visual arts teacher. Introduce the concept of masquerades during session 1. People throughout the world and throughout history have enjoyed making masks or decoratively painting their faces. Show students pictures of masks and painted faces. Ask them why they think people made these masks. (To pretend to be somebody or something else.) We call that *empathizing,* transforming yourself from the person you really are into a different creature or person. And it's a lot of fun! It's what actors and actresses do. They become different characters in a play, a film, or a dance. When and where do people in our culture enjoy using masks and costumes to transform themselves? (New Year's eve, costume parties, Halloween, Mardi Gras, Disney World.)

Tell the students that they will use materials to make masks. As they decorate the masks they have chosen, they can determine ahead of time what character or creature it might be, or they can just decorate the mask and then decide its personality based on how it looks when it is finished. When all students have completed their masks, they'll put them on and transform themselves into the characters of the masks.

THE MOVING ADVENTURE

Session 1
Each student selects a mask and decorates it.

Session 2
When all masks are completed, have the students list a written description of the character that the mask represents. Is it good? Mean? Magical? Humorous? Happy? Is it short, tall, gigantic, invisible? This exercise gives the students an opportunity to define the character in written form, which they can then refer to as they develop movement and shapes for it.

Session 3
1. If time permits, this session can immediately follow session 2 while creative juices are still flowing. Instruct students to go to a scattered formation. As they try on their masks, encourage them to explore through movement and shape how their character might act. Might it move heavily and sluggishly? Lightly and serenely? Distorted in its body? Curious? Cautious? ⚙ **Empathizing**

2. Each student should develop three shapes reflective of the mask's character and memorize them. ⚙ **Body Thinking**

3. Each student should also develop three traveling movements reflective of the mask's character that he or she can use between making the shapes. Suggest traveling at different levels and in different directions.

4. Masquerade dance: The structure of the dance is movement 1, shape 1, movement 2, shape 2, movement 3, shape 3. Students begin by standing anywhere at the edges of the dance space. Start the music and tell the students they may begin whenever they feel ready by using their first traveling movement to enter the dance space. At some point after traveling for a while, they must stop and make shape 1, holding it until they feel ready to do the second traveling movement and then the second frozen shape. Repeat process for third movement and shape. Dancers choose a traveling movement for exiting the space.

5. Repeat the dance and suggest that the students interact with another mask wearer while dancing by using the traveling movement to follow and chase, circle, or complement another character. Or they can make memorized shapes directed at or close to another character.

ASSESSMENT
- How did your mask turn out? Do you like what you created?
- Who was the character you created? Could you give it a descriptive name?
- What does it mean to transform yourself? Did you think you were successful in transforming into your character? Do you think we can learn about someone or something else by becoming that character?
- Did your dance tell a story with a beginning, middle, and end?

Assessment Forms

- Movement Study Assessment form, for teacher use and for student evaluation of the performance.
- Participation Assessment form.
- Self-Assessment form (version appropriate for students' level). Add these factors to the form: I used different levels and directions well; I remembered my movements and shapes accurately; I remembered the order of the dance well (travel, shape, travel, shape); I transformed into my character well; the movements and shapes I chose for my character were appropriate to its personality; I tried to interact with other characters during the dance.
- Peer Assessment form. Perform the dance with half the class dancing and half observing (share through performance). Observers should comment to the performers on the interactions and movements they found interesting, or they can use the written Peer Assessment form with questions similar to those in the Self-Assessment form.

Extensions

- Trade masks with someone else, developing a new character and dancing it.
- Repeat exercise wearing the mask in an unexpected way or on another body part.
- Wear two masks, one on the back of the head, one on the face. Closure questions could include the following: Did you feel more like the mask character when the mask covered your head, or when it was on a different body part? Why? How did you feel with two masks on?
- Create a story about how this character came to be, and write it down. Write how it felt to be that character and what happened when it met other characters. Include a copy in student portfolios.
- Take students on a field trip to see an art exhibit on masks, or take them to a live performance by a dance or theater troupe that uses masks or puppets during their presentation.

Everyday Life
in Faraway Times

USING ANCIENT GREEK ART
TO UNDERSTAND CULTURE, TIME, AND PLACE.

GRADES: 3 TO 5 **LENGTH:** TWO OR THREE 30-MINUTE SESSIONS

Materials

- Numerous pictures of art and sculpture from ancient Greece depicting images of people in passive and active pursuits (dancing, worshiping, wrestling, eating and drinking, playing instruments). Many of the pottery items are in black-and-gold colors, circling the edges of urns, vases, and plates. Others are three-dimensional sculptures and decorative implements or friezes on the sides of temples.
- Photographs of Isadora Duncan or Vaslav Nijinsky, famous dancers who danced scenes and images from ancient Greek art.

National Standards

Visual Arts: 4

Social Studies: 1, 2, 3

Dance: 1, 2, 3, 7

Objectives

The students will be able to do the following:

- Recognize specific works of art that belong to the culture of ancient Greece.
- Recognize that a civilization can be revealed through its works of art.
- Interpret visual art through dance using shapes and movement.

INTRODUCTION

As with many cultures and civilizations throughout history, the ancient Greeks used scenes from their everyday lives to decorate their art. They painted these scenes on their pottery, carved them in stone to make wonderful sculptures, and decorated their temples. And, because pieces of their artwork are in museums all over the world, we can get an understanding of how they lived. Let's look at some of these pictures of Greek art.

After the students have had a chance to study an image, ask them, "What is going on in this picture?" followed by "What do you see that makes you say that?" so that they can back up their interpretations with evidence. Paraphrase what is said, pointing to what is mentioned as a student gives an opinion. Here's where you can link related answers, help them construct meaning and historical context, and introduce vocabulary. (This type of discussion uses Visual Thinking Strategies. See References, p. 302, for more information.)

Tell students that they have learned a lot about the everyday lives of ancient Greeks through their artwork. Now it's time to bring their history to life!

THE MOVING ADVENTURE

Session 1

1. Have each student select three images from the pictures to inter-pret through dance. These three images will become frozen shapes that they create with their bodies. Encourage them to select images with varying levels, directions, and actions. (Some images will be selected by more than one student, so you may want to have black-and-white photocopies of the images on hand. Or post them on the wall, if possible, for their reference.) ⚙ Observing

2. Instruct students to organize their three shapes into a set sequence: shape 1, shape 2, shape 3. Working in self-space, students should practice each shape and memorize the details of each. Encourage *silent practice,* kinesthetic imaging while remaining frozen in the shape. When all have completed prac-ticing, ask them to show you their shape 1. (The room should look like a sculpture garden with many different shapes.) Repeat with shape 2, then shape 3. If they need more practice, allow more time and rehearse the sequence again.

Session 2

1. Review tasks from session 1. Now ask the students to develop movement to connect the shapes, which in dance terminology are called *transitions.* The transitions should reflect movement the students think happened right before the person in the image was depicted. Lead their thinking with questions such as, "How did the person get into that shape? Was she lifting the goblet to her lips, or was she setting it down after drinking? Was he stalking the animal before he knelt to draw back the arrow, or had he already shot an arrow at high level and then knelt to shoot again? Create the moment before the shape. You decide the story!" ⚙ Empathizing

2. Help the students rehearse their shapes and transitions as needed. They should hold the shapes for at least 5 counts before starting a transition. The final structure of the dance should be shape 1, transition, shape 2, transition, shape 3.

3. Add music! Classical music works well. *Ancient Airs and Dances* by Ottorino Respighi is especially serene and beautiful, but you may prefer one of your own favorite pieces of clas-sical music. Slow to moderate tempo works best. The sequence can be set exactly to the music through rhythm, but it is certainly not necessary. Students can all do their transitions at the same time through a musical signal you give, such as a strike on a triangle, or you can let them do their transitions whenever they choose. Students remain in final pose until all have finished.

ASSESSMENT

- How do we recognize the art of the ancient Greeks? (Through the use of black-and-gold colors, clothing and hairstyles of the people, friezes—whatever was reinforced during introduction section of this lesson.)
- Did the dance you created bring a part of the everyday life of the ancient Greeks to life for you?
- Do you think that we could learn about other ancient civilizations if we investigated their art?
- How and where are movements from our everyday life depicted in art today?

Assessment Forms

- Movement Study Assessment form, for teacher use and for student evaluation of the performance. Add these factors to the form: clear shapes, clear transitions, confidence in performance.
- Peer Assessment form. Split the class in half or thirds and have the students share through performance, reinforcing appropriate audience skills. At the conclusion of each performance, students should give written or oral comments on aspects of the dance they found interesting or that they enjoyed.

Extensions

- This dance can be especially beautiful to watch, especially if students are arranged to replicate the form of a frieze. To do this, move the students to the back of the space and line them up side by side with just enough room for them to move without touching. (If the line is too close to the viewers, they cannot see the frieze effect clearly.)
- Share this dance with other classes or at an evening function for parents or school board. If it feels too brief, extend the dance by using four or five groups, each of which performs the entire sequence and then freezes in a group shape that is easy to hold while the next group begins, dances, and freezes. For togas, use large white T-shirts belted with gold or white rope.
- Repeat this activity using other ancient civilizations, perhaps ones that reinforce your current curriculum objectives or those that students suggest. Students could work in small groups to investigate a different civilization and then share their findings with the other groups, using art works, dance, music, and costumes.
- Have students draw a picture of a simple pose from their own everyday life. Display the finished artwork in a linear format to represent a frieze. This could be developed into a dance about their own everyday lives in present time, using the same structure described previously.

97 Point-Line-Plane

INSPIRED BY WASSILY KANDINSKY.

GRADES: 3 TO 5   **LENGTH:** TWO 30-MINUTE SESSIONS

Materials

- Drawing paper
- Watercolor markers
- Kandinsky print (find an example at your local library or from your art teacher)
- Triangle, drum, woodblock
- Audio playback system

National Content Standards

Visual Arts: 1, 3

Math: 5

Dance: 1, 2, 3, 7

Objectives

The students will be able to do the following:

- Use improvisation to discover, invent, and solve movement problems.
- Demonstrate an understanding of points, lines, and plane in dance, mathematics, and visual arts.
- Use visual structures in art to communicate ideas.

INTRODUCTION

Introduce the students to the Kandinsky print and look closely to find the points, lines, and planes designed within his work. Share a brief biography of Wassily Kandinsky, the Russian painter who is considered the father of abstract painting. Suggest that the students imagine the space around them as the dancers' canvas. Explore the idea of point as a dancer's starting point in space, an ending point, or a point in between. Then, discuss how a dancer takes a line through space and have the students walk along straight or zigzag lines. Finally, ask the students how they might interpret a plane through body shape and try making a flat shape on the vertical plane (up and down), horizontal plane (parallel to the horizon line), or diagonal plane (on an angle, connecting nonadjacent corners).

THE MOVING ADVENTURE

Point-Line-Plane Dance

The students are now ready to create a masterpiece of point, line, and plane through space. They each begin by finding self-space in a scattered formation and then creating and memorizing a shape that represents their point in space. From their starting points, they move forward along a line in space as you beat the drum. Through any two points, there is one line. Each student may follow a straight or zigzag line or any combination. If the student comes to a wall or an obstacle, he or she should turn away and continue to move forward on a new path. Sound the triangle and instruct students to make a flat shape on a vertical, horizontal, or diagonal plane. Continue to design the space on a new line with drum accompaniment. If you play the woodblock, they are to freeze into the memorized "point" shape. Repeat the new line of travel and plane design.

You may want to put on music and ask the students to randomly and spontaneously create their point, line, plane movements and shapes. Following an improvisational structure requires dancers to be aware of the movement of the group through general space.

Variations

- Travel with locomotor movements other than walking, such as galloping or skipping.
- Travel along a line backward or sideways.
- Make a plane shape with a partner or group.

Kandinsky Art and Math

The dancers should now work with partners. Each partner team will need a shared piece of 11- by 14-inch drawing paper. Partners select three colored markers for their design, find a shared personal space, and seat themselves so that both partners can have access to the paper at the same time. They begin creating points and lines using their selected markers. Planes will result in closed shapes where lines intersect as the partners work. The surface between the lines and points must be been filled in to become a plane. Think of a plane as a surface containing all straight lines, flat with no thickness. Mathematicians would draw a plane on paper the same as they would draw a tabletop. The partners must determine how to design the planes that they have created. They can add stripes, polka dots, other patterns, or solid colors to their selected planes. ⚙ **Transforming**

ASSESSMENT

- Did you feel confident in the creation of your point, line, and plane movement?
- How did your Kandinsky-style art evolve with your partner?
- Did the geometry concepts of points, lines, and planes become clearer with this exploration of movement and art?

Assessment Forms

- Participation Assessment form, for teacher use.
- Movement Study Assessment form.
- Peer Assessment form.

Extensions

- Share through performance: The partners can take their completed art and choreograph movement that follows the design. They can begin with one sequence of point, line, plane, making a partner shape when the lines intersect to make a plane. Add musical accompaniment and have the students perform their compositions for each other.
- Study the Kandinsky print again and select a point, line, plane within his work. Create a movement phrase that represents the chosen point, line, plane. Select three or four students to perform their movement phrases at the same time, and notice the relationships that develop as the separate phrases complement each other.

Reprinted by permission from Linda Z. Smith, Point-Line-Plane, Michigan Council for Arts and Cultural Affairs Annual Meeting.

98 Tempo, Pattern, Accent

CREATING A TEMPO, PATTERN, AND ACCENT DANCE.

GRADES: 3 TO 5   **LENGTH:** THREE 30-MINUTE SESSIONS

Materials

MOVEnture CD track 7
- Audio playback system
- Hand drum
- Paper and pencil

National Standards

Music: 5

Math: 2

Dance: 1, 3

Objectives

The students will be able to do the following:

- Describe the three principles of time: tempo, rhythmic pattern, and accent.
- Demonstrate the three principles of time: tempo, rhythmic pattern, and accent.
- Choreograph and perform a movement composition emphasizing elements of space and time.

INTRODUCTION

Explain to students that they will explore the element of time in music and movement. They will cover three aspects of time:

- Tempo is how fast a movement or movement phrase is completed; it is the speed of the movement.
- Rhythmic pattern is the regulation of tempo and duration of beats or movements into ordered sets.
- Accent is the emphasis within the rhythmic pattern of movements. It is the strongest and most significant movement in a movement phrase.

THE MOVING ADVENTURE

Students are in scattered formation. Use the following cues to guide students' movement.

Tempo

1. Move your arm as slowly as you can. Now move your arm as fast as you can.
2. Now move your legs, head, shoulders.
3. Moving through general space, start moving very slowly and then gradually get faster. Change from one speed to another.
4. Try different locomotor movements.
5. Select three nonlocomotor movements and perform them at various tempos. For example, use a slow bend, a medium twist, and a fast shake.

Rhythmic Pattern

1. Show the students a note-value tree (see drawing). At the top is the whole note; half notes, quarter notes, and eighth notes follow.

2. Assume that the whole note has 4 beats per measure. Have students clap the rhythm of each level of the note-value tree where the whole note gets 4 beats, the half note gets 2 beats, the quarter note gets 1 beat, and the eighth note gets half a beat.

- A whole note receives 4 beats. Clap once for each whole note and say aloud, "One, two, three, four."
- A half note receives 2 beats. Clap once for each half note and say aloud, "One, two, three, four."
- A quarter note receives 1 beat. Clap once for each quarter note and say, "One, two, three, four."
- An eighth note receives half a beat. Clap once for each eighth note and say, "One and two and three and four and."

Reading Rhythms

Clap the following note value diagrams:

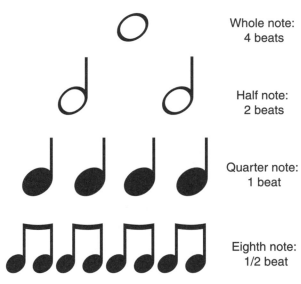

People As Musical Notes

1. Form groups of four.
   - One person is the whole note.
   - One person is the half note.
   - One person is the quarter note.
   - One person is the eighth note.
2. Walking in place, students perform 4 measures of 4 beats. (Use a drum to keep the beat of the quarter note.)
3. Use other body parts to maintain the rhythm. Now switch places.
   ⚙ Forming Patterns, Transforming

Patterning

1. In self-space, students create a rhythmic pattern that is 8 counts long using a combination of whole, half, quarter, or eighth notes.
2. Make a diagram of the rhythmic pattern first.
3. Try clapping the pattern and then creating the same patterns with movement.
4. See if you can perform the pattern more than once without altering it.
5. Repeat the rhythmic pattern; add 8 counts more that include some silences.
6. Add a third rhythmic pattern and practice this pattern using sound. For example, use body sounds such as slaps, swipes, finger snaps, and fists pounding on the chest to create a range of sounds. Try to repeat this pattern with movement alone.

Accenting

1. Find a way to move by accenting a different beat in each measure.
2. Walk through general space: 1, 2, 3, 4; 1, 2, 3, 4; 1, 2, 3, 4; 1, 2, 3, 4.
3. Repeat, using a different body part for the accent.
4. Repeat, changing levels for the accent.
5. Freely explore accenting.

Creating

Direct students to create a movement phrase with the following components:

1. Begin with a specific body shape before count 1 of the first movement sequence.
2. Develop an 8-count movement sequence using nonlocomotor movements performed in self-space.
3. Design an 8-count movement sequence using a locomotor movement with changes in accent.
4. Design an 8-count movement sequence with tempo changes.
5. Return to the first 8-count movement sequence and perform it on a different level.
6. End the composition with a specific body shape on count 8 of the last sequence.

ASSESSMENT

- Describe tempo.
- Describe rhythmic pattern.
- Describe accent.
- Students notate their compositions using music and movement terminology.

Assessment Form

Movement Study Assessment form, for teacher use. Videotape students and assess their ability to maintain the beat as they perform their compositions.

Extensions

- Students manipulate tempo, pattern, and accent in a movement study.
- Students develop a score for a dance. They use percussion instruments to play the score.
- Students create a rhythmic pattern from math problems. For example, 2 + 6 = 8 (2 jumps + 6 twists = 8 twisting jumps).

Composition and Choreography

CREATING MUSIC AND DANCE.

GRADES: 3 TO 5 **LENGTH:** TWO OR THREE 45-MINUTE SESSIONS

Materials

- Computer software for composition
- Blank CDs
- Copies of several short poems

National Standards

Music: 5
Language Arts: 6
Dance: 2

Objectives

The students will be able to do the following:

- Choreograph a dance inspired by a poem within the structure of theme and variation.
- Compose a musical selection based on the structure of the dance (theme and variation) and the mood of the poem.

INTRODUCTION

A music composer creates and arranges sound, and a choreographer creates and arranges movement to express a variety of messages, including emotions and moods. In this assignment, students will become composers, choreographers, and performers.

Each student will select a poem on which to base a dance. The poem will be read and then the dance and music will be performed. The poem is an inspiration for the dance and music. Students are required to use the structure of theme and variation for both choreography and composition.

Definitions

- Movement phrase is a series of movements that complete an idea. It is similar to a sentence in music. An example is three walks forward, turn right, stretch up, and collapse.
- Theme and variation is a movement phrase with several variations on the original theme. Variations should have some resemblance to the original theme. Variations include changing the direction of the theme, inverting the theme, and speeding up or slowing down the theme.

THE MOVING ADVENTURE

Choreographing

1. Students are in scattered formation. Direct students to read a poem, think about movements that will express the ideas in the poem, and then explore poetry individually. Each person will spend three minutes improvising a movement phrase based on or inspired by the poetry. (Instruct students to use the movement concepts of space, time, dynamics, and body movement to develop their movement phrases.) ⚙ **Transforming**
2. All students perform the first phrase together on signal. (Signal start and stop.)

261

3. The students improvise the first variation. (Instruct them to maintain the original phrase but change it by changing the space, time, or dynamics or by reversing the order of the movements for the first variation.)

4. Students perform theme and first variation. (Signal start and stop.) Students take five minutes to create second variation. (Instruct them to maintain the original phrase but vary it by changing the space, time, or dynamics or by adding additional movements for the second variation.)

5. Students perform the theme and first and second variations. (Signal start and stop.)

Music Composition

1. Instruct students to determine the rhythmic structure of their dances (for example, the theme is 8 counts, first variation is 8 counts, second variation is 16 counts).

2. On a computer, students compose a theme and variation of sounds to accompany their dances. (Instruct students to use a variety of sounds and maintain the mood of the poem. Burn a CD of the music composition for each performer.)

3. If computer software for music composition is unavailable, they can use a variety of rhythmic instruments. In this case, they can teach the compositions to other students, or students can form partners, with one student creating a music composition that matches the movements and mood of the dance. ⚙ **Recognizing Patterns and Forming Patterns**

Performing

Dancers recite their poems and then perform their solo theme and variation dances to the music compositions.

ASSESSMENT

- Describe the choices you made for the choreography. Describe the choices you made for the music.
- What are the similarities and differences between composers and choreographers?
- Videotape the assessment.

Assessment Form

Movement Study Assessment form for teacher use.

Extension

Choreograph a dance and compose music using other forms such as ABA, canon, or rondo (ABACAD).

100

Writing and Dancing a Play

COMBINING MOVEMENT AND DIALOGUE.

GRADES: 3 TO 5   **LENGTH:** THREE 30-MINUTE SESSIONS

Materials

Paper and pencil for each student

National Standards

Theater: 1

Language Arts: 1

Dance: 2

Objective

The students will write and dance a short play that includes the elements of dialogue, character, and action.

INTRODUCTION

Ask the students whether they have seen a play. Ask them what happens during a play. (Dialogue and action happen in a play.) What are the people in a play called? (Characters.) Explain that each student will write and then dance a short play.

THE MOVING ADVENTURE

Session 1: Writing the Dialogue

1. Instruct students to write the number 1 at the center of the top of a sheet of lined paper. Ask them to skip the next line and then write the number 2. They should continue this pattern on the page as follows: 1 (line), 2 (line), 1 (line).

2. Inform the students that they will write a short play that will be a conversation between two people. The play begins with character 1 saying, "Hey, did you see that . . ." Instruct the class to write 1's line beneath the number. For example:

   1

   Hey, did you see that . . .

3. Tell the class that it is their job to finish the first line any way they like. Perhaps "Hey, did you see that runaway train?"

4. They should then supply the response of character 2 and then the reply of character 1 and so on. Have students fill the page with dialogue. Tell them not to worry about how interesting it is or how much sense it makes; they should just keep the voices of the characters distinctive and the points of view different. Their job is to fill up one side of a page in 15 minutes. Start the clock!

5. When 15 minutes is up, let them finish the final line. Inform the class that they have just written a play.

6. Ask students to read their plays aloud.

Session 2: Developing the Characters

1. Students form partners and combine ideas or choose one play to structure into a movement duet.

2. Instruct students to develop a better understanding of each of their characters by determining information about the character, such as the following:

   • Age of the character

   • Education and cultural background

   • Interests

   • Physical appearance and health

   • Members of the character's family

   • Personality

3. Instruct the students to explore their characters through movement. Guide the students through a review of the qualities of movement listed in chapter 2 and in lesson 17, Express Yourself!, in chapter 3. ⚙ **Empathizing**

   • Percussive movement has a distinct beginning and ending. Have students move fingers, then arms, legs, and whole body percussively in self-space and in general space.

   • Sustained movement is smooth, constant, even flow of energy. Have students select a partner and begin mirroring activity. The students should face each other, with one student designated as the leader. The partners perform sustained movements (change levels, use the torso, focus).

   • Vibratory movement is shaking movement with starts and stops in energy. Have students begin vibrating hands and then add arms, head, whole body.

   • Swinging movement is pendular. Direct students to swing forward and backward, then side to side. Have them travel through general space while swinging.

   • Suspended and collapsed movement occurs when the body or body part rises to a height and then falls back on itself. Direct students to suspend an arm and then collapse it, suspend upper body and then collapse it, and suspend the whole body and then collapse to the floor.

4. Have students connect characters' personalities to movement quality. For example, quiet characters use sustained movement; happy characters use swinging movement; angry characters use percussive movement.

5. Instruct students to explore energy qualities performed by their characters in the play.

6. Direct students to start at the beginning of the play and perform all appropriate energy qualities of the characters. For example, an excited character would use percussive movement; a happy character would use swinging movement; a sad character would use suspended and collapsed movement.

7. Have students work with their partners in an energy dance drama.

8. Direct students to learn their lines before the next session.

Session 3: Combining Movement and Dialogue

1. Direct students to perform the play using movement (energy qualities) only.

2. Have the students perform the play using dialogue and movement.

3. Direct the students to perform the play with dialogue in a realistic manner.

4. Duets perform the movement play for an audience.

ASSESSMENT

- Were you surprised at how quickly you were able to create characters and dialogue and come up with a play?

- Describe your ability to connect movement qualities to the dialogue.

- Evaluate the students' ability to identify appropriate movement qualities, connect the movement qualities to the dialogue, and perform the play in a believable manner.

- Evaluate play for elements of action and character development.

Assessment Form

Comprehensive Assessment form.

Extension

Students select a monologue, analyze the character using movement, and perform the monologue with and without movement.

101

Dance of the Four Elements

A MOVEMENT LESSON USING RHYTHMIC CHANTING.

GRADES: 3 TO 5   **LENGTH:** THREE 30-MINUTE SESSIONS

Materials

MOVEnture DVD
• Hand drum

National Standards

Music: 1
Language Arts: 8
Dance: 1, 2, 7

Objectives

The students will be able to do the following:

- Identify the four elements of ancient Greek culture.
- Sing or chant with a group, maintaining a steady tempo.
- Sing or chant expressively with appropriate dynamics.
- Perform a sequence of movement repetitively while chanting.
- Speak (chant) and listen in a variety of contexts.

INTRODUCTION

Enlist participation of the music teacher.

In ancient times, the Greek people believed there were four elements: earth, wind, fire, and water. They thought that all things were made up of these elements. For instance, animals (including humans) and plants were made of earth. Rivers, streams, rain, and snow were all made of water. Breezes, tornadoes, and the air they breathed were made of wind. Then there was the element of fire: the sun and stars, the cooking hearth. Now we know that these four elements cannot describe everything. Our world is not so simple. Yet it was an understandable way for people to try to make sense of the world around them.

Explain to students that they will explore the four elements of earth, wind, fire, and water through movement. In addition, they will add their voices to the movements, chanting in rhythm together. So it will be a group effort to bring these four elements to life!

THE MOVING ADVENTURE

Session 1

1. Start with students seated comfortably on the floor in a circle formation.
2. Teach the chant first. The four elements are arranged as follows: water, wind, earth, fire. Each element chant will use a 4-beat measure. (See the Element Chant Beat Chart.)
3. Students chant each element phrase repeatedly, using their voices expressively (high and light, breathy, low voice, playful) and maintaining the tempo. ⚙️ **Recognizing Patterns**
4. Sequence all four phrases into one long phrase, keeping the rhythm throughout: a silly likki poko / oom bwaa shhh! / duh! / clap / clap duh! / zzzzzzzzzzzzzzzzZing!

Element Chant Beat Chart

		Beats in the measure and breakdown of syllables						
Elements	**&**	**1**	**&**	**2**	**&**	**3**	**&**	**4**
Water (a silly likki poko) high, light voice	a	sil	ly	lik	ki	po		ko
Wind (oom bwaa shhh!) breathy voice		oom		bwaa		shhh!		
Earth (duh! [clap] [clap] duh!) low voice		duh!		[Clap]	[Clap]			duh!
Fire (zing!) playful voice		zz	zz	zzzzzz	zzzzz	Zing!		

Session 2

Now add movement! Have the students stand up to learn. ⚙ **Body Thinking**

- **Water.** Legs start apart, slightly wider than the hips, toes forward. On each of the first two beats, students reach upward with all fingertips pinching to thumb, forming a raindrop with their hands, which they can pull downward: Right hand on count 1 (silly); left hand on count 2 (likki); slap right hand on right thigh (po); slap left hand on left thigh (ko). Rehearse repeatedly until students can move and vocalize clearly within the rhythm. If desired, you can make this movement more interesting by pivoting a quarter turn to the right on the first beat of each measure (sil).

Movement Chart

Elements	Beats in the measure and movements for each							
	&	1	&	2	&	3	&	4
Water (a silly likki poko)		Right pinch		Left pinch		[Slap]		[Slap]
Wind (oom bwaa shhh!)		Arms up		Arms at chest		Left step & push		
Earth (duh! [clap] [clap] duh!)		Right stamp		[Clap]	[Clap]			Left stamp
Fire (zing!)		Running		Running	Running	Zing!		

- **Wind.** Pull back arms with palms open just above head (oom); bring hands down by chest (bwaa); take a step forward, lunging on the left leg, as arms push strongly forward like a powerful flame (shhh!). Bring legs together and repeat arm action, stepping forward with the right leg. This movement can travel by continually alternating feet, or it can stay in one place by pulling the leg back from the lunge each time. Rehearse!

- **Earth.** (This rhythm is the most challenging because of the hold on count 3.) Stamp right foot to the right with legs bent on count 1 (duh!); clap hands twice quickly on counts 2 &; hold count 3; stamp left foot to the left on count 4 (duh!). The tricky part of this pattern is stamping on count 4 and then immediately on count 1 again. This movement can travel gradually by stepping on the forward diagonal with each stomp. Rehearse!

- **Fire.** Zing! likes to be airborne, like a spark from a flame. Students run briefly on the zzzz on counts 1 & 2 &, then jump lightly any way they choose with arms also into the air, on the word *zing!* on count 3. Hold count 4. Running can be in any direction: forward, sideways, backward, or diagonally. (See the Movement Chart.)

Session 3

1. The Dance of the Four Elements may now begin.

2. Determine which students, through observation during sessions 1 and 2, are most able to perform the different sequences.

3. Place the students in four groups, one for each element.

4. Place the first three elements around a large semicircle, facing forward. Zingers start in the middle of the semicircle.

5. Keeping the basic rhythmic beat on the hand drum, the water students start the sequence by performing their chant and movement once, followed immediately by the wind chant, the earth chant, and the fire chant, all without breaking the rhythm.

6. Zingers can travel anywhere in the general space.

7. Repeat from the beginning. This is a conversation, a structure in which different participants take turns speaking and listening to each other.

ASSESSMENT

- What were the four elements that the ancient peoples of Greece believed composed all things?
- Were you able to chant the different elements while moving your body and still keep a steady rhythm? Did you chant with an expressive voice?
- How successful do you think you were as a whole class in doing the Dance of the Four Elements? Did you all keep a steady tempo?
- Which element was your favorite to chant and dance? Why?

Assessment Forms

- Movement Study Assessment form, for teacher use and for student evaluation of the performance. Add these factors to the form: steady tempo, expressive voice, overall performance.
- Self-Assessment form (version appropriate for students' level). Add these factors to the form: I kept a steady tempo; I used my voice expressively.

Extensions

- Pass out paper and instruct the students to draw or color and label the four elements.
- Have the students write out the entire chant, using their own phonetic way of spelling.
- Try these other options for the structure of Dance of the Four Elements:
  - Each element group performs their chant and movement at the same time so that their vocalizations are layered on top of each other. (Do layered vocals first, then add movement.) This option is similar to a choral work in music or a dramatic reading in which many parts are sung or spoken at the same time to create a harmonic outcome, one that does not drown out each other's voices.
  - All students perform the entire sequence of elements together in unison (not divided into four groups) with chanting and movement. This option reflects a dramatic poetic recitation.
  - Drumming the tempo steadily, tell the students to perform the dance sequence without chanting (but thinking it in their heads). This option underscores that dance is communication mostly through movement, not through words.
  - Related lesson: Everyday Life in Faraway Times, lesson 96.

appendix A
Assessment

Assessment is an integral part of the teaching and learning process. Our goal as educators is to create an environment for learning in which students can grow and develop their potential. By incorporating a variety of evaluation tools that are standards based and objective focused, the teacher and student can measure progress in skill development and growth in knowledge.

The three domains of learning (cognitive, affective, and psychomotor) provide a structure for authentic assessments that are essential to learning. *Cognitive* assessment can take place during the closing moments of each class through the asking of questions specific to the content of the class. Student journals allow students to respond to questions in a written format. *Affective* assessment, or assessment of feelings and attitudes, can be determined through the use of student journals and checklists designed for that purpose. *Psychomotor* assessment can occur through teacher and peer assessments.

Assessment Tools

The lessons in this text are aligned with national standards and benchmarks to ensure the content is in sync with educational goals set by the nation, states, and schools. Appropriate assessments allow us to determine whether or not the objectives set forth in the lesson have been achieved. Various formats of authentic assessment are included within the lessons: journal writing, interviewing, drawings, portfolio development, and performance assessments.

- **Journal writing.** Journal writing allows students to record their feelings, perceptions, and reflections of the materials covered in class. Journal writing promotes self-analysis and can indicate the depth of student learning, a reflection of how each student processes information. The questions listed in the "Assessment" sections of the lessons could be assigned as journal entries.

- **Interviewing.** Requiring students to conduct interviews allows them to connect their course work with their families and the larger community. For example, in the lesson Dances of the 1920s (lesson 60, chapter 6), students are required to interview parents and grandparents about dances they performed in social settings when they were young.

- **Drawings.** Students' drawings can reveal their understanding of a curricular concept (for example, the life cycle of a spider) or an emotional response to a story. Drawings are especially appealing to students in kindergarten through second grade. As an example, Shape, Shape, Shape, lesson 39 in chapter 5, includes the following assessment: "For homework, students may observe and draw pictures of objects in their homes that are round, triangular, square, or rectangular."

- **Portfolios.** Portfolios are recommended as a concise method of compiling and showcasing the interdisciplinary connections put forth in this text. Portfolios can provide a place to document learning that occurs over time. For example, a science portfolio could include a listing of the standards, with the corresponding learning experiences documented through student writing; drawing; self-assessment checklists, teacher checklists, and peer checklists; pictures; and videotape examples. Examples in the text include Levers and Games (lesson 87) and The Kaleidoscope of Life (lesson 62).

- **Performance assessments.** Students' performance, judged with the use of assessment forms, drawings, interviews, and portfolios, is evaluated with the use of rubrics. Rubrics are broken down into several levels. The highest level is the ideal, a challenging but realistic goal for students. The other levels include criteria that are sequentially less optimal than the top layer. For example, in scoring with the Movement Study Assessment, page 278, the number 3 represents an above-standard performance, the number 2 represents an at-standard performance, and a 1 represents a below-standard performance. The teacher must determine and inform the students of the specific nature of the scoring criteria based on the objectives of the lesson and the abilities of the students in the class.

Assessments

Teacher and student assessment forms and templates are included in this appendix. Not all criteria apply to every lesson, so these forms are adaptable. They include blank lines for you to fill in additional factors for assessment—either those suggested in the specific Moventure lesson, or evaluation criteria of your own. When students are a part of the assessment process, they learn to be good observers, and they can apply the performance criteria to improve their own performance. Peer assessments can also aid students' learning. By administering a peer assessment, the student learns how to give helpful comments.

Assessments can be scored via checking or circling identified criteria. The following are provided in this appendix:

- **Action Word Chart, page 273.** This chart can be used with Action Words (lesson 27).
- **Action Word Worksheet, page 274.** This assessment can be used with Action Words (lesson 27).
- **Comprehensive Assessment, page 275.** This comprehensive rubric can be used for assessing specific lessons in movement, cognitive, creative, and social categories.

- **Group Evaluation Form, page 276.** This form is useful in assessing the effectiveness of group work.
- **Movement Concept Chart, page 277.** This is a blank version of the charts used to help connect interdisciplinary concepts to dance. This can be used by teachers to create posters or overhead materials, or it can be passed out to students as an assessment form.
- **Movement Study Assessment, page 278.** This assessment can be used by teachers and by students. This instrument can be used during a live or videotaped performance. Students may use the same form to assess their peers.
- **Participation Assessment, page 279.** This checklist was developed specifically for assessing behaviors and attitudes. Teachers may add additional criteria.
- **Partner Assessment of Movement Qualities, page 280.** This assessment can be used with Express Yourself! (lesson 17).
- **Peer Assessment, page 281.** This peer assessment may be used for most composition evaluations. Additional criteria may be added.
- **Peer Assessment: Change of Direction Dance, page 282.** This assessment is used for Changes (lesson 44).
- **Probability Dance Worksheet, page 283.** This chart can be used with Probability Dance (lesson 53).
- **Seed to Flower Assessment, page 286.** This chart can be used with Seed to Flower (lesson 72).
- **Self-Assessment, page 287.** This smiley-face version of the self-assessment form is for students in kindergarten through second grade.
- **Self-Assessment, page 288.** This version was created for students in third through fifth grade.

Action Word Chart

Run	Shake	Wiggle	Skate	Undulate	Pop
Jump	Bend	Stretch	Spin	Turn	Freeze
Skip	Vibrate	Shiver	Twirl	Burst	Open
Hop	Swing	Reach	Sneak	Close	Slink
Leap	Squirm	Fidget	Shuffle	Prowl	Fling
Walk	Twist	Wring	Roll	Grow	Rise
Step	Bounce	Spring	Pounce	Swell	Shrink
Slide	Fall	Collapse	Squeeze	Explode	Flick
March	Drop	Melt	Dab	Tap	Press
Stamp	Fold	Crumple	Punch	Float	Glide
Crawl	Compress	Contract	Slash	Splatter	Stab
Slither	Inflate	Deflate	Explode	Bump	Push
Gallop	Recede	Advance	Pull	Slam	Kick

From *Interdisciplinary Learning Through Dance: 101 MOVEntures*, by Lynnette Overby, Beth Post, and Diane Newman. 2005. Champaign, IL: Human Kinetics.

Action Word Worksheet

Name(s)_____ Class _____

List action words expressed through movement.

_____

_____

_____

1. Clear expression of words?   Yes   No

2. Strong and clear starting shape?   Yes   No

3. Variety of movements in self-space and general space?   Yes   No

4. Strong and clear ending?   Yes   No

 From *Interdisciplinary Learning Through Dance: 101 MOVEntures,* by Lynnette Overby, Beth Post, and Diane Newman. 2005. Champaign, IL: Human Kinetics.

Comprehensive Assessment

Scoring

4 = Fulfilled all requirements and showed a deep understanding of the skills and concepts.

3 = Fulfilled all requirements but does not have a deep understanding of the skills and concepts.

2 = Did not fulfill all requirements.

1 = Did not complete the work to a satisfactory level.

0 = Did not try or was uncooperative.

Skills	Scoring
Movement skills	
1. Performs with good form	4_____3_____2____1____0_____
2. Clear demonstration of dance vocabulary	4_____3_____2____1____0_____
3. Performs movement expressively	4_____3_____2____1____0_____
	Total possible = 12 **Student total** _____
Cognitive skills	
1. Knowledge of dance vocabulary	4_____3_____2____1____0_____
2. Knowledge of _____ vocabulary	4_____3_____2____1____0_____
	Total possible = 8 **Student total** _____
Creative skills	
1. Strong and clear beginning	4_____3_____2____1____0_____
2. Use of appropriate body shapes	4_____3_____2____1____0_____
3. Moves in self-space	4_____3_____2____1____0_____
4. Moves in general space	4_____3_____2____1____0_____
5. Demonstrates creative problem solving	4_____3_____2____1____0_____
	Total possible = 20 **Student total** _____
Social and affective skills	
1. Works effectively in groups	4_____3_____2____1____0_____
2. Demonstrates self-discipline	4_____3_____2____1____0_____
3. Enthusiastic and positive learner	4_____3_____2____1____0_____
	Total possible = 12 **Student total** _____

From *Interdisciplinary Learning Through Dance: 101 MOVEntures,* by Lynnette Overby, Beth Post, and Diane Newman. 2005. Champaign, IL: Human Kinetics.

Group Evaluation Form

Names_____ Class _____

1. We all talked in our group.   Yes   No

2. We kept track of time and got our task done.   Yes   No

3. We listened to each other.   Yes   No

4. We praised each other when we had good ideas.   Yes   No

5. To be a better group next time we might _____

_____

_____

_____

_____

 From *Interdisciplinary Learning Through Dance: 101 MOVEntures,* by Lynnette Overby, Beth Post, and Diane Newman. 2005. Champaign, IL: Human Kinetics.

Movement Concept Chart

Individual or Group Name_____ Class _____

Movement concepts				
Space: place, levels, directions, pathways				
Time: slow, medium, fast				
Force: energy, weight, flow				
Body movement: locomotor, nonlocomotor, shapes				

From *Interdisciplinary Learning Through Dance: 101 MOVEntures,* by Lynnette Overby, Beth Post, and Diane Newman. 2005. Champaign, IL: Human Kinetics.

Movement Study Assessment

Individual or Group Name_____ Class _____

Rating Scale

      1 = Below standard   2 = At standard   3 = Above standard

1. Strong and clear beginning	1	2	3
2. Use of appropriate body shapes	1	2	3
3. Moving in self-space	1	2	3
4. Moving in general space	1	2	3
5. Use of appropriate dynamics	1	2	3
6. Use of appropriate time	1	2	3
7. Strong and clear ending	1	2	3
8. _____	1	2	3
9. _____	1	2	3
10. _____	1	2	3
11. _____	1	2	3
12. _____	1	2	3
13. _____	1	2	3
14. _____	1	2	3

Comments

_____

_____

_____

 From *Interdisciplinary Learning Through Dance: 101 MOVEntures,* by Lynnette Overby, Beth Post, and Diane Newman. 2005. Champaign, IL: Human Kinetics.

Participation Assessment

Individual or Group Name_____ Class _____

Evaluation Key

1 = Below standard   2 = At standard   3 = Above standard

Names	Listening	Imagination	Appropriate movement	Attitude							

From *Interdisciplinary Learning Through Dance: 101 MOVEntures,* by Lynnette Overby, Beth Post, and Diane Newman. 2005. Champaign, IL: Human Kinetics.

Partner Assessment of Movement Qualities

Name_____ Teacher_____

Partner_____ Date_____

1. Sustained   Good   Very good   Needs more work

2. Percussive   Good   Very good   Needs more work

3. Swinging   Good   Very good   Needs more work

4. Vibratory   Good   very good   Needs more work

5. Suspend   Good   Very good   Needs more work

6. Collapse   Good   Very good   Needs more work

 From *Interdisciplinary Learning Through Dance: 101 MOVEntures,* by Lynnette Overby, Beth Post, and Diane Newman. 2005. Champaign, IL: Human Kinetics.

Peer Assessment

Peer Name(s)_____ Evaluator_____

1. Did your peer(s) include a clear beginning, middle, and ending?   Yes   No

2. Did your peer(s) have good focus and presentation?   Yes   No

3. _____   Yes   No

4. _____   Yes   No

5. _____   Yes   No

Peer Assessment:
Change of Direction Dance

Peer Name(s)_____ Evaluator_____

1. Did your peer(s) include 3 different locomotor movements and 3 different times?   Yes   No

2. Did your peer(s) move in 3 different directions?   Yes   No

3. Did your peer(s) have a strong beginning and ending shape?   Yes   No

From *Interdisciplinary Learning Through Dance: 101 MOVEntures,* by Lynnette Overby, Beth Post, and Diane Newman. 2005. Champaign, IL: Human Kinetics.

Probability Dance Worksheet

Names_____ Class _____

Complete the worksheet with all of the items listed as a group. Select one item from each set of items on the worksheet, then determine whether or not the item is equally likely to be selected or not equally likely to be selected. Next, develop a ratio of your desired outcome to the total outcome.

Circle one item in each section.

Section 1: Select one floor plan from the list of 10 floor plans.

Begin at Center Stage move to Upstage Right and end at Downstage Left.

Begin Center Stage Left move to Center Stage end Center Stage Right.

Begin Upstage Right move to Downstage Center end Center.

Begin Upstage Center move to Downstage Center end Downstage Right.

Begin Downstage Right move to Downstage Left end Upstage Left.

Begin Downstage Left move to Downstage Right end Upstage Right.

Begin Downstage Center move to Upstage Center end Downstage Right.

Begin Upstage Left move to Downstage Right end Downstage Center.

Begin Center move to Downstage Left end Upstage Center.

Begin Center Stage Right move to Upstage Center end Center Stage Left.

1. How likely is it that you will select this floor plan from the box of 10 floor plans?

      Equally likely   Not equally likely

2. What is the probability that you will select this floor plan from the box of 10 floor plans? (Write in a ratio)_____

(continued)

(continued)

Section 2: Select one locomotor and nonlocomotor movement sequence.

Jump, twist, run, swing, leap, run, slide.

Slide, reach, skip, turn, gallop, leap, collapse.

Run, jump, hop, leap, twist, bend, stretch.

Leap, turn, slide, twist, reach, lunge.

Twist, swing, hop, jump, run.

1. How likely is it that you will select this locomotor and nonlocomotor movement sequence from the box of 5?

   Equally likely   Not equally likely

2. What is the probability that you will select this locomotor and nonlocomotor movement sequence from the box of 5? (Write in a ratio)

   _____

Section 3: Select one beginning and ending group shape.

Straight and round

Symmetrical and asymmetrical

Balanced and reaching

Wide and round

Square and triangle

Curved and angular

Narrow and wide

Low and high

1. How likely is it that you will select these beginning and ending shapes from the box of 8?

    Equally likely   Not equally likely

2. What is the probability that you will select these beginning and ending shapes from the box of 8? (Write in a ratio) _____

Probability Dance

Beginning and ending shapes

Floor plan and stage directions

Locomotor and nonlocomotor movement sequence

From *Interdisciplinary Learning Through Dance: 101 MOVEntures*, by Lynnette Overby, Beth Post, and Diane Newman. 2005. Champaign, IL: Human Kinetics.

Seed to Flower Assessment

Have students complete the following chart by drawing their interpretation of the written items.

Flowers are living things.

All flowers need certain things to grow:

Sunshine   Water

Soil   Minerals

 From *Interdisciplinary Learning Through Dance: 101 MOVEntures*, by Lynnette Overby, Beth Post, and Diane Newman. 2005. Champaign, IL: Human Kinetics.

Self-Assessment

Name_____ Class _____

1. I have good self-control.   😊 😐 ☹️

2. I follow directions.   😊 😐 ☹️

3. I am a good listener.   😊 😐 ☹️

4. I cooperate.   😊 😐 ☹️

5. I put forth my best effort.   😊 😐 ☹️

6. I like to dance.   😊 😐 ☹️

7. _____   😊 😐 ☹️

8. _____   😊 😐 ☹️

9. _____   😊 😐 ☹️

10. _____   😊 😐 ☹️

11. _____   😊 😐 ☹️

12. _____   😊 😐 ☹️

13. _____   😊 😐 ☹️

14. _____   😊 😐 ☹️

15. _____   😊 😐 ☹️

From *Interdisciplinary Learning Through Dance: 101 MOVEntures*, by Lynnette Overby, Beth Post, and Diane Newman. 2005. Champaign, IL: Human Kinetics.

Self-Assessment

Name_____ Class _____

Evaluation Key

1 = Below standard   2 = At standard   3 = Above standard

1. I have good self-control.	1	2	3
2. I follow directions.	1	2	3
3. I use my imagination.	1	2	3
4. I work well with others.	1	2	3
5. I put forth my best effort.	1	2	3
6. I enjoy dance.	1	2	3
7. _____	1	2	3
8. _____	1	2	3
9. _____	1	2	3
10. _____	1	2	3
11. _____	1	2	3
12. _____	1	2	3
13. _____	1	2	3
14. _____	1	2	3
15. _____	1	2	3

From *Interdisciplinary Learning Through Dance: 101 MOVEntures,* by Lynnette Overby, Beth Post, and Diane Newman. 2005. Champaign, IL: Human Kinetics.

National Standards

The Moventure lessons have been developed to help you address nine sets of curricular national standards with your students: dance, physical education, language arts, mathematics, social studies, science, music, theater, and visual arts. These standards represent the body of knowledge that each student should acquire during their elementary and secondary school years.

National Standards for Dance Education

Standard*	MOVEnture Implications
Standard 1: Performing—Identifying and demonstrating movement elements and skills in performing dance.	The content of dance is presented in this standard. The content includes movement skills (locomotor and nonlocomotor movements), movement principles (alignment and balance), and movement elements (space, time, and force).
Standard 2: Choreographing—Understanding choreographic principles, processes, and structures.	Dance making is the focus of this standard. Choreographic processes include theme and variation, ABA, rondo, canon, and narrative.
Standard 3: Creating—Understanding dance as a way to create and communicate meaning.	To meet this standard, students, as dancers and choreographers, will clearly communicate meanings and intentions.
Standard 4: Critical Thinking—Applying and demonstrating critical-thinking and creative-thinking skills in dance.	The focus of this standard is critically analyzing dance by applying criteria used to define a dance work, including elements of space, time, and force as well as technical components, such as lighting, sound, and costumes. The dance work could be a solo classroom project or a performance by a world-renowned dance company.
Standard 5: Culture and History—Demonstrating and understanding dance in various cultures and historical periods.	This standard provides for the inclusion of dances that provide a view into a culture and time period. Examples include folk and square dances, as well as the Charleston, a U.S. social dance of the 1920s.
Standard 6: Healthful Living—Making connections between dance and healthful living.	Students are encouraged to explore the health and well-being of a dancer in relation to the impact of psychological and sociological constraints. For example, many dancers suffer from eating disorders and injuries. Students should be encouraged to explore these problems and develop plans for achieving a healthy lifestyle.
Standard 7: Interdisciplinary Connections—Making connections between dance and other disciplines.	Dance is a discipline that connects with many other disciplines. Identification and elaboration of these connections promote a deeper understanding of content and concepts that cross disciplines.

*National Dance Standards 1-7 (pp. 6-9)—These quotes are reprinted from the *National Standards for Arts Education* with permission of the National Dance Association (NDA) an association of the American Alliance for Health, Physical Education, Recreation, and Dance. The source of the National Dance Standards (*National Standards for Dance Education: What Every Young American Should Know and Be Able to Do in Dance*) may be purchased from: National Dance Association, 1900 Association Drive, Reston, VA 20191-1599; or telephone (703) 476-3421.

National Standards for Physical Education

Standard 1: Uses a variety of basic and advanced movement forms.

Standard 2: Uses movement concepts and principles in the development of motor skills.

Standard 3: Understands the benefits and costs associated with participation in physical activity.

Standard 4: Understands how to monitor and maintain a health-enhancing level of physical fitness.

Standard 5: Understands the social and personal responsibility associated with participation in physical activity.

Reprinted, by permission, from Mid-Continent Research for Education and Learning (MCREL), 2004, *Standards and Benchmarks* (Aurora, CO: MCREL). [Online] Available: www.mcrel.org/compendium?Standard.asp?SubjectID=18 [October 8, 2004].

National Standards for Language Arts

Writing:

Standard 1: Uses the general skills and strategies of the writing process.

Standard 2: Uses the stylistic and rhetorical aspects of writing.

Standard 3: Uses grammatical and mechanical conventions in written compositions.

Standard 4: Gathers and uses information for research purposes.

Reading:

Standard 5: Uses the general skills and strategies of the reading process.

Standard 6: Uses reading skills and strategies to understand and interpret a variety of literary texts.

Standard 7: Uses reading skills and strategies to understand and interpret a variety of informational texts.

Listening and Speaking:

Standard 8: Uses listening and speaking strategies for different purposes.

Viewing:

Standard 9: Uses viewing skills and strategies to understand and interpret visual media.

Media:

Standard 10: Understands the characteristics and components of the media.

Reprinted, by permission, from Mid-Continent Research for Education and Learning (MCREL), 2004, *Standards and Benchmarks* (Aurora, CO: MCREL). [Online] Available: www.mcrel.org/compendium?Standard.asp?SubjectID=18 [October 8, 2004].

National Standards for Mathematics

Standard 1: Uses a variety of strategies in the problem-solving process.

Standard 2: Understands and applies basic and advanced properties of the concepts of numbers.

Standard 3: Uses basic and advanced procedures while performing the processes of computation.

Standard 4: Understands and applies basic and advanced properties of the concepts of measurement.

Standard 5: Understands and applies basic and advanced properties of the concepts of geometry.

Standard 6: Understands and applies basic and advanced concepts of statistics and data analysis.

Standard 7: Understands and applies basic and advanced concepts of probability.

Standard 8: Understands and applies basic and advanced properties of functions and algebra.

Standard 9: Understands the general nature and uses of mathematics.

Reprinted, by permission, from Mid-Continent Research for Education and Learning (MCREL), 2004, *Standards and Benchmarks* (Aurora, CO: MCREL). [Online] Available: www.mcrel.org/compendium?Standard.asp?SubjectID=18 [October 8, 2004].

National Standards for Social Studies

Standard 1: Culture—Social studies programs should include experiences that provide for the study of culture and cultural diversity.

Standard 2: Time, Continuity, and Change—Social studies programs should include experiences that provide for the study of ways human beings view themselves in and over time.

Standard 3: People, Places, and Environments—Social studies programs should include experiences that provide for the study of people, places, and environments.

Standard 4: Individual Development and Identity—Social studies programs should include experiences that provide for the study of individual development and identity.

Standard 5: Individuals, Groups, and Institutions—Social studies programs should include experiences that provide for the study of interactions among individuals, groups, and institutions.

Standard 6: Power, Authority, and Governance—Social studies programs should include experiences that provide for the study of how people create and change structures of power, authority, and governance.

Standard 7: Production, Distribution, and Consumption—Social studies programs should include experiences that provide for the study of how people organize for the production, distribution, and consumption of goods and services.

Standard 8: Science, Technology, and Society—Social studies programs should include experiences that provide for the study of relationships among science, technology, and society.

Standard 9: Global Connections—Social studies programs should include experiences that provide for the study of connections and interdependence.

Standard 10: Civic Ideals and Practices—Social studies programs should include experiences that provide for the study of ideals, principles, and practices of citizenship in a democratic republic.

Reprinted, by permission, from National Council for the Social Studies, 2004, *Social Studies National Standards*. [Online]. Available: http://www.socialstudies.org/standards/strands/ [October 4, 2004].

National Standards for Science

Earth and Space Sciences:

Standard 1: Understands atmospheric processes and the water cycle.

Standard 2: Understands Earth's composition and structure.

Standard 3: Understands the composition and structure of the universe and the Earth's place in it.

Life Sciences:

Standard 4: Understands the principles of heredity and related concepts.

Standard 5: Understands the structure and function of cells and organisms.

Standard 6: Understands relationships among organisms and their physical environment.

Standard 7: Understands biological evolution and the diversity of life.

Physical Sciences:

Standard 8: Understands the structure and properties of matter.

Standard 9: Understands the sources and properties of energy.

Standard 10: Understands forces and motion.

Nature of Science:

Standard 11: Understands the nature of scientific knowledge.

Standard 12: Understands the nature of scientific inquiry.

Standard 13: Understands the scientific enterprise.

Reprinted, by permission, from Mid-Continent Research for Education and Learning (MCREL), 2004, *Standards and Benchmarks* (Aurora, CO: MCREL). [Online] Available: www.mcrel.org/compendium?Standard.asp?SubjectID=18 [October 8, 2004].

National Standards for Music

Standard 1: Sings, alone and with others, a varied repertoire of music.

Standard 2: Performs on instruments, alone and with others, a varied repertoire of music.

Standard 3: Improvises melodies, variations, and accompaniments.

Standard 4: Composes and arranges music within specified guidelines.

Standard 5: Reads and notates music.

Standard 6: Knows and applies appropriate criteria to music and music performances.

Standard 7: Understands the relationship between music and history and culture.

Reprinted, by permission, from Mid-Continent Research for Education and Learning (MCREL), 2004, Standards and Benchmarks (Aurora, CO: MCREL). [Online] Available: www.mcrel.org/compendium?Standard.asp?SubjectID=18 [October 8, 2004].

National Standards for Theater

Standard 1: Demonstrates competence in writing scripts.

Standard 2: Uses acting skills.

Standard 3: Designs and produces informal and formal productions.

Standard 4: Directs scenes and productions.

Standard 5: Understands how informal and formal theater, film, television, and electronic media productions create and communicate meaning.

Standard 6: Understands the context in which theater, film, television, and electronic media are performed today as well as in the past.

Reprinted, by permission, from Mid-Continent Research for Education and Learning (MCREL), 2004, Standards and Benchmarks (Aurora, CO: MCREL). [Online] Available: www.mcrel.org/compendium?Standard.asp?SubjectID=18 [October 8, 2004].

National Standards for Visual Arts

Standard 1: Understands and applies media, techniques, and processes related to the visual arts.

Standard 2: Knows how to use structures (e.g., sensory qualities, organizational principles, expressive features) and functions of art.

Standard 3: Knows a range of subject matter, symbols, and potential ideas in the visual arts.

Standard 4: Understands the visual arts in relation to history and cultures.

Standard 5: Understands the characteristics and merits of one's own artwork and the artwork of others.

Reprinted, by permission, from Mid-Continent Research for Education and Learning (MCREL), 2004, *Standards and Benchmarks* (Aurora, CO: MCREL). [Online] Available: www.mcrel.org/compendium?Standard.asp?SubjectID=18 [October 8, 2004].

appendix C

Thinking Tools

abstracting—Discovering simplicity in complexity by eliminating all but one essential characteristic. The ability to abstract allows the dancer to be clear and concise.

analogizing—Discovering functional similarities between structurally different things. Imagine the movement of a swing on a playground. Dancers can apply that image to the body and its parts as they swing forward and back with the arms, legs, and whole body. The swing and the swinging body part are functionally similar yet structurally different.

body thinking—Engaging actively and primarily in learning the vocabulary of body movement and expression. Dancing enhances body thinking, and the ability to think with the body enhances the dancer's skills.

dimensional thinking—Being able to translate between two and three (or more) dimensions (for example, between a blueprint and an invention, a sketch and a sculpture, or an equation and a physical process). Dancers employ dimensional thinking when they think about the body's pathways through space and explore the body's position in space or time.

empathizing—Becoming the thing one studies, be it animate or inanimate. As dancers experience the persona of an object, including its feelings, movements, and structure, they are able to communicate it in a realistic manner.

forming patterns—Creating or discovering new ways to organize things. The ability to form patterns is necessary for choreographing dances.

imaging—Creating mental images using any and all senses. The ability to image allows dancers to create mental pictures, sounds, smells, textures, and feelings that can enhance movement and expression.

modeling—Creating a simplified or miniaturized analogue of a complex thing in order to test and modify its properties. Students (often in groups) build a model of a thing with many bodies and imitate some process, as in a flower that opens and closes, or the water cycle. Modeling is at work when students re-create something that can't readily be seen or sensed because it is too large or too small or too conceptual.

observing—Honing all of the senses to perceive acutely. Observing through sight, hearing, touch, taste, and smell provides dancers with material for understanding and expression.

playing—In cases of unrestrained improvisation, a goalless activity performed for fun that develops skill, knowledge, and intuition. Improvisation is a form of playing in dance that leads to the development of knowledge and skill.

recognizing patterns—Perceiving similarities in structure or properties of different things. The ability to recognize patterns promotes learning of dance sequences.

synthesizing—The result of using multiple tools for thinking is that one can know things in multiple ways simultaneously—bodily, intuitively, sensually, and subjectively as well as mentally, intellectually, and objectively.

transforming—1. Going from one "language" to another to include interpreting and expressing in dance a concept taken from some nonmovement discipline. 2. Expressing one's own ideas in one form (visual, mathematical, verbal, bodily) and then another. Dancers often transform a poem into a dance or music into movement.

See Root-Bernstein, R. and Root-Bernstein, M. 1999. *Sparks of genius: The Thirteen thinking tools of the world's most creative people.* New York: Houghton Mifflin.

293

Vocabulary of Dance and Movement

The following list has been developed as an introductory reference to dance terminology and concepts for the novice movement teacher.

Space: The Where of Dance

directions—Forward, backward, right side, left side, up, down, clockwise, and counterclockwise.

general space—The total space in the gymnasium, classroom, studio, or outdoor area designated as moving space.

levels—Low, middle, and high.

negative space—Space not being used, or empty space.

pathways—Straight, curved, and zigzag.

positive space—Space that is being used or filled by a person's body.

self-space (also known as personal space)—The space surrounding one person; a stationary location in space.

Time: The When of Dance

accent—Stress placed on one or more beats.

counterpoint—Contrasting sets of beats.

felt time—Personal rhythm, i.e., breath.

pulse—The underlying beat.

rhythm—Arrangements of beats.

tempo—Speed.

Force or Dynamics: The How of Dance

energy—Sharp and smooth.

flow—Bound and free.

qualities of movement—Sustained, percussive, vibratory, swing, collapse, suspend.

weight—Strong and light.

The Body: The What of Dance

body shapes—Curved, straight, angular, twisted, wide, narrow, symmetrical, asymmetrical, open, closed.

locomotor skills—The eight basic movements that travel across general space: walk, run, jump, hop, leap, gallop, slide, skip.

nonlocomotor skills—Movements that stay in personal space: rotate, stretch, bend, push, pull, shake.

other locomotor skills—Rolling, crawling, scooting.

Relationships: The Setting of Dances

with others or objects—Between, around, through, in front of, behind, beside, under, over, above, below.

with partners or groups—Leading (moving ahead); following (moving behind); meeting (moving toward); parting (moving away from).

Creating: The Design of Dance

ABA—A represents a movement phrase; B represents a different movement phrase; A represents a return to the first movement phrase.

canon (also known as round)—A single movement phrase that is layered and restated at successive intervals.

chance dance—Movement phrases performed in random order.

improvisation—Creative problem solving through movement.

movement phrase—A series of movements that complete an idea.

narrative—A dance story.

rondo—A movement phrase with three or more movement themes; starts with a main theme and moves to another theme, then returns to the main theme at intervals: ABACADAE.

shape, move, shape—Start in a shape, move, end in a shape.

theme and variation—A movement phrase followed by several variations on the original theme.

MOVEnture CD Song List

Track	Song title	Corresponding MOVEnture(s)	Track length and notes
1	Pachebel's Canon	5 Mirroring 12 Ahh! Relaxation	2.01 min. Adagio; slow movement
2	Emotion Medley	6 How Are You Feeling?	2.02 min. Four segments: sad, happy, scared, and mad; sustained, swing, vibratory, percussive
3	Skating	8 Flower Dance 70 Shadows 72 Seed to Flower	1.02 min. Melodic with sustained quality
4	Winter Portrait	12 Ahh! Relaxation 68 The Snowflake Dance	2.00 min. Adagio; slow movement
5	Danish Folk Dance	15 Seven Jumps	2.52 min. Traditional folk dance
6	Open Horizons	3 Strong and Light 9 Over, Under, Around, and Through . . . Where Are You? 18 Towers	2.03 min. Upbeat rhythm
7	Jumping Bean Funk	2 Silly Dance 19 Jump, Everybody, Jump! 98 Tempo, Pattern, Accent	2.00 min. Steady rhythm
8	A Sunny Day	11 Do the Locomotion! 20 Bouncing Buddies 67 Traveling in Many Directions 87 Levers and Games	2.00 min. Light, swing tempo
9	Street Vibe	23 Alphabet Soup 52 Pizza Portions	1.58 min. Brassy and fast
10	Tribal Day	29 African Folktale 58 Expedition	1.59 min. Galloping, skipping, marching rhythm
11	Sweet Sorrow of Yesterday	33 Dancing Dreams	2.28 min. Melancholy piano melody followed by somber mood
12	Taste of the Orient	34 Haiku Dances	1.58 min. Free-form flute
13	Technomotion	35 Too Much TV 53 Probability Dance	1.29 min. Strong, moderate tempo
14	Touch of Ivory	17 Express Yourself! 36 Dance Me a Story 91 A Spider's Life	2.54 min. Swinging and swaying tempo
15	Wacky Sax	39 Shape, Shape, Shape	1.00 min. Marching and clapping rhythm with vaudeville flavor
16	Beanbag Bop	41 Beanbag Boom!	1.49 min. 32 beats, pause; repeated many times
17	Pop Rhythm	50 Equation Creations	1.25 min. Running, jogging tempo
18	Moonscape	45 1-3-5, 2-4-6	1.56 min. Fast and techno
19	Happy Daze	54 Universal Circle Dance	0.37 min. Slow gallop tempo

From *Interdisciplinary Learning Through Dance: 101 MOVEntures,* by Lynnette Overby, Beth Post, and Diane Newman. 2005. Champaign, IL: Human Kinetics.

Track	Song title	Corresponding MOVEnture(s)	Track length and notes
20	My Baby's Foxtrot	60 Dances of the 1920s	1.58 min. Charleston
21	Lost Ones	61 A Native American Poem	2.00 min. Slow flute and drum
22	Bebop Beat	62 The Kaleidoscope of Life	0.48 min. Strong, steady beat
23	Animals on the Hoof	64 Time Scrolls 92 The Animal Tale 95 Masquerade	2.15 min. Swing and sway percussion
24	Chopin's Nocturne in Eb—Opus 9, No. 2	65 20th-Century Celebration, Ballet	1.04 min. Classical piano
25	Reeling Along	65 20th-Century Celebration, Virginia Reel	3.36 min. Folk dance fiddling
26	Ol' Soft Shoe	65 20th-Century Celebration, Tap Dance	1.31 min. Slide whistle, happy melody
27	Francesca	65 20th-Century Celebration, Waltz	1.55 min. Traditional waltz
28	Benny's Boogie	65 20th-Century Celebration, Swing	1.30 min. Big band sound
29	The Blue Skirt Polka	65 20th-Century Celebration, Polka	1.18 min. Accordion polka
30	Be-Bop Party	65 20th-Century Celebration, Twist 65 20th-Century Celebration, Mashed Potato	1.18 min. Early rock 'n roll sound
31	Do the Jerk	65 20th-Century Celebration, Jerk	1.23 min. Motown style with vocals
32	On the Disco Line	65 20th-Century Celebration, The Hustle	1.21 min. Disco style
33	Michael-Jean	65 20th-Century Celebration, Moonwalk	1.30 min. Michael Jackson style
34	Space Jive	44 Changes 65 20th-Century Celebration, Contemporary Jazz and Hip-Hop dance	1.27 min. Funky beat
35	Mirage	71 The Fall Season	1.42 min. Three segments, each ending with a falling sound
36	Integrator	56 The Speaker for the Trees 74 The Water Cycle	2.25 min. Percolating pipes followed by a steady beat
37	Glass Mountain	79 Dinosaurs	1.56 min. Percussion with environmental sounds
38	Living Canopy	80 Save the Rainforest	2.02 min. Environmental sounds with melody
39	Horizons	83 Microscopic World	2.00 min. Water sounds and melody
40	Kentucky Rose Bach's Bouree Heat Seekers Toon Time	94 Dance TV	1.58 min. Toe-tapping country Court dance Outer space lasers Cartoon theme
41	Solar Power	General 16 Straight, Curved, Zigzag, Dot!	0.39 min. Walking tempo
42	In the Hood	General	0.42 min. Running, jogging tempo
43	Clubland	General 11 Do the Locomotion!	0.37 min. Running tempo

From *Interdisciplinary Learning Through Dance: 101 MOVEntures,* by Lynnette Overby, Beth Post, and Diane Newman. **297** 2005. Champaign, IL: Human Kinetics.

References and Resources

Chapters 1 and 2 References and Resources

Bonbright, J., and S. McGreevy-Nichols. 1999. *Arts Education Policy Review*. Volume 100, Issue 6, pp. 27-33.

Bushner, C. 1994. *Teaching children movement concepts and skills*. Champaign, IL: Human Kinetics.

Consortium of National Arts Education Associations. 2002. *Authentic connections: Interdisciplinary works in the arts*. Author.

Gardner, H. 1983. *Frames of mind*. New York: Basic Books.

Gardner, H. 1987. Developing the spectrum of human intelligence. *Harvard Education Review* 57: 187-193.

Mansilla, V., W. Miller, and H. Gardner. 2000. On disciplinary lenses and interdisciplinary work. In *Interdisciplinary curriculum: Challenges to implementation*, eds. S. Wineburg and P. Grossman. New York: Teachers College Press.

Martin, D. 1997. *Elementary science methods: A contructivist approach*. Albany: Delmar.

National Association for Sport and Physical Education. 1995. *Moving into the future: National standards for physical education: A guide to content and assessment*. St. Louis: Mosby.

National Dance Association. 1994. *National standards for dance education: What every young American should know and be able to do in dance*. Reston, VA: Music Educators National Conference for the National Dance Association.

Root-Bernstein, R., and M. Root-Bernstein. 1999. *Sparks of genius: The thirteen thinking tools of the world's most creative people*. New York: Houghton Mifflin.

Root-Bernstein, R., and M. Root-Bernstein. 2000. Learning to think with emotion. *Chronicle of Higher Education*, June 13, A64.

U.S. Department of Education. December 2002. www. nochildleftbehind.gov. A comprehensive Web site with information about standards, funding, and policy issues related to the No Child Left Behind legislation.

von Glaserfeld, E. 1995. A constructivist approach to teaching. In L. Steffe and J. Gale (eds). *Constructivism in education*, pp. 3-16. New Jersey: Lawrence Erlbaum Associates, Inc.

MOVEnture Resources

Chapter 3:
MOVEntures in Physical Education

3 Strong and Light

Green Gilbert, A. 1992. *Creative dance for all ages*. Reston, VA: American Association for Health, Physical Education, Recreation and Dance.

7 Diana's Walk

Hutchins, P. 1968. *Rosie's walk*. New York: Aladdin.

11 Do the Locomotion!

Chappelle, E. *Music for creative dance: Contrast and continuum*. Seattle, WA: Ravenna Ventures, 206-527-7799 or NDA/AAHPERD, 800-321-0789.

Graham, G., S. Holt/Hale, and M. Parker. 1998. *Children moving*. 4th ed. Mountain View, CA: Mayfield.

Roberton, M.A., and L.E. Halverson. 1984. *Developing children: Their changing movement*. Philadelphia: Lea & Febiger.

Wickstrom, R. 1983. *Fundamental motor patterns*. 3rd ed. Philadelphia: Lea & Febiger.

15 Seven Jumps

Pangrazi, R. 1992. *Dynamic physical education for elementary school children*. New York: Macmillan.

Weikert, P. 1997. *Teaching folk dance*. Ypsilanti, MI: High Scope Press.

17 Express Yourself!

Sabatine, J. 1995. *Movement training for the stage and screen*. New York: Back Stage Books.

21 Rockin' To The Oldies

Music for Little People. 1998. *A Child's Celebration of Dance Music*. Redway, CA: Rhino Records.

Best of Rock 'n Roll of the 50s. Canada: Madacy 21 Winners.

Chapter 4:
MOVEntures in Language Arts

23 Alphabet Soup

Martin, B. Jr., and J. Archambault. 1989. *Chicka chicka boom boom*. New York: Simon & Schuster.

Mendoza, G. 1970. *The Marcel Marceau alphabet book*. Garden City, NY: Doubleday.

Purcell Cone, T. 1994. *Teaching children dance: Becoming a master teacher*. Champaign, IL: Human Kinetics.

27 Action Words

Purcell Cone, T. 1994. *Teaching children dance: Becoming a master teacher*. Champaign, IL: Human Kinetics.

29 African Folktale

Lewis, B. 1992. *Primitive truth*. Los Angeles: Ikauma Records.

McDermott, G. 1972. *Anansi the spider: A tale from the Ashanti*. New York: Henry Holt.

32 Cliché Studies

Morgenroth, J. 1987. *Dance improvisations*. Pittsburgh: University of Pittsburgh Press.

33 Dancing Dreams

Hughes, L. 1994. *The collected poems of Langston Hughes*. New York: Alfred A. Knopf.

34 Haiku Dances

Musical Heritage Society. *Like waves upon the sand or lyrical melodies of Japan*. 1710 Highway 35, Oakhurst, NJ 07755 *www.musicalheritage.com*.

Rentschler, R.J. 1980. *Michigan four seasons*. Ann Arbor, MI: Braun-Brumfield.

35 Too Much TV

Silverstein, S. 1974. *Where the sidewalk ends*. New York: Harper & Row.

36 Dance Me a Story

Ryder, J. 1996. *Earthdance*. New York. Henry Holt.

38 Imaginative Thinking Tools

Root-Bernstein, R., and M. Root-Bernstein. 1999. *Sparks of genius: The thirteen tools of the world's most creative people*. New York: Houghton Mifflin.

Chapter 5:
MOVEntures in Mathematics

43 Thinches and Toe Rulers

Myller, R. 1962. *How big is a foot?* New York: Scott, Foresman.

44 Changes

Fuller, R. and N. Lyons. 1977. *Moving box*. Santa Rosa, CA: The Footprint Press.

52 Pizza Portions

Isaac, K. 1996. *Math + Pizza = Dance*. Movement Me? Why Not! Workshop for 5-9th grade math teachers. Workshop materials.

53 Probability Dance

Payne, J. et al. 1985. *Mathematics*. New York: Scribner.

Chapter 6:
MOVEntures in Social Studies

56 The Speaker for the Trees

Seuss, T. 1971. *The lorax*. New York: Random House.

57 Room to Move

Coleman, E. 1996. *White Socks Only*. Morton Grove, IL: Albert Whitman.

Curtis, C.P. 1995. *The Watsons Go to Birmingham—1963*. New York: Delacorte Press.

Taylor, M.D. 1976. *Roll of Thunder, Hear My Cry*. New York: Dial Press.

58 Expedition

Lewis, B. 1992. *Primitive truth*. Los Angeles: Ikauma Records.

60 Dances of the 1920s

Schroeder, A. 1989. *Ragtime tumpie*. Boston: Little, Brown.

61 A Native American Poem

Babcock, C.M., ed. 1973. *The planting song: Walk quietly the beautiful trail*. Kansas City, MO: Hallmark Cards.

62 The Kaleidoscope of Life

Kids Against Pollution. www.kidsagainstpollution.org. This Web site is the home of an organization of children called Kids Against Pollution (KAP). KAP is a multinational organization of active youth dedicated to solving and preventing pollution problems through interactive educational projects and events with the goal of protecting children's health and the environment. The site includes the following:

- A variety of environmental links
- Opportunities to pen-pal with member students
- Chances to join KAP and participate in activities

Minnesota Pollution Control Agency. 2004. The MPCA kid's page. www.pca.state.mn.us/kids.
This Web site contains a link titled "Student Guide to Environmental Information." Clicking on the link leads to a wealth of information written in kid-friendly language about the following subjects: air pollution, water pollution, land pollution, and methods of cleaning up pollution.

One World. Tiki the penguin: For kids and our planet Earth. www.oneworld.net/penguin.
Tiki's Web site features environmental information in kids' own language. The site features the following:

- Environmental quizzes
- Fun pages with jokes, puzzles, and riddles
- Guides to working with the environment
- Chance to pen-pal with Tiki himself

Overby, L., and Kinetic Energy Company. Spring 2002. *The kaleidoscope of life.* Michigan Elementary Schools.

65 20th-Century Celebration

Anderson, J. 1974. *Dance.* New York: Newsweek Books.

Graham, G., S. Holt/Hale, and M. Parker. 1998. *Children moving.* 4th ed. Mountain View, CA: Mayfield.

Grau, A. 1998. *Dance.* New York: Eyewitness Books, Dorling Kindersley.

Harris, J., A. Pittman, and M. Waller. 1955. *Dance a while.* Minneapolis: Burgess.

Johnson, A.E. 1999. *Jazz tap: From African drums to American feet.* New York: Rosen.

Martin, J.J. 1963. *John Martin's book of the dance.* New York: Tudor.

Penrod, J., and J.G. Plastino. 1998. *The dancer prepares: Modern dance for beginners.* Mountain View, CA: Mayfield.

Sorell, W. 1981. *Dance in its time: The emergence of an art form.* Garden City, New York: Anchor Press/ Doubleday.

Chapter 7:
MOVEntures in Science

67 Traveling in Many Directions

Chappelle, E. *Music for creative dance: Contrast and continuum.* Seattle: Ravenna Ventures, 206-527-7799 or National Dance Association/AAHPERD, 800-321-0789.

Gilbert, A. 1992. *Creative dance for all ages.* Reston, VA: National Dance Association/ AAHPERD.

Purcell Cone, T. 1994. *Teaching children dance: Becoming a master teacher.* Champaign, IL: Human Kinetics.

69 In the Cloud Crowd

Shaw, C.G. 1947. *Sometimes it looked like spilt milk.* New York: Scholastic.

70 Shadows

Alexander, M. 1969. *Light and sight.* Englewood Cliffs, NJ: Prentice Hall.

Benzwie, T. 1987. *A moving experience: Dance for lovers of children and the child within.* Tucson: Zephyr Press.

Overby, L., and Kinetic Energy Company. Spring 2002. *Spark and pop: The adventures of light and sound.* Michigan Elementary Schools.

Ridiman, B. 1973. *What is a shadow?* New York: Parent Magazine Press.

Rowan, B. 1963. *Learning through movement.* New York: Teachers College Press.

Stevenson, R.L. 1885. *My shadow.* New York: Oxford University Press.

72 Seed to Flower

The following Web sites are links to unit plans that include experiments, worksheets, and activities related to growing plants:

- Plants: http://kindergartenclass.netfirms.com/plants.htm.
- Thematic units: www.libsci.sc.edu/miller/plants.htm.
- Growing Plants Unit: http://commtechlab.msu.edu/sites/letsnet/noframes/subjects/science/b2u3.html.

73 Wacky Weather Forecast

James, C., B. Steffen, and G. Lessons. United States Weather, West Michigan Edition, WZZM-TV 13.

74 The Water Cycle

Barron, R. 1996. Water cycles: Integrating dance and science. ARTSEDGE curriculum Unit/Lesson Plan. http://artsedge.kennedy-center.org.

Branklyn, F. 1982. *Water for the world*. New York: Crowell.

Martin, D. 1997. *Elementary science methods: A constructivist approach*. Albany: Delmar.

Overby, L., and Kinetic Energy Company. Spring 2000. *Water works: Tales of the hydrosphere*. Michigan Elementary Schools.

79 Dinosaurs

http://dinosaurs.eb.com

This site offers a wealth of information about dinosaurs and their environment and behavior. It includes theories of extinction.

http://www.enchantedlearning.com/subjects/dinosaurs/

This site includes information about a variety of dinosaurs, dinosaur anatomy, and theories of dinosaur extinction.

81 Ecosystem Explorers

www.desertusa.com

This is an online directory to the desert regions of the American southwest; providing a look at desert life, plants, and animals.

82 The Kelp Community

National Wildlife Federation. *Diving into oceans*. 1998. New York: McGraw-Hill.

Overby, L., and Kinetic Energy Company. Spring 2000. *Water works: Tales of the hydrosphere*. Michigan Elementary Schools.

Swanson, D. 1994. *Safari beneath the sea*. North Vancouver, British Columbia: Whitecap Books.

83 Microscopic world

Overby, L., and Kinetic Energy Company. Spring 2002. *The kaleidoscope of life*. Michigan Elementary Schools.

R. Russell, C. McGowan, and S. Tellschow. 1999. *The microbe zoo*. Michigan State University. (An educational resource about ecology and microbiology. CD-ROM includes information about microbes and the habitats they dwell in.)

http://commtechlab.msu.edu/site/dlc-me/zoo.

84 Roller Coaster

Asimov, I. 1975. *How did we find out about energy?* New York: Walker.

Hewitt, P. 1997. *Conceptual physics*. Menlo Park, CA: Addison-Wesley.

Overby, L., and Kinetic Energy Company. Spring 1999. *Kinetic energy*. Michigan Elementary Schools.

86 Spaceship Ahoy!

Coffelt, N. 1993. *Dogs in space*. New York: Harcourt Brace.

87 Levers and Games

Anderson, N. 1975. *Investigating science using your whole body*. New York: McGraw-Hill.

Overby, L., and Kinetic Energy Company. Spring 2002. *The kaleidoscope of life*. Michigan Elementary Schools.

Spolin, V. 1986. *Theater games for the classroom*. Evanston, Illinois: Northwestern University Press.

Stinson, S. 1988. *Dance for young children: Finding the magic in movement*. Reston, VA: National Dance Association of the American Alliance for Health, Physical Education, Recreation and Dance.

Chapter 8:
MOVEntures in Music, Theater, and Visual Arts

89 Color Me

O'Neill, M., and J. Wallner. 1961. *Hailstones and halibut bones: Adventures in color*. Garden City, New York: Doubleday.

Seuss, T., S. Johnson, and L. Fancher. 1996. *My many colored days*. New York: Knopf.

90 Rain Dance

American Indian Dance Theatre cue sheet for students. John F. Kennedy Center for the Performing Arts, Washington D.C. A supplement to American Dance Theatre in performance.

91 The Spider's Dance

Davis, J., and M. Evans. 1987. *Theatre, children and youth*. New Orleans: Anchorage Press.

Ryder, J., and R.J. Blake. 1981. *The spider's dance*. New York: Harper & Row.

92 The Animal Tale

Fuller, R., and N. Lyons. 1977. *The moving box*. Santa Rosa, CA.: Footprint Press.

95 Masquerade

Percussion music: A variety of albums by Brent Lewis, Mickey Hart, or Gabrielle Roth and the Mirrors.

Alkema, C. *Mask making*. 1981. New York: Sterling.

Nobleman, R. 1979. *Mime and masks*. Rowayton, CT: New Plays.

96 Everyday Life in Faraway Times

The process described in this lesson uses the visual thinking strategy developed by Visual Understanding in Education, a visual arts program for elementary school students, which is based on the premise that finding meaning in works of visual art involves a rich range of thinking skills. Web site for VTE is www.vue.org.

98 Tempo, Pattern, Accent

Fuller, R., and N. Lyons. 1977. *The moving box*. Santa Rosa, CA.: Footprint Press.

Sabatine, J. 1995. *Movement training for the stage and screen*. New York: Back Stage Books.

99 Composition and Choreography

Adams, A., ed. 1972. *Poetry of the earth*. New York: Charles Scribner.

Lowden, M. 1989. *Dancing to learn*. Bristol, PA: Falmer Press.

Sandburg, C. 1970. *The Carl Sandburg treasury: Prose and poetry for young people*. New York: Harcourt Brace Jovanovich.

100 Writing and Dancing a Play

Sabatine, J. 1995. *Movement training for the stage and screen*. New York: Back Stage Books.

101 Dance of the Four Elements

Rius, M., C.S. Vendrell, and J.M. Parramón. 1984. *The four elements*. Barcelona: Alvagraf.

Pictured left to right, Beth C. Post, Diane Newman, and Lynnette Young Overby.

Lynnette Young Overby, PhD, is the director of the Program for Interdisciplinary Learning Through the Arts at Michigan State University. She has taught dance, theater, and physical education across multiple disciplines in public school and university settings for 30 years, and she has created several dance and theater productions that teach curricular content. Overby has served as president and conference director of the National Dance Association, a board member of Dance and the Child International, and conference director and founding member of the National Dance Education Organization.

Beth C. Post, MS, is a creative arts teacher for K-5 students in Williamston, Michigan. Post has extensive teaching experience in public schools using an interdisciplinary approach to learning. She has designed and implemented an interdisciplinary creative arts curriculum for grades K-5 and is an advocate for movement education in the schools,

having presented at state and national teacher professional development conferences. Post is a veteran member of the Happendance Professional Contemporary Dance Company, working as a dancer, choreographer, director, and educator. She was named Michigan Dance Teacher of the Year in 1998.

Diane Newman, MA, is the founder and director of the Happendance Professional Contemporary Dance Company, which serves up to 10,000 students per year. She developed a 10-level curriculum of ballet training and instituted a progressive syllabus for creative dance and dance composition for Happendance students. She also has taught dance and conceptual learning through movement in various settings for more than 30 years. Newman is a popular presenter at dance, dance education, service learning, and K-12 teachers' professional development conferences. She was named Michigan Dance Teacher of the Year in 1981.

You'll find
other outstanding
dance resources at

www.HumanKinetics.com

In the U.S. call

1-800-747-4457

Australia.. 08 8277 1555
Canada 1-800-465-7301
Europe... +44 (0) 113 255 5665
New Zealand....................................... 0064 9 448 1207

HUMAN KINETICS
The Information Leader in Physical Activity
P.O. Box 5076 • Champaign, IL 61825-5076 USA